D1550889

Health
in the
Headlines

HEALTH
IN THE
HEADLINES

The Stories Behind
the Stories

STEPHEN KLAIDMAN

New York Oxford
OXFORD UNIVERSITY PRESS
1991

Oxford University Press

Oxford   New York   Toronto
Delhi   Bombay   Calcutta   Madras   Karachi
Petaling Jaya   Singapore   Hong Kong   Tokyo
Nairobi   Dar es Salaam   Cape Town
Melbourne   Auckland

and associated companies in
Berlin   Ibadan

Copyright © 1991 by Stephen Klaidman

Published by Oxford University Press, Inc.,
200 Madison Avenue, New York, New York 10016

Oxford is a registered trademark of Oxford University Press

Library of Congress Cataloging-in-Publication Data
Klaidman, Stephen.
Health in the headlines : the stories behind the stories / Stephen Klaidman.
p.   cm.
Includes bibliographical references and index.
ISBN 0-19-505298-6
1. Health risk assessment in the press—United States.
2. Health risk communication—United States.
3. Public health—Reporting—United States.
4. Environmental health—United States—Reporting.
5. Health—Social aspects—United States—20th century.
6. Health in mass media—United States.
I. Title.
PN4784.M4K55 1991 070.4′49613—dc20 90-19297

2   4   6   8   9   7   5   3   1

Printed in the United States of America
on acid-free paper

Acknowledgments

A number of persons and institutions have made this book possible. The Institute for Health Policy Analysis of Georgetown University, the Media Studies Project of the Woodrow Wilson International Center for Scholars, the Esther A. and Joseph Klingenstein Fund, and the Josiah Macy Jr. Foundation provided substantial support. Edward J. Burger, M.D., director of the IHPA, encouraged me in the early stages of my research and writing. Cheryl Pleasant-Bey introduced order into an often chaotic environment. Philip Cook, director of the Media Studies Project, offered intellectual guidance and made available all of the resources of the project. Bruce Napper of the Wilson Center relieved my frustration almost daily, especially when I was baffled by the mysteries of WordPerfect. My two research assistants, Eric Gorovitz and Kevin Leahy, provided invaluable assistance. Without them there would be no book. Jeffrey House, my editor at Oxford University Press, raised a host of relevant questions and improved the manuscript substantially. My family, and especially my son, Danny, provided sustenance all along the way. But most of all I thank David B. McCallum, director of the Risk Communication Program of the IHPA, who was involved in the conception of the work, who raised funds to support it, and whose ideas are embedded, otherwise unacknowledged, throughout it.

Contents

Health
in the
Headlines

1

Knowing When to Be Afraid

SUSAN Cohen, while a 22-year-old senior at Columbia University, said she was worried about AIDS. "I think so many people—men and women—are going to be dying in ten or fifteen years, people I know, that it scares me a lot," she said. But Cohen did not think she or her contemporaries would use condoms, the most reliable way of reducing the spread of the disease through sexual intercourse. "I don't think people are going to use all these sterile methods," she said. "It hurts the whole point of sex."[1] Cohen, in other words, thought she had read or seen enough about AIDS to know essentially what the trade-offs were and concluded that she and her friends were probably willing to take the low (for people of their background) but deadly risk of contracting the AIDS virus because of the high value they place on unimpeded sexual pleasure.

Some people have stopped eating beef, butter, and eggs; others have reduced their consumption of these foods, which, the news media have repeatedly reported, contribute to unhealthily high cholesterol levels. Others still eat as much fatty food as they did before the media began saturating the marketplace with coverage of the risks involved. Like Cohen, these people have concluded that the trade-off—in this case an increased likelihood of cardiovascular disease and premature death—is worth it; or they don't believe or understand the often confusing media reports; or they have been living in their own media-free zone and remain completely unaware of the prevalent view in the medical community about the risks related to eating foods high in saturated fat; or they simply deny what they read or see on television.

Many people bake in the sun despite the reasonably well-documented and widely reported risk of skin cancer from overexposure to ultraviolet rays; others use sunscreens that run all the way up to number 30, and still others stay out of the sun altogether.

Some have their homes tested for radon, and others don't. A study conducted at Rutgers University indicated that people were more concerned about what radon in their basements does to the value of their property than about its potential hazard to their health. At Love Canal, a heavily covered news story and a watershed event in precipitating the Environmental Protection Agency's Superfund program to clean up toxic wastes across the country, residents panicked at the dire predictions of cancer and chromosomal damage resulting from chemical waste. These results, from a quick EPA "pilot" study, were leaked to *The New York Times* and published, prompting fear and trembling and the sale of Love Canal real estate to the U.S. government, the only available buyer. But an outside review of the EPA study, issued almost simultaneously, found "inadequate basis for any scientific or medical inferences . . . concerning exposure to mutagenic substances because of residence in Love Canal." Later studies suggested that the danger to those living near Love Canal may have been negligible.[2]

Simply speaking, people like to pick their risks. They prefer to decide for themselves, usually in seat-of-the-pants fashion, whether the payoff in pleasure or profit is worth the risk. And they sometimes make their decisions based on information that is incomplete, confused, misleading, or wrong. Moreover, even when accurate and substantially complete information is available to them from the news media and other sources, they may make irrational choices. In the words of Aaron Wildavsky, "What to favor and what to fear are cultural constructs that enable us to walk right past snarling monsters and run away from little-bitty things. If we want to know why we are fearful about what and whether we should be, this is equivalent to asking the cultural question: How should we live?"[3]

Even when the press pays a great deal of attention to health risks, this does not guarantee that readers and viewers will know when to be concerned about them. And even when consumers of news are reasonably well informed and concerned about these risks, this does not guarantee that individuals will change their behavior. People often hold strong views about what they want to do that are not easily swayed by awareness that their chosen activities are risky; conversely, they may be outraged by trivial risks that are imposed on them. Moreover, many of us have a strong and comforting tendency to underestimate our own personal risk. One survey found that 54 percent of respondents believed that a serious illness "couldn't happen to them." At the same time, some people believe that "everything causes cancer" and therefore "there is no way to avoid cancer."[4] The implicit message in both cases is that many people think it is pointless to alter personal behavior. In addition, the messages about risk delivered by the press and other sources, including scientific experts, may be ambiguous or even in direct conflict with one another. How could it be otherwise when each source of health-risk information has a perspective shaped by its frequently narrow and sometimes politicized history and objectives, and all of the sources and channels of information operate in a universe of scientific uncertainty and professional constraints? Under these circumstances, there is no way to determine precisely the influence that press coverage of health risks has on individuals.[5] It is possible, however, to show that media coverage of health risks has an impact on public policy. The EPA has found that budgetary and other priorities for regulating environmental hazards often correlate more closely with public opinion than they do with the priorities of professional risk assessors and managers. Intuitively, public opinion, to a greater or lesser degree depending on the specific issue, would appear to be influenced by what people read in newspapers and magazines, hear on the radio, or watch on television. To demonstrate this clearly in the field of health, however, it is necessary to unravel a complex web of interrelated motives, influences, activities, and institutions and to discuss the ways in which health risks are perceived by risk analysts and risk managers, by policymakers and environmental activists, by scientists who work for industry and those who work for government. Each of these and other perspectives is taken into account in the policy process, or rather the political process that leads to policy formation. It may be, however, that the most influential perspective in shaping policy is the public perspective, or public opinion. Fred L. Smith, a former EPA official, made this point succinctly when he said that EPA "finds itself selecting projects based on their political and public relations value."[6] But how well people grasp any risk, irrespective of politics and public relations, depends on how well they understand three fundamental concepts: uncertainty, comparability, and acceptability.

Elements of Risk

Uncertainty

Vernon Houk of the Centers for Disease Control in Atlanta has said that "the difference between risk assessment and a five-year weather forecast is that at least with the weather forecast, if you wait five years you find out whether you were right."[7] As Houk suggests, a lot of what scientists know about health risks they do not know, and may never know, for sure. But this does not always prevent them from sounding as if they are sure. Thus, one credible scientist may recommend in the most authoritative fashion that older women should take calcium supplements to avoid osteoporosis, and another equally credible scientist may assert in an equally authoritative manner that calcium supplements are probably useless. Or there may be widespread agreement among scientists that formaldehyde in drinking water can cause cancer, but little agreement about how much formaldehyde it takes to do so.

This scientific uncertainty presents a problem for the press and the public, especially when, as frequently happens, the scientific data do not provide a causal link between a risk factor and a disease. For example, what should a well-informed layperson make of the following sequence? The general press reported on a scientific paper in the *New England Journal of Medicine* by Dr. Brian MacMahon of the Harvard School of Public Health indicating that there was an association between drinking coffee and getting cancer of the pancreas.[8] Some press accounts accurately and precisely portrayed the study as saying that there was "an *unexpected association* of pancreatic cancer with coffee consumption."[9] Another account said: "Harvard University scientists have found a *suspicious and alarming association* between coffee drinking and cancer of the pancreas, one of the fastest killing of all cancers."[10] Still others blurred the distinction between a statistical association between the presence of the risk factor and the occurrence of the disease, which is what the MacMahon study suggested, and causation, which was not demonstrated by the study and is generally difficult to prove in science. Even without the blurring, however, most laypersons do not recognize the relevant difference between an association, whether "unexpected" or "suspicious and alarming," and a cause-effect relationship. It would probably not occur to most people, for example, to ask whether the MacMahon study controlled for a whole range of other possible causes of pancreatic cancer, such as smoking (it did), which has a known association with the disease. The point is that tobacco smoke could be the causal agent, or there could be a synergistic effect between coffee and tobacco smoke that causes pancreatic cancer, or possibly neither coffee nor tobacco smoke causes pancreatic cancer. In any event, many persons almost certainly concluded from the press coverage that drinking a lot of coffee meant an increased risk of pancreatic cancer. Even a very carefully written story and headline are susceptible to that interpretation, because the distinction between association and causation is not clear in most people's minds and because news stories frequently are not carefully read.

Subsequent less well-covered studies produced no evidence of a link between coffee drinking and pancreatic cancer. And then, MacMahon himself, in letters to the *New England Journal of Medicine*, described follow-up work that did not support his group's original findings.[11] These letters received no press coverage.[12]

It is in these uncertain waters that reporters and editors, many of whom lack the proper intellectual instruments, must navigate. "So much of the [health risk] news is contradictory," one reporter wrote, "so much of it is incomplete, so much of it is disproven by other reports later on that it's hard for a person without a Ph.D. in biochemistry to know what to do."[13] Indeed, the same might be said even for someone *with* a Ph.D. in biochemistry.

The risk-assessment and risk-management processes can amplify the uncertainty surrounding policy-making and public information about health hazards because these processes depend on widely varying assumptions as well as data that are often softer than researchers might like. For example, "estimates of the cancer risk to individuals exposed to 1 part per million of vinyl chloride 24 hours a day for 70 years range from one in ten to one in a hundred million (U.S. EPA, 1983)."[14] When the EPA submitted five new risk-assessment guidelines to the Office of Management and Budget (OMB) for review, Wendy Lee Graham, head of OMB's office of information and regulatory affairs, responded with this familiar complaint: "If worst-case assumptions and upper-bound estimates are used and repeatedly combined, they will produce a final risk estimate that is almost certain to amplify the real risk hundreds or thousands of times."[15] On the other hand, when chemical manufacturers promote a new product or defend an old one, they often use methods or assumptions that may understate the risk associated with the product.

In health matters, people are looking for answers to tough questions about what to do and what not to do; what to eat and what not to eat; what, in other words, is safe and what is unsafe. Sometimes science can provide the answers. After many years of research, for example, science has spoken clearly on the unambiguous health threat of smoking. Science can say with certainty that exposure to radiation at certain levels for certain periods of time will prove fatal. But when the answers are less certain—as for shorter exposures to radiation at lower levels—the public still demands unambiguous recommendations. Is it safe to live half a mile from the landfill? Yes or no? The radon reading in my basement studio is 12 picocuries. Am I going to get lung cancer? Should I buy biscuit mix if there might be a trace of EDB in the flour? Will I get cancer from the dioxin in toilet paper? That series of questions, each of which seems to demand a yes-or-no answer but cannot be adequately answered yes or no, leads logically to the two remaining key concepts framing the subject of health risks: comparative risk and acceptable risk.

Risk Comparison

"From the risk analyst's point of view," as a pair of wry observers have put it, "it might be said that the object of living is to die!"[16] Over the long term, all lives are terminal. The overall, lifetime risk of dying is 100 percent; the risk is absolute.

In the short term, however, risk is relative, not absolute. It may be safer to sleep late than to spend the morning practicing free-fall parachuting, but sleeping in does not eliminate, among other things, the risks of radon, robbers, or rapists. Most people know that, if only intuitively. Yet they are often fuzzy about how to compare one risk to another. There are those who smoke two packs of unfiltered cigarettes a day, consume a case of beer a week, and commute two hours a day to and from work, but are unwilling to live near a nuclear power plant or perhaps even to drink tap water or eat a peanut butter sandwich. One thing this implies is that some people have no idea that the daily risks they run vastly outweigh other risks they would not dream of taking or accepting. Survey results indicate that people consistently overestimate the role of some causes of death (accidents, botulism, fires, and homicide) and consistently underestimate others (diabetes, stomach cancer, lightning, and stroke).[17]

Relative riskiness is rarely a person's sole guide to action, but knowing how one risk compares to another can provide a decision-making perspective that is often either lacking or distorted. There are numerous kinds of relevant comparisons. For example, people who are afraid of flying could be told that not only are the chances of death by air travel slim, but on a trip of equal mileage, they are twenty-nine times less than the chances of being killed in an automobile.[18] On the other hand, if one compares air travel and car travel by the number of trips taken instead of the number of miles traveled, then the chance of fatal injury is six times greater in an airplane.[19]

An example involving automobile seat belts provides another perspective on the the mileage-multiple trip comparison:

> [P]eople's reluctance to wear seatbelts voluntarily might be due to the extremely small probability of incurring a fatal accident on a single automobile trip. Since a fatal accident occurs only once in every 3.5 million person trips and a disabling injury only once in every 100,000 person trips, refusing to buckle one's seatbelt may seem quite reasonable. It looks less reasonable, however, if one adopts a multiple-trip perspective and considers the substantial probability of an accident on some trip. Over 50 years of driving (about 40,000 trips), the probability of being killed rises to .01 and the probability of experiencing at least one disabling injury is .33. In a pilot study, Slovic, Fischhoff, and Lichtenstein showed that people asked to consider this lifetime perspective responded more favorably toward seat belts (and air bags) than did people asked to consider a trip-by-trip perspective. Whether the favorable attitudes toward seat belts induced by a lengthened time perspective would be maintained and translated into behavior remains to be seen.[20]

In other words, depending on which end of the telescope one looks through, the risk appears greater or smaller. This illustrates, among other things, the political dimension of the concept of relative risk. The method or perspective selected to evaluate or characterize a risk inevitably influences how the public responds to it. For example, an airline regulator with libertarian leanings who favors free choice in matters such as the wearing of seat belts or motorcycle helmets might select the single-trip perspective, while a paternalistic regulator might pick the multiple-trip perspective.

The press plays an influential mediating role in the policy process by selecting, packaging (which may or may not substantially distort meaning), and passing on to the public risk assessments generated and framed by scientists, the government, industry, and advocacy groups, and by reflecting back to these groups the public's response.

Therefore, journalists need to understand concepts such as relative risk and the ways in which they can be manipulated.

Acceptable Risk

While views of comparative risk may have a political dimension, the notion of acceptable risk is entirely value-driven and therefore substantially political. "Acceptable risk" is the answer to the question "What is safe?" William Lowrance of Rockefeller University has phrased it, "A thing is safe if its risks are judged to be acceptable."[21] Lowrance's definition embraces the axiomatic point made above that nothing is risk-free, but it also implies that the word *safe* may mean different things to different people, and different things in different circumstances. The idea of acceptability also suggests that there are trade-offs involved in determining whether a risk is worth taking that have nothing to do with safety. Sky divers and coal miners know they engage in high-risk enterprises even though they may not know precisely how great the risk is of getting sick, injured, or killed. But the thrill of jumping out of airplanes in one case and the need for a job in the other provide a rational basis for accepting the risk. In other words, if the benefit is seen as outweighing the cost or, alternatively, if the cost is borne by someone else, the risk is likely to be viewed as more acceptable.

Policymakers must also decide what risks are acceptable, but they are required to do so for a diverse public whose collective views about what constitutes acceptable risk must be divined in a variety of ways that include public meetings, surveys, news coverage, and expert and lay opinions expressed through the media and other channels. Over the last twenty or thirty years, standards have been established, although by no means firmly fixed, that represent the government's effort to define socially acceptable risk. One such standard for nuclear power plants says: "Societal risk to life and health from nuclear power plant operation should be comparable to or less than the risk of generating electricity by viable competing technologies and should not be a significant addition to other societal risks." The Nuclear Regulatory Commission policy statement goes on to provide the following quantitative objectives:

> The risk to an average individual in the vicinity of a nuclear power plant of prompt fatalities that might result from reactor accidents should not exceed one-tenth of one per cent (0.1 percent) of the sum of prompt

fatality risks resulting from other accidents to which members of the
U.S. population are generally exposed.

The risk to the population in an area near a nuclear power plant of
cancer fatalities that might result from nuclear power plant operation
should not exceed one-tenth of one percent (0.1 percent) of the sum of
cancer fatality risks resulting from all other causes.[22]

In other words, risk to life from cancer in the vicinity of a nuclear plant
must not be increased by more than one-tenth of 1 percent because
of the operation of the plant.

Another such attempt, known as the Delaney amendment (to
the Food and Drug Act of 1958) for James J. Delaney, the Democratic congressman who introduced it, says in a fashion that is at
once categorical and imprecise, "no [food] additive shall be deemed
to be safe if it is found... to induce cancer in man or animal."[23] The
NRC and Delaney approaches are based on the assumption that people
"do not want facts but instead the assurance that they are being protected. That is, whatever the risks may be, they are in line with government policy."[24] The Food and Drug Administration has been the
government pacesetter in developing concepts such as *de minimis* risk,
the notion that product and other safety risks should be reduced to as
close to zero as possible. The EPA has a shorter history and has promoted a patchwork of regulation and legislation. Some statutes require
zero levels, such as the standards set by the EPA under the Safe
Drinking Water Act for contaminants such as arsenic, nitrate, and
mercury, while others, such as those dealing with pesticides, mandate
only that the benefit should exceed the risk. Other agencies such as
the Department of Health and Human Services (DHHS) have statutory
authority and have implemented policies to reduce risks such as strokes
related to high blood pressure that a few decades ago were seen as
irreducible given the state of medical science.

Lowrance also provides what he calls "an array of considerations
influencing safety judgments."[25] These include factors such as
whether the risk is borne voluntarily, whether the effects are immediate, whether there are alternatives, whether a risk evokes dread,
whether a hazard is encountered on the job, and whether the consequences of the risk are reversible. No item on this list is a risk
factor as such, but each is an element in the constellation of concerns surrounding risk. Some smokers (despite the habit-forming
properties of tobacco smoke, smoking is treated here as a voluntary
activity) will strongly object to the siting of a landfill in their com-

munity because, even though they understand that the risks are minimal, they simply don't want the disposal site in their neighborhood when it could be in someone else's. Some people will engage in risky sexual behavior despite awareness of how AIDS is spread because the pleasure is immediate and disease symptoms may not turn up for years, which makes denial (that they will become infected) easier. Uranium miners may continue their risky work because there are no other jobs available and they feel there is no alternative but to accept the risk. Many people oppose nuclear power without any idea of what the real risks are because the potential for a catastrophic disaster, even though minuscule, fills them with dread. Construction workers will walk beams twenty stories above the ground because it is part of their job. And people of all ages will participate in downhill skiing, in part because the pleasure of the activity offsets the risk of breaking a bone, but also because few skiing accidents cause death or permanent damage.

Peter Sandman, an expert on risk communication at Rutgers University, has observed that people are more concerned about what he calls the "outrage factor" than about the hazard itself. Outrage might result from the fact that the risk is imposed rather than elected, as in the siting of an unwanted nuclear plant in one's community. Hazard and outrage bound the policymaker's task. If the risk is both hazardous and perceived as outrageous, then the political will to confront it is high. Politicians can safely ignore low-hazard, low-outrage risks. The other two combinations—high-hazard, low-outrage and low-hazard, high-outrage—are the real problems.[26] In other words, for individuals, safety is subjective. In making public policy, however, the goal is to objectify it as much as possible, which is what risk analysts and risk managers are paid to do.

The Expert's Perception of Risk

Risk analysts are responsible for characterizing hazards and quantifying risk. Risk managers devise plans to minimize a particular risk's potential for harm. Often the official in charge of risk management is a policymaker who, with his or her staff, develops a management plan. The professional's approach to risk is systematic, but the disciplines of risk analysis and risk management are in their infancy, their instruments are crude, the data risk analysts receive are often unreliable, and the analysts are not always competent to evaluate them as opposed to simply plugging them into a statistical model, which may have conceptual flaws or may not fit the situation. According to Vincent Covello of Columbia University:

> uncertainties in risk assessment derive [from] four generic sources: (1) statistical randomness or variability of nature (e.g., variability due to differences between individuals in their susceptibility and responses to toxic substances); (2) lack of scientific knowledge about the mechanisms by which particular toxic chemicals produce particular adverse health effects, including cancer and reproductive impairments; (3) lack of scientific data (e.g., lack of laboratory and epidemiological data about the toxicological effects of synthetic chemicals); and (4) imprecision in risk assessment methods (e.g., imprecision due to variations in laboratory protocols for the conduct of animal bioassays).[27]

With respect to Covello's last point, C. F. Wilkinson, professor of insecticide chemistry and toxicology at Cornell University, has observed that "often animals are selected [for particular experiments] because of their sensitivity to carcinogens."[28] Indeed, EPA guidelines mandate that experiments done for risk-assessment purposes be done with the most sensitive strain of the species selected for the experiment. A flaw specific to this case of selecting animals for experiments that goes beyond the obvious statistical bias of the method is "that although rats get nasal cancers from formaldehyde and appear to be the species that is most sensitive to it, rats are unusual because they can breathe only through their noses. In contrast, other animals, notably humans, can breathe through the mouth and this would reduce significantly the estimate of cancer risk from formaldehyde in humans."[29] This conservative system of selecting experimental animals, which was questioned by OMB under the Reagan administration, reflects the U.S. government's regulatory philosophy. It is worth noting because its effect is multiplied as it is applied throughout the experimental, analytical, and policy-making stages of risk assessment and risk management.

In addition to being chosen for maximum sensitivity, the animal is given the maximum tolerable dose (MTD) of the chemical, which is just below the level that would kill it over the term of the experiment. Moreover, Wilkinson said, "the model for extrapolating high dose to low dose is usually very conservative."[30]

These choices, using the most sensitive species and strain and the maximum tolerable dose, plus uncertainties about the amounts of light, humidity, noise, and stress to which the animals were exposed, make it extremely difficult to get a precise result regarding the likely effects in humans. The experts know this, and so should the policymakers, at least those whose attention has been directed to a study called *Determining Risks to Health: Federal Policy and Practice*, which was prepared by the Task Force on Health Risk Assessment of the Department of Health and Human Services. With respect to the difficulty of extrapolating accurately from animal to human doses, for example, it says:

> When human health risk estimations are based on laboratory animal data, the doses must be converted to equivalent doses in humans. The interspecies conversion is complex and a source of substantial uncertainty because of the many species-specific physiologic, metabolic, and genetic factors that may cause the responses of the test animal to differ from those of humans. Moreover, the three mathematical models [commonly used to extrapolate doses from animals to humans] can arrive at substantially different estimates of risk based on the same data. For example, in estimating from rat data the human risk for cancer from saccharin consumption at a dietary intake corresponding to 0.12 g/day, the results from different models range from 0.0034 percent to 0.1 percent, a 300-fold difference (NRC, 1978).[31]

In other areas, a Department of Energy (DOE) study estimated that the number of fatalities associated with emissions from coal-fired power plants in a year would be between 1 and 305, and the Nuclear Regulatory Commission (NRC) estimated that the risk of the core melting at a nuclear reactor ranged from 1 in 10,000 to 1 in 1,000,000.[32] Since chemicals provide social benefits, as do nuclear and coal-burning power plants, and since estimates of the level at which they may be human carcinogens vary by orders of magnitude, what are risk managers and policymakers to do? They decide because that is their job. And they use a conservative approach even though such an approach might not always be the most technically sound, because the consensus among policymakers has long been that this approach is in the public interest. There is no simple equation for balancing benefits such as safety and jobs when they are in conflict with one another, so policymakers must make do with rules of reason operating in a highly politicized universe. Policy actions such as not banning saccharin and banning EDB reflect not only risk analysis and risk management but the will of some very vocal corporate and public citizens.

The Role of the Media

Journalists, of course, are not just passive conveyors of information about health risks. They decide—usually according to more or less well-established journalistic conventions—what to publish (or air) and when to publish (or air) it, they decide how long the story will be and where to put it in the paper or on the air, they interpret and comment on the policy debate and the decisions that flow from it, and more and more they explain the science itself and comment on it. In recent years a handful of reporters and editors have recognized the importance of the risk-assessment and risk-management processes and have studied them and reported on them. Simply by exercising its prerogatives, the press influences public policy, on health or anything else. What is less clear is the extent to which it does so, the extent to which it does so intentionally and systematically as opposed to unintentionally and hap-hazardly, the impact on policy of manipulation of journalists by sources, the degree to which the media set the public agenda in contrast to simply reacting to public opinion about the importance of health-risk issues, the extent to which journalism's preoccupation with controversy polarizes policy issues, and the different ways in which the print and electronic media exert their influence.

Studies relying on crude techniques such as content analysis have failed to provide satisfactory answers to these questions.[33] As a result, the influence of news coverage on health policy remains poorly understood. A few things, however, are fairly obvious. News coverage contributes directly to the opinions of policymakers, virtually all of whom read news publications and watch television news programs; it plays a role in setting the agenda of public concerns as a consequence of what is published or aired and what is left out; and it helps shape public opinion by continuous, reinforcing coverage of issues it deems interesting or important. There is no reliable way to separate the media's influence from the variety of other influences with which it co-exists (such as government publications, public hearings, advertising and public relations campaigns, and public-interest and other kinds of lobbying), and there is no precise way to quantify it. But nonmedia players such as government, industry, and public-interest groups devote a lot of time, money, and energy to trying to place their messages in the press and manipulate coverage. They seem convinced that the press is a powerful instrument for influencing policy.

In trying to meet the public's need for full and accurate information about health risks, journalists come up against a variety of obstacles, some of which are of their own making. Moreover, the key imperatives of journalism are sometimes in direct conflict with the key imperatives of science and medicine. In their concern to reach the public, journalists look for concrete, emotional anecdotes to make their stories accessible and compelling to an audience that is pretty close to scientifically illiterate. In television, where the emotional impact of pictures can be far more powerful than words, the availability of pictures often dictates the selection of anecdotes. This sometimes produce forceful but misleading stories. Consider the following two examples, the first provided by Holly Atkinson, a physician who is also an experienced television journalist:

It was... a story about antipsychotic drugs.... The reporter interviewed the parents of a young girl, I think she was about 7 years old, who developed not only a side-effect from the antipsychotic drug, but a permanent result from this side-effect. The chances of that [happening] are extremely small. What you saw was a 100-percent case of something that was probably only [a] .1 percent chance in reality. What happened was that people all over the United States taking antipsychotic drugs were extremely stressed by that piece. Now that is a problem, because if you have only got three minutes and you show one story, that story is 100 percent, and I do not care if the reporter says in there it is .1 percent, the viewer walks away with an emotional gestalt of 100 percent. I think that is a serious problem.[34]

Don Berreth, director of public affairs for the Centers for Disease Control, added this account:

Talking about anecdotes, I guess the thing that really brought that home to me was "20/20" several years ago did a follow-up story on a problem with an infant formula called Neo-Mull-Soy, which was, for "20/20," a reasonably straightforward account of the problem. But out of the 20 minutes or so that they devoted to it, about 20 seconds said that some parents believed that there may be long-term brain damage as a result of Neo-Mull-Soy, whereupon they showed a picture of a brain-damaged child—not from Neo-Mull-Soy, because there were no brain-damaged children from Neo-Mull-Soy.
At the end of the show, they did another thing that was even more irresponsible. They said, 'if you want more information about this, call the CDC,' and gave my number. Now we had thousands of calls and nearly every one was on that 20-second segment on brain damage.[35]

A specific case chosen to represent a general scientific proposition cannot possibly account for the range of qualifications, uncertainties, and exceptions that are characteristic of scientific findings; and the emotional elements, while involving the reader or viewer in the story, may cloud his or her understanding of the scientific facts. But an account that is qualified to the satisfaction of most scientists is likely to be soporific and therefore either ignored or misunderstood by most laypersons.

Realistically, these imperatives are going to remain in conflict. The truth is, science does not translate precisely into lay language. The best journalists in the field, however, popularize science with remarkable success. Their reports often zero in on the essence of the story, are readable, and do not significantly mislead the audience. Of course, reporters with the training and talent to perform at the high level of physician-journalists such as Lawrence K. Altman of *The New York Times*, Susan Okie of *The Washington Post*, and Timothy Johnson of ABC News, or experienced science and medical reporters such as David Perlman of *The San Francisco Chronicle* and Ruth SoRelle of *The Houston Chronicle* are still relatively few in number and limited mainly to the large metropolitan newspapers and television networks that can afford the luxury of specialization.

Reporters for small and medium-sized newspapers and local radio and television stations, few of whom have any special expertise in science and medicine, must cover everything from toxic spills to AIDS, radon in the basement, gaps in the ozone layer, and carcinogens in all their guises. They must contend with sources who rarely have the whole story and sometimes cannot or will not explain the health risks involved. There is enough spin on most health-risk stories to induce vertigo in all but the best-balanced reporters. Health-risk stories often contain all of the standard elements of other news stories, such as conflicting financial, political, personal, and social interests, but there is also the science, which is usually complex. Most general-assignment reporters have training or experience that qualifies them to deal with the nonscientific aspects of health-risk stories, but they are often at a loss when it comes to reporting on the science. They do not know what dose-response curves are, nor have they ever heard of mathematical exposure models or confidence limits. This inability to evaluate scientific information has nothing to do with lack of intelligence or scientific aptitude. It has to do with lack of education, training, and experience. In other words, it can be corrected.

A quick fix, however, is unlikely. Although there are now roughly 600 to 800 science and medical reporters in the United States, that is hardly enough to provide coverage for the almost 12,500 radio and television stations[36] and more than 1,650 daily newspapers. As a result, scientists and physicians who will talk to reporters and are adept at translating the science into lay language are in a strong position to influence media coverage and thereby public opinion and, ultimately, policy. Sometimes scientists such as Carl Sagan get so good at this that they become spokespersons on issues that fall well outside their areas of professional competence. For example, Sagan's views on nuclear winter, an area in which his expertise as an astronomer is not particularly helpful, have been widely covered by the media. The psychiatrist Robert Jay Lifton has been quoted in the press as saying that nuclear technology is "unsafe."[37] How does he know? What does he mean by it? And what qualifies him to render a judgment? Such statements are well attended to by the press not because they are authoritative but because they are expressed concisely, felicitously, and comprehensibly by celebrities with academic credentials, even if irrelevant ones. It stands to reason that the public would be better informed and less confused about health risks if reporters were knowledgeable enough to properly screen sources for the public and to characterize their expertise and biases, as well as to explain the assumptions and methods that underlie scientific findings. The Altmans and Okies, Philip Boffeys (*The New York Times*), Victor Cohns, and Cristine Russells (*The Washington Post*) can do this, and their stories are widely available through the news services of their respective papers. Moreover, the three networks have skillful science and medicine reporters—George Strait (ABC), Susan Spencer (CBS), and Robert Bazell (NBC)—whose stories (generally brief but accurate) are accessible to anyone with a television set. The wire services also have science and medicine reporters, as do the national news magazines. These specialized reporters have access to high-level science and policy sources, they have the facilities to keep extensive files, and they have access to substantial libraries and a number of on-line data bases. The newspaper reporters among them are often given adequate space in the paper to provide readers with sufficient information. It is therefore possible for anyone who cares to take the time and trouble to be reasonably well informed about health risks. But polls indicate that despite the fact that most people consider these issues to be very important, relatively few make the effort to become as informed as they might.

Sometimes, however, the press's influence is exerted in a relatively organized and thorough manner so that almost everyone is exposed to an issue, as in the case of AIDS coverage since mid-1985. Developments were being covered so thoroughly, in fact, that the columnist Charles Krauthammer argued in 1987 that the disease's impact on society was being blown out of proportion.[38] At the same time, the biologist Stephen Jay Gould wrote that Americans had underestimated the likely impact of AIDS.[39] Gould's view and that of Krauthammer, a nonpracticing physician, represented the reasonable bounds of the debate on the seriousness of AIDS as a societal problem. Both viewpoints deserved to be published prominently, as they have been. Only additional science can resolve a genuine scientific controversy, but people can keep up to date on what the experts are saying about AIDS by reading a good newspaper regularly. Since Rock Hudson's death from AIDS, the coverage in the best American papers has been "substantially complete."[40]

Few health-risk stories hold the attention of the press and the public for as long as the AIDS story has. Most, like cholesterol, dip in and out of the spotlight, and the pattern of coverage is much more dependent on events such as the publication of an article in an influential medical journal, a major press conference, or the report of a blue-ribbon panel.

A reporter for a major newspaper indicated the vagaries to which decisions about how to write a story that may influence the public policy debate on cholesterol are subjected. The reporter had been "saving string," newspaper jargon for collecting material for a story to be written later. He was on the verge of writing a story based on several interviews and recent studies. Its thrust would be either that some leading researchers were reporting that the threat of cholesterol at levels that were not wildly elevated was not nearly as great as the public had been led to believe, or that the preponderance of available evidence continued to show that elevated cholesterol levels constituted a major health risk. He was holding off because he was not sure what weight to give recent material challenging earlier findings on the dangers of cholesterol. He slept on it and wrote the story more or less in the form of a debate, but one in which, by his own guesstimate, he gave a 60–40 advantage to the position that the risk was not as great at minimally elevated levels as had been previously thought. Two weeks later, he could not remember precisely how he had arrived at that particular solution to his dilemma. He did say, however, that he had gone for a physical and had his cholesterol level checked. Did the article give a slight nudge to the policy debate because of its 60–40 tilt toward minimizing the risks of slightly elevated cholesterol levels? Reporting on health risks is rarely simple and straightforward. It requires considerable inventiveness on the part of journalists to convert sometimes mind-numbing, confusing material into compelling, readable stories. This alchemy can result in exaggeration of risks or of scientific progress, it can promote overemphasis of emotional or political elements of essentially technical or scientific stories, and it can result in inaccuracies and important omissions. Nevertheless, the rewards of transmuting base science into journalistic gold can be a powerful incentive for reporters and editors. The news sources who understand this best and use it most effectively are the ones who have the most impact on policy.

NOTES

1. "*Newsweek* on Campus," April 1987, p. 12.

2. Robert W. Crandall, "Fleeing the Love Canal," *Wilson Quarterly*, Autumn 1987, pp. 76, 77.

3. Aaron Wildavsky, "No Risk Is the Highest Risk of All," *American Scientist*, Vol. 67, January–February 1979, p. 36.

4. David B. McCallum and Elaine B. Arkin, "Risk Communication to the Public," Institute for Health Policy Analysis, Washington, D.C.

5. Polling data and experimental studies indicate some influence on attitudes and behavior.

6. Robert W. Crandall, "Learning the Lessons," *Wilson Quarterly*, Autumn 1987, p. 73.

7. Dale Hattis and David Kennedy, *Technology Review*, May–June 1986, p. 62.

8. Brian MacMahon, M.D., et al., "Coffee and Cancer of the Pancreas," *New England Journal of Medicine*, March 12, 1981, pp. 630–33.

9. Matt Clark with Phyllis Malamud, "Coffee—a Cancer Culprit?" *Newsweek*, March 23, 1981, p. 87. Emphasis added.

10. Victor Cohn, "Coffee, Harvard Scientists Find Link to Pancreatic Cancer," *Washington Post*, March 12, 1981, p. A9. Emphasis added.

11. Brian MacMahon et al., "Coffee and Pancreatic Cancer (Chapter 2)," *New England Journal of Medicine*, February 19, 1987, pp. 587–89.

12. A search of the Nexis data base revealed nothing.

13. Peggy Brown, "What's a Body to Believe," *Newsday*, August 25, 1985, p. 13.

14. Vincent Covello, "Risk Comparisons and Risk Communication: A Critical Assessment," unpublished draft.

15. David Hanson, "EPA Releases Guidelines for Risk Assessment of Chemicals," *Chemical and Engineering News*, September 15, 1986.

16. Edmund A. C. Crouch and Richard Wilson, *Risk/Benefit Analysis* (Cambridge, Mass.: Ballinger, 1982), p. 166.

17. Barbara Combs and Paul Slovic, *"The Register-Guard, The Standard-Times," The Journalist*, September 1984, p. 10.

18. National Safety Council, statistics on passenger death rate for automobile and airplane, 1980–1985.

19. Covello, "Risk Comparisons," p. 21.

20. Paul Slovic, Baruch Fischhoff, and Sarah Lichtenstein, "Facts versus Fears: Understanding Perceived Risk," *Judgment under Uncertainty: Heuristics and Biases,* Daniel Kahneman, Paul Slovic, and Amos Tversky, eds. (New York: Cambridge University Press, 1982).

21. William Lowrance, *Of Acceptable Risk* (Los Altos, Calif. William Kaufmann, 1976), p. 8.

22. Nuclear Regulatory Commission, "Safety Goals for the Operation of Nuclear Power Plants; Policy Statement," republication, *Federal Register*, Vol. 51, No. 162, August 21, 1986, pp. 30028–29.

23. Food and Drug Act of 1958, Public Law 85–929 (72 Stat. 1786).

24. National Research Council, *Improving Risk Communication* (Washington, D.C.: National Academy Press, 1989), p. 284.

25. Lowrance, *Of Acceptable Risk*, p. 87.

26. Workshop on the Role of Government in Health Risk Communication and Public Education, Alexandria, Va., January 1987.

27. Covello, "Risk Comparisons," pp. 18, 19.

28. Christopher F. Wilkinson, professor of insecticide chemistry and toxicology, Cornell University, interview, Ithaca, N.Y., February 11, 1987.

29. Hanson, "EPA Releases Guidelines," p. 19.

30. Wilkinson interview.

31. U.S. Department of Health and Human Services, Task Force on Health Risk Assessment, *Determining Risks to Health: Federal Policy and Practice* (Dover, Mass.: Auburn House, 1986), pp. 17–18.

32. Covello, "Risk Comparisons," pp. 18–19.

33. See, for example, the Report of the Public's Right to Information Task Force to the President's Commission on the Accident at Three Mile Island, October 31, 1979.

34. Stephen Klaidman, "Health Risk Reporting," Institute for Health Policy Analysis, 1986, pp. 7–8.

35. Ibid.

36. Federal Communications Commission. Numbers as of August 1, 1987.

37. Cal Turner, *Harrisburg News*, February 11, 1983, p. D3.

38. Charles Krauthammer, *Washington Post*, June 12, 1987, Section 1, p. 15.

39. Stephen Jay Gould, "The Terrifying Normalcy of AIDS," *New York Times Magazine*, April 19, 1987, p. 33.

40. A story can be considered substantially complete if it contains "enough information to satisfy the needs of an intelligent nonspecialist who wants to evaluate the situation" that is being reported on. This definition is taken from Stephen Klaidman and Tom L. Beauchamp, *The Virtuous Journalist* (New York: Oxford University Press, 1987), p. 35.

2

How EDB Spoiled
Bill Ruckelshaus's
Christmas

A T Christmastime in 1983, William Ruckelshaus was eight months into his second tour as head of the Environmental Protection Agency. His return to the agency was viewed by many career employees as the return of a true white knight of the bureaucracy. Ruckelshaus's record in the Nixon administration was widely admired, not only at EPA where in 1972 he banned all uses of DDT and implemented the Clean Water Act, but also at the Justice Department where he followed Attorney General Elliott Richardson's lead and resigned as deputy attorney general over President Nixon's order that he fire Watergate Special Prosecutor Archibald Cox. Ruckelshaus had responded to a call for help from President Reagan to rehabilitate EPA in the wake of a series of scandals involving the multibillion-dollar Superfund for toxic waste cleanup. These scandals culminated in the resignation of Ruckelshaus's predecessor as EPA administrator, Anne Gorsuch Burford. By late December, traditionally a quiet time in Washington, matters seemed sufficiently in hand so that he felt comfortable going to Florida to visit his mother.

Ruckelshaus had already succeeded in dramatically improving the

morale of the agency, and there were no obviously explosive problems
on the horizon. There was one issue, however, that would turn into a
long-term headache for EPA and its administrator: regulation of the
pesticide ethylene dibromide, better known as EDB. Ruckelshaus had
no recollection at all of EDB from his first term as head of the environmental agency, but he became aware of it as a possible source of
trouble even before officially succeeding Gorsuch in May. Shortly before taking office, Ruckelshaus and his longtime aide Philip Angell
went to New York to have lunch with CBS News anchorman Dan
Rather, one of a series of steps taken by Ruckelshaus to begin improving the soiled public image of his agency. (Another was the ini-
tiation of regular brown-bag lunches with the administrator for
reporters who covered EPA.) Toward the end of the lunch with Rather,
Angell recollected, the CBS anchorman asked what environmental
issues might develop into national news stories. "EDB," Angell said,
although he can no longer explain his prescience. When asked how
Rather responded, Angell said, "Just blank. It wasn't a public issue,"[1]
By the middle of 1984, however, when the EDB story had finally wound
down, its impact on the American public; U.S. trade with Japan, the
Soviet Union, and several Caribbean nations; interstate trade; several
federal and state agencies; and the personal lives of numerous individuals had been substantial, indeed in some cases devastating. This
useful but necessarily toxic substance, which Ruckelshaus couldn't
remember having heard of at the time, was destined to become the
source of one of the knottiest problems he had to deal with in his two
tours at EPA.

Ethylene dibromide is a clear, colorless, nonflammable petroleum-
based heavy liquid (at room temperature) with multiple uses. In 1983,
about 300 million pounds of it were being produced annually, of which
all but about 20 million pounds went into leaded gasoline as an anti-
knock agent. The other 20 million pounds were used for a variety of
agricultural purposes, but mainly for preplant fumigation by injection
into the soil to kill nematodes, or root worms, before they kill plants.
Citrus, pineapples, soybeans, tobacco, and about thirty other fruit,
vegetable, and nut crops were protected in this way. About 1 million
pounds a year were used for fumigation of stored grain and grain-
milling machinery to protect against insect infestation. Other uses
included quarantine fumigation of citrus fruit awaiting shipment in
interstate or international commerce, treatment of felled logs, termite
control, and fumigation of storage vaults and beehives.[2] EDB had been
in use in the United States since 1948, and it was popular because of

its versatility and its volatility, the latter term signifying not that it was explosive but that it dissipated quickly and was thought to leave no residue that might—in soil fumigation, for example—leach into groundwater. Indeed, in 1956 it had been granted an exemption from residue limitations by the Food and Drug Administration because of this property.

EDB's toxicity was first recognized in 1927, and by 1973 a number of studies indicated that it was mutagenic (capable of causing mutation) and caused reproductive damage in laboratory animals. It was the toxicity, of course, that made EDB an effective pesticide. There was insufficient evidence until 1974 to label it a potential carcinogen in either animals or humans. But that year, the National Cancer Institute issued a "memorandum of alert" warning that EDB was a potential carcinogen, and in 1975 the NCI issued a preliminary notice indicating that EDB induced cancer (squamous cell carcinomas of the stomach) in laboratory animals and should be considered a potential human carcinogen. In 1977, additional evidence confirmed that EDB posed risks of cancer, mutations, and adverse reproductive effects in animals.[3] How great were these risks to humans? To this day no one can satisfactorily answer that question, partly because of the uncertainty involved in extrapolating from animal results to humans and partly because of the unknowns and unpredictable variables that confound the models used to project risk. How great were the benefits of EDB? The answer to that question, too, though more susceptible to quantification than the health risk, is heavily dependent on one's perspective. A citrus grower or grain miller, for example, is likely to value the chemical's benefits more than a consumer with a family history of cancer. For policymakers such as Ruckelshaus, however, there are several obligations that both determine and circumscribe their actions. These include a duty to protect the public health, a legal obligation to weigh the social costs and benefits of using a particular chemical (disputed by the Natural Resources Defense Council in a current court case), and an EPA approach to carcinogens favoring a zero level for human exposure.

At a hearing of a House of Representatives subcommittee in 1984, Ruckelshaus explained the policymaker's dilemma. His explanation was both comprehensive and eloquent:

> As I see it, our primary mission is the reduction of risk to public health or the environment. Only rarely do we encounter an air or water pollutant, a waste product, a pesticide, or an industrial chemical which

poses such acute hazards that immediate action to eliminate all exposure is the necessary and obvious solution.

Far more often, EPA encounters the situation posed by EDB, in which evidence generated in laboratory studies of animals indicates that long-term exposure to the substance imposes increased risks of a chronic effect, such as cancer or adverse reproductive effects. It is then EPA's responsibility first to assess how dangerous the substance may be to people and, second, to decide how to manage that risk to achieve acceptable levels of protection for our society.

Cancer risk assessments pose their own special set of problems—first in conducting them, and second, in explaining them. To begin with, in animal tests for cancer, the doses given are extremely high, often close to the level the animals can tolerate for a lifetime without dying from non-cancer effects. Environmental exposures are typically much lower.

So in order to determine what the risk of cancer is at such low exposures, we must extrapolate down from the high-dose laboratory data. There are a number of statistical models for doing this. But choosing the "right model" and interpreting the results are the subject of frequent and vigorous debate. A critical part of this debate centers on how to estimate risks at the very low doses.

Next, we must deal not only with the uncertainty of extrapolating cancer data from animals to man, but also with uncertainty about exposure. We have to determine, usually on the basis of very scant data, and very elaborate mathematical models, how much chemical is being produced, how it is being dispersed, changed, or destroyed by natural processes and how the actual dose that people get is changed by behavioral or population characteristics.

Historically, EPA has thought it prudent to make conservative assumptions about risk; that is, we couch our conclusions in terms of a plausible upper bound. I think it is important to bear this in mind in looking at our risk numbers. This means that when we generate a number that expresses the probability or risk of a substance causing a disease, we know that the number is only an indicator of risk and not a hard prediction. We can, however, state, that it is very unlikely that the actual risk is greater than our estimate.

When risks estimated through such assessments are substantial, as with EDB, the stacking of conservative assumptions one on top of another becomes a problem for the policymakers. If I am going to propose controls that may have serious economic and social effects, I need to have some idea how much confidence should be placed in the estimates of risk that prompted these controls. I need to know what is likely to happen in the real world if I fully ban a substance, partially control it, or do nothing. Only then can I apply the balancing judgments that are the essence of my job.[4]

In December 1977, just six years before Ruckelshaus's Florida vacation, the EPA began a review of the risks and benefits of EDB under one of those ineptly named processes that give bureacracy a bad name. The process is known as *rebuttable presumption against registration.* It requires those favoring the use of a designated chemical to demonstrate that the substance is safe to use. Predictably, this took a long time. Moreover, it was only the evaluation stage, and it came a decade and a half after, in the words of Rep. Ted Weiss (D-N.Y.), "FDA, the agency principally responsible for monitoring for pesticide residues in edible food products, [knew] that significant amounts of EDB could persist in ready-to-eat foods. Despite this, FDA did not begin to sample for EDB residues in products such as bread and quarantine-fumigated citrus until several years after the National Cancer Institute had confirmed the extraordinarily potent carcinogenicity of EDB."[5] What Weiss did not say was that at the levels to which humans were being exposed to the pesticide, no one knew whether it was carcinogenic at all.

By December 1980, three years after the process began, Jimmy Carter's EPA recommended the cancellation of EDB use on stored grain, milling machinery, and timber and a phase-out on its use as a quarantine fumigant over roughly two years. But nothing happened. The recommendation for soil fumigation, the principal agricultural use of EDB, was that it be continued with certain limitations because there was no firm evidence that it leached into groundwater thereby resulting in significant human exposure.

The agency's recommendation pleased neither the agricultural industry nor the manufacturers of the pesticide. These interests knew, however, that they were likely to get a more sympathetic hearing from the incoming Reagan administration. The president's new EPA chief, Anne Burford, appointed Dr. John Todhunter, a toxicologist who had been a professor of biology at the Catholic University of America and a member of Maryland's Hazardous Waste Facilities Siting Board, to head the Office of Pesticides and Toxic Substances, where he inherited the responsibility for EDB. Todhunter resigned shortly after Burford did over the Superfund controversy. There is widespread agreement inside EPA that under Todhunter action to ban or limit the uses of EDB stalled. For one thing, he slashed the staff of the office that reviewed chemicals such as EDB from 128 employes to about 20.[6] And according to Todhunter's subordinate, Dr. Edwin L. Johnson, head of EPA's Office of Pesticide Programs, in June 1982 Todhunter ordered a new EDB risk assessment to be completely recomputed to

correct what Johnson said were "unimportant" technical errors. Johnson also said that Todhunter met frequently with citrus industry representatives and pro-EDB members of Congress such as senators Paula
Hawkins (R-Fla.) and Lawton Chiles (D-Fla.), and that although he
was in office only fourteen months, he effectively stalled the EDB ban
for eighteen months to two years.[7] Moreover, "Todhunter unaccount-
ably requested the SAP [the agency's independent Scientific Advisory
Panel] to review the EDB regulatory package again in 1983," although
a review had been completed in 1981.[8]

   This, then, was the situation with respect to EDB that Ruckelshaus
had to contend with when he rejoined the agency. Residues of the
pesticide had turned up in groundwater in Georgia in March 1982.
And shortly after he arrived, residues were found in groundwater in
California, where a monitoring program had been in effect since 1980
when tests suggested that EDB could leach into groundwater. But
these findings had attracted little or no national press coverage and
were not a high priority for the administrator of a vast federal agency
with a multitude of concerns. Likewise, the dispute within EPA between Todhunter and career employees such as Richard Johnson, who
headed the EDB task force, and Edwin Johnson, who ran the Office
of Pesticide Programs, had attracted little outside attention except from
the interested industries and federal agencies and a handful of environmental groups such as the Audubon Society and the Natural Resources Defense Council. As far as the national media were concerned,
the issue simply was not news.

   The discovery of EDB in groundwater was considered significant
by those in EPA who were responsible for dealing with it. It changed
the risk-benefit equation because it provided another route of human
exposure. When the Georgia contamination was discovered, EPA and
the U.S. Geological Survey conducted an investigation; but the two
agencies could not determine whether the groundwater contamination
resulted from soil fumigation or from leaking fuel storage tanks. More
than 90 percent of the EDB produced in the United States, after all,
was used as a gasoline additive, and much of that gasoline was stored
in underground tanks. The discovery in June 1983 of contaminated
groundwater in areas of California where the soil had been fumigated
led to stopping EDB use in four counties. Shortly thereafter, wells in
Hawaii and Florida were also found to be contaminated. The California
finding and the subsequent discoveries in these two other agricultural
states made it sufficiently clear that soil fumigation was responsible
for the groundwater contamination, so that by September 30, EPA

ordered an immediate nationwide suspension of the soil fumigation use of EDB. A suspension is the strictest action EPA can take. Sale and distribution of EDB were halted immediately. There is an appeal process that can take years to complete, but use of the product is prohibited during the appeal.[9]

The Florida Story

It may be that if groundwater contamination had been discovered only in Georgia, California, and Hawaii, the story of EDB would have unfolded quietly outside the glare of publicity. But it was also found in Florida groundwater, and that discovery was to make a significant difference for Ruckelshaus, the EPA, farmers, food manufacturers, the national media, and ultimately just about everyone in the United States. Why was Florida different? The answer to that question may hinge in part on the craftiness of a state politician, although that suspicion, which is widely held by the EPA officials who dealt with the Florida EDB situation, remains unproved. What seems beyond challenge, however, is that some combination of Florida officials and the state press, working in the odd relationship of adversity and dependency that characterizes the government-media symbiosis, raised the issue to one of national concern.

While Ruckelshaus was visiting his mother in Florida over Christmas, Angell was also spending his holiday in the sun visiting family in California. He recalls:

It really began around Christmastime where I used to carry a portable computer with me. And we had an electronic clipping service at EPA that I used to sign on to every morning.... You just saw this rash of stories beginning in Florida, wire stories, concern about EDB in foodstuff, pulling food off shelves, statements from the state officials down there about their concern with threat to public health because of EDB in food.... I was obviously in close contact with the Washington office, and the man who ran the press office for us was telling me that he was getting a lot of inquiries about this.[10]

Meanwhile, in Florida, Ruckelshaus was watching the EDB story unfold on local television and the network news:

I was watching it on television and seeing the kind of potential public panic... that could result.... The focus was on the supermarket itself and people coming in and hauling this cake mix and other things off the shelf, which needless to say is not reassuring to the public. . . . It seemed to me at least to have the potential for creating widespread public panic because there was always a kind of open-ended question at the end of the story of how much more of this material is on the shelves that we don't know about. If it's in Aunt Jemima cake mix, how do we know it isn't in every other cake mix? Now what effect that had on the average viewer, I don't know. But it was clear to me that we had a serious problem. If not a public-health problem, then a public-relations problem.[11]

The extent to which EDB constituted a public-health problem remains in dispute. The extent to which it was a public-relations problem does not; nor does the importance assigned to the media by Angell (witness his traveling electronic clipping service that even accompanied him on his Christmas holiday) and Ruckelshaus. To explain how EDB got to be a public-relations problem, which is to say a media problem for EPA, requires a review of what happened in Florida from the summer of 1983 when EDB was first found in drinking water to late December when it was found in grain-based products and hauled off supermarket shelves in front of television cameras.

The discovery of EDB in California groundwater in June 1983 was reported in various newspapers and came to the attention of Florida officials, who concluded that if the chemical was in California's drinking water supply it might well be in Florida's. The reasons for this were not obscure. State officials had known since the end of 1980 that EDB might be able to leach into groundwater; large amounts of the pesticide were injected into the soil to kill root worms in citrus groves, on golf courses, and elsewhere; and Florida was almost entirely dependent on groundwater for its drinking-water supply. George Fong, who ran a testing laboratory for the state Department of Agriculture, remembers beginning testing and finding positive samples in early July 1983. Fong said the first tests were conducted around citrus groves where EDB had been injected into the soil to prevent the spread of the root worms from infested to uninfested areas.[12] In fact, tests begun on July 5 turned up traces of EDB in a 125-foot-deep well 125 feet from a buffer zone at a commercial citrus grove in Lake County. Samples taken between July 5 and July 13 showed levels between 5 and 7 parts per billion in the water. At the time, no federal or state standard existed for EDB in drinking water. Samples from a second Lake County well also appeared positive, according to a press release issued by the Florida Department of Agriculture and Consumer Services on July 21. The department's press release attracted almost no attention, however.

The state agriculture agency had been injecting EDB into barrier zones for citrus growers for decades to control the microscopic worms that if left uncontained could devastate Florida's billion-dollar citrus industry. The specter of losing the use of the pesticide, with no certain substitute on the horizon, was not pleasant for growers to contemplate. And in 1983 it was especially unpleasant, because productivity had been low, and Brazil and other countries were underselling Florida producers. Moreover, there had been a bad freeze that spring, further endangering industry profits.[13]

The man who had been responsible for the EDB barrier zone program for almost twenty years at the time was the commissioner of agriculture, Doyle Conner, a considerable force in Florida politics who was speaker of the Florida House of Representatives at the age of 28 and has a boulevard in the state capital named after him. Conner is a man of generally serious demeanor, but with a politician's gift for spinning a yarn and turning a melodramatic phrase. In an interview five years after the EDB affair first became perceptible as a burgeoning problem for Conner, he said, "Even though ... it was scientifically, professionally prescribed by responsible agencies, all of a sudden I was the guy with a pitchfork and horns, pouring poison in drinking water."[14]

The fact is, Conner acted quickly to test Florida drinking water once there appeared to be a reason to do so, and on September 16 he suspended the injection of EDB into barrier zones between citrus groves, the use that was the likely cause of contamination. This was just three and a half weeks after the discovery of traces of the chemical in a Lake County well. He also asked the state health officer, Dr. Stephen H. King, to recommend tolerance levels for EDB in drinking water in the absence of a federal standard. In a letter dated September 15, King recommended that the level be set at 1 part per billion (1 ppb), which was the smallest amount of EDB that could be detected with existing technology.[15] At this stage, the Florida media reported Conner's suspension action in a straightforward fashion with little comment. King's recommendation of a 1 ppb tolerance level for EDB in groundwater was not reported at all.

Within the state bureaucracy, however, there was reason to believe that trouble could be on the way, especially if the press began investigating the Agriculture Department's role as a contractor to the citrus industry. According to a chronology dated August 31, 1983, that was prepared for King, "For many years FDACS [Florida Department of Agriculture and Consumer Services] ... had been treating buffer zones around nematode infested groves with EDB at high rates of application (50 g/acre)."[16] What the chronology did not say, but everyone involved knew, was that those "high rates" were greater than labels placed on EDB containers by the federal government allowed.

In a report from Washington on September 27, Victoria Churchville, a young reporter for the *Orlando Sentinel* who had been following the EDB story from the start, wrote that "Federal officials are investigating whether Florida illegally used EDB in its chemical war against rootworms." Churchville's article, which appeared on page 1 of the *Sentinel*, went on to say:

> Stuart Cohen, a chemist with the EPA pesticides programs office, said Florida's sandy porous soil and "the method of application in the Central Florida ridge," the core of the state's citrus groves, had caused unprecedented pollution.
>
> "My initial reading is that the state use is not legal," Cohen said.
>
> Florida Agricultural Commissioner Doyle Conner said ... "I don't know anything about it being illegal but nothing is a shock to me anymore."
>
> Since the early 1960s the Florida Department of Agriculture and Consumer Services has been injecting 10 times more than the federally approved dose into 422 "barrier zone" acres around groves. State and federal officials believe that these megadoses are largely responsible for contaminating the drinking water supplies of an estimated 10,000 Floridians.[17]

By November 6, Churchville was reporting that

> Florida agriculture officials applied massive doses of a cancer-causing pesticide to 10 times more land [4,268 acres] in the state's citrus midsection than they first reported. ... Viewed together, the new information and missing facts highlight what one state health official called "an invisible threat" far greater than the widespread water contamination uncovered since July, when Florida began the most extensive effort to test drinking water for pesticides in state history.[18]

EDB had already been found in four city water systems and hundreds of wells. And the 4,268 acres treated with large doses of EDB as citrus buffer zones were only part of the rapidly emerging problem. The chemical was also being used to protect peanut and

soybean crops and to kill mole crickets on golf courses. Maggy Hur-
challa, a Martin County commissioner, said, "There are more golf
courses than new farms springing up in the state. In South Florida
there are over 150."[19] According to Churchville's November 6 article,
the fact that Florida was the only state with a large-scale problem
involving EDB in drinking water had been linked to "the Agriculture
Department's frequent and high-volume use of the pesticide." Churchville wrote in the *Sentinel*:

> EPA is investigating whether that use violated a federal environmental
> law that has regulated pesticides since 1972. Before that misusing pes-
> ticides did not violate any federal or state laws.
>   The federal label states that only 15 gallons of an 83 percent EDB
> formula may be applied in groves or orchards once before trees are
> planted, never where there are mature trees. The state Agriculture De-
> partment says it used higher, more frequent doses on the recommen-
> dation of the U.S. Department of Agriculture.
>   "Based on what we know, the evidence points toward the conclusion
> that the state of Florida overused the product," said Frank Wheeler, a
> spokesman for Great Lakes Chemical Co., one of the nation's four EDB
> producers.
>   "There's literally been hundreds and hundreds of wells tested outside
> the state of Florida and only a handful have shown EDB. Most of the
> handful is due to improper use, such as spills."
>   ... Like moats around castles, barrier zones were dug near citrus
> groves to protect the trees from nematodes. First, 50 gallons of EDB per
> acre were injected into the soil. Every six months, half that amount was
> applied to the barrier zone for as long as it was active....
>   In a second state-run program, only one massive dose of EDB was
> used but thousands of acres were treated.[20]

In the spring of 1988, Conner was somewhat vague about why his
department had failed to follow the instructions on the federal label.
He suggested that there might have been some confusion between
standards for the "broadcast" and "barrier" uses of the chemical, but
EDB was never applied to citrus groves by the broadcast (spraying)
method. He did not say specifically that the U.S. Department of Agriculture had recommended the doses used in the buffer zones, but
rather suggested that "federal and land-grant college people ... the
Department of Agriculture ... assist[ed] our people in establishing" the
amounts of EDB applied.[21]

With these new discoveries about the "misuse" of EDB by the state
Department of Agriculture, the EDB affair was taking a distinctly

unpleasant turn from Conner's perspective. "Where we were involved in the instance of citrus," Conner said, "we were accused... of misuse—and that's pretty damaging... and then you get down to the political part of it and saying, 'Doyle Conner misused pesticides,' and when it gets that personal, then you begin to think perhaps it is political to some extent."[22] According to King, "It was a very critical issue for Florida politics. People feel very sensitive about their water."[23]

By mid-November, EDB politics had burst into the open. "Big" Sid Martin, a conservative Democrat like Conner who was perhaps best known for showing up on the floor of the House in "a tent-sized orange sport coat" to boost his alma mater, the University of Florida, sharply criticized the agriculture commissioner for his handling of the EDB issue. A *St. Petersburg Times* account, quoting Martin, said:

> "[A]ny prudent man" would have tested for groundwater contamination earlier, since Agriculture officials applying EDB to the soil were using more than twice the dosage recommended on the product label. But "he didn't have the common sense."
>
> "Doyle Conner, with state employees, put out... this stuff.... He has done a great harm to the people of Florida by polluting their water."
>
> Now that EDB contamination has been found in at least 238 Florida wells, which need to be cleaned up, Conner wants to "run away from it... where he can hide." It's time for Conner to "start telling the truth ... quit hiding and start helping these poor people."[24]

Martin's accusations about Conner were sharp, and his feelings surfaced again during an exchange in a House hearing among him, Rep. Chuck Smith, and Roy G. Davis of the Florida Nurserymen and Growers Association. The discussion was about setting tolerance levels for EDB. Smith questioned the validity of a 7 ppb level, and Martin asked him if he would drink water containing that level of EDB. Smith replied, "I've seen nothing to establish any link to cancer. Certainly I'd drink the water." Later, Martin recognized Davis, who said that he, too, would drink the water, to which Martin replied; "If you want to drink that water, you go ahead. I hope you get cancer from it."[25]

By this time EDB had become a major environmental and political story in Florida, and Conner's contention that he was being portrayed as "the guy with a pitchfork and horns" was approaching the truth. The story was getting almost daily coverage in the print press and on television, and Conner was facing the greatest challenge of his long political career. A possible solution to his problem was to get the spotlight off drinking water. One way to do that was to shift the focus to food, especially grain-based products for which Conner and his agency could bear no responsibility because Florida was not a grain-producing state. It is here that the story becomes a bit murky. There is no conclusive evidence that Conner contrived to divert the press's (and thereby the public's) attention to grain products, but the logic of such a strategy is sufficiently compelling so that virtually every EPA official interviewed for this chapter speculated or passed on as rumor the suggestion that he had done so.

Vincent Giglio, director of the Division of Inspection under Conner, said "the commissioner felt that we should be looking at the food products. And I think 90-some samples were collected initially, of which all of them [were] nondetects except two. And both of them were grain products. And when the commissioner was apprised of this, he suggested—or directed, rather—that we look at food products in the marketplace, which we did."[26] Looking at food products in the marketplace, which is to say on the supermarket shelf, was to be the action that triggered wide national press coverage of the EDB situation and finally forced the EPA to act. Before products were dramatically pulled from the shelves in front of TV cameras, though, George Fong's Agriculture Department laboratory quietly tested processed grain and products derived from animals that might have ingested EDB-treated grain. It did not test products made from fruit grown in Florida. Fong said that "during the first week of December, 1983, residues in excess of 1.0 ppb were found in 14 samples, ranging from 1.05 to 75.10 ppb of EDB." Since EDB was exempted from federal tolerance requirements, Fong said, Florida was obliged to set its own standard for acceptable levels of the pesticide in both food and water.[27]

The fact that the Agriculture Department was testing food "was kept very quiet," King said. "George himself was going down to the grocery store and buying stuff and bringing it back and really kind of running it himself."[28] While Fong's food-testing program was being carried out without any publicity, Conner and his agency were coming under increasing pressure because of water contamination. When asked in an interview about the role of the press at this point, King said:

I'm very confident that the press became particularly important [during this period]. And Victoria [Churchville] was the main person at that time. Victoria was on us like a duck on a bug.... If I wasn't in my office, she'd immediately find out where Commissioner Conner was. And if we were both in the same place she would go there and catch us.... I'd come

home and my wife would say Victoria called. And she called Conner.
She teased him about his polyester suits.... You talk about the impact
of the press, he began to wear tweed coats with leather patches as a
result of Victoria.... She struck a chord in a bunch of 40-year-old-plus
guys. And she had a way of making us feel good.[29]

    Churchville might have made them feel good personally, but at the
same time, she and her colleagues in the Florida press corps were
putting their feet to the fire. For example, on September 19, the *St.
Petersburg Times* had this to say in an editorial about Conner's sixty-
day suspension of EDB as a soil fumigant: "Late may be better than
never, but simply stopping the use of EDB will not cancel its festering
legacy of pollution." Moreover, the *St. Petersburg Times* editorial cited
a report by Churchville noting that laboratory animals had developed
cancer just fifteen days after inhaling EDB.[30] A few days later, Churchville made it into *The New York Times* with an unsigned article from
Orlando headlined "Pesticide Inaction Prompts Inquiry." This story
about an upcoming congressional investigation of EDB use was important partly because it was in the *Times*, an agenda setter for national
television and other national publications, but also because Churchville
wrote about EDB as a food contaminant. In particular, she cited EPA
tests in 1980 showing that EDB-tainted bread was being served to
children in the federal school-lunch program. In the *Times* article she
also quoted L. Vernon White, director of research and government
relations for the Great Lakes Chemical Company, the leading producer
of EDB for agricultural purposes, as saying that his company would
"not defend the huge amunts used in Florida in citrus grove barrier
zones or its use as a post-harvest fumigant to stop fruit fly infestation."[31]
Conner had been publicly abandoned by the company that had the
most to gain from the continued use of EDB.
    Conner's sixty-day ban on the soil-fumigant use of EDB received
scant coverage in the national media. *The New York Times* buried it
in the middle of a September 18 news roundup on page 20. The story
was five paragraphs long, and half of it was devoted to the lifting, with
restrictions, of the suspension on another pesticide with the trade name
Temik. By mid-November, Churchville had written her long article in
the *Sentinel* charging that ten times as much acreage had been over-
treated with EDB as the state had said, and John Harwood's article
with Sid Martin's scathing criticisms of Conner had appeared in the
St. Petersburg Times. EPA had also announced immediate suspension

of the pesticide as a soil fumigant and its cancellation or phase-out for most other uses. The pressure on Conner was mounting daily.

On December 9, however, the focus shifted abruptly. Vincent Giglio, Conner's director of inspections, announced to the press that EDB had been detected in packaged grits, cornmeal, and hush puppy mix, and the Grocery Manufacturers of America filed suit against Florida in an effort to prevent the state from banning the sale of food containing detectible amounts of EDB. Giglio said that the level of EDB found in thirteen commercial food products was not dangerous since 80 percent of it would dissipate during cooking. "But it's there, and we don't want it in there.... I wouldn't make a diet of it now.... I'd take it back to the store where I'd bought it."[32] Within two weeks the list of tainted products included those manufactured by giant national food corporations such as Pillsbury, General Mills, Procter and Gamble, and Quaker Oats.

Shifting the focus on EDB from drinking water to food turned it from a local story in a handful of states into a major national story, diverting Floridians' attention away from their drinking water problem in the process. The reason for that was simple. The "cancer-causing pesticide," as it was often labeled without qualification in news stories, was turning up in products that were widely sold in every supermarket in America. EDB had become everybody's problem, and everybody was on the verge of knowing about it as it hit the networks' evening newscasts and the front pages of leading newspapers. By now, it was fast becoming William Ruckelshaus's number one problem.

EPA Responds

For years EDB had been one of a dozen or more chemicals representing a source of concern for EPA career staffers such as Edwin L. Johnson, who ran the Office of Pesticide Programs, and Richard Johnson, who led the EDB team at EPA. Both men had believed for years that EDB was a "bad actor" that should be removed from the food chain, and both had done battle with Dr. John Todhunter, the Reagan administration official who kept putting roadblocks in front of a suspension or cancellation of use of the product. At the end of September 1983, their view that something had to be done finally prevailed with EPA's order to suspend, cancel, or phase out most uses of the pesticide. This action resulted from a combination of factors including press reports from

Florida about EDB in drinking water and the results of EPA's joint study with California, which showed "contamination [of groundwater] with EDB . . . and a couple of other things that were beginning to suggest that the chemical would likely survive as a constituent in groundwater for some time."[33]

The September 30 EPA action received national coverage on the networks, the "MacNeil-Lehrer News Hour," and the national newspapers. It was bracketed for a day or two before and after with news stories. But then it dropped off the national screen until EDB was found in food in Florida.

During that month, two other television news programs had been devoted to EDB. One was a sixteen-minute segment on a short-lived NBC magazine-format program called "First Camera," and the other was on WDVM-TV, CBS's affiliate in Washington. The WDVM segment aired on September 12 on the station's 11:00 P.M. news program called "Nightcast." It was titled "EDB: The Hidden Hazard," the reporter was Ellen Kingsley, and it was billed as the result of a two-month investigation. EDB was identified in the voice-over as "one of the most potentially hazardous pesticides known to man," with pictures of schoolchildren eating sandwiches in the background. The piece went on to detail laboratory data on the carcinogenic, mutagenic, and teratogenic (birth-defect-inducing) qualities of the chemical, and it presented spokespersons for the EPA, the agriculture industry, and the environmental movement. Al Myerhoff, a San Francisco-based staff attorney for the Natural Resources Defense Council, talked provocatively about "time bombs in our food" and called EPA's handling of the EDB matter "a classic case in malfeasance," while Jack Burkhalter, a representative of Cargill, the giant grain company, droned on about productivity. This confrontation was typical of those on television between Myerhoff, who was articulate, well prepared, and absolutely clear in his presentation, and the various spokespersons for industry and the EPA. Against Myerhoff's polished performance, which was especially disarming because of his relaxed appearance, EPA and industry spokespersons often seemed inept.

All of this was interesting but probably would have been quickly forgotten even though it was aired in the nation's capital. WDVM went a step further in this program, however. The station had hired American Medical Laboratories of Fairfax, Virginia, to test food for EDB, and of sixteen grocery samples tested half were found to contain EDB at levels ranging from 2 to 16 ppb. Apparently as a result of the Ellen

Kingsley report on WDVM, the Food and Drug Administration began testing "on-the-shelf grain products" for EDB.[34]

No such result can be attributed to the "First Camera" piece on NBC, which was introduced by anchorman Lloyd Dobyns and reported by correspondent Mark Nykanen on September 25. But if there came to be something approaching general panic among the public, as William Ruckelshaus believed at the time, or if, as Harold Sharlin wrote, "The situation in regard to EDB on national television. . . . was that of being a 'typhoid Mary' of sorts and spreading the contagion of public anxiety,"[35] then the "First Camera" segment is a classic example of how fear can be spread by television. Dobyns introduced the piece by saying:

> Given to laboratory rats in normal doses, EDB does not cause them to get cancer: it causes them to drop dead instantly. Correspondent Mark Nykanen says that EDB can be found in some drinking water, some fruit and flour for the school lunch program. And the Environmental Protection Agency knew all that; it just didn't tell you.
>
> There is poison in paradise. Where Kilauea erupts and flowers are bathed in the gentle mist of the tropics, a deadly pesticide has seeped into the earth and poisoned drinking water; it cannot be seen, it cannot be tasted. The pesticide is ethylene dibromide—EDB. It has poisoned drinking water in Hawaii and on the mainland 2,500 miles away.
>
> EDB also has become a danger in the workplace. Almost a year ago today, EDB killed two workers at this chemical plant near Bakersfield, California. Robert Harris and James Harris (no relation) died gruesome deaths after they were exposed to a fraction of an ounce of EDB in this tank. As Robert Harris was rushed to a hospital, paramedics stripped James Harris to his underwear and hosed him down with water to try to save his life. He died seventy two hours later.
>
> In Superior, Wisconsin, Bob Kauther suffers from severe nerve damage. He spent twelve years using EDB and other pesticides on grain. Kauther's nerve damage is so bad he can't even sign his name.
>
> *Bob Kauther* [appears onscreen and says]: "I have a lot of blurred vision. A lot of head pressure. Boiling blood, where I have to get up at two, three, or four in the morning and take a cold shower and try to get back to sleep."

Nykanen's voice over James Harris being hosed down in his underwear and Bob Kauther trying to give an interview while shaking uncontrollably were made for television. They had the drama of theater, or at least of the kind of soap opera that consistently wins high ratings and large audience shares. But what about the relationship of these images to the broader truth about EDB? Or their relevance as news? Or the fear they must have produced in viewers? The two Harrises, who worked with large quantities of EDB, died from massive doses of the chemical compared to what an ordinary individual would encounter over a seventy-year lifetime of exposure (let alone a single dose) through food and drinking water, even in central Florida. And Kauther worked with many pesticides. There was no evidence at all that EDB even played a role in his nerve damage. Just moments before, however, Dobyns had referred to rats dropping dead from exposure to "normal" doses of EDB. What did he mean by normal? A viewer could surely be forgiven for thinking that the amount to which he might be exposed by eating a stack of Aunt Jemima pancakes was a normal dose.

After inaccurately but effectively presenting EDB as more like a nuclear warhead than a time bomb in the nation's food and water supply, Nykanen proceeded to characterize EPA's Edwin Johnson as an apologist for an evil agency and product in an interview edited down to just the right set of sound bites, as discrete segments of TV or radio matter are called in the trade. Then "First Camera" went on to say that a laboratory had found "significant amounts of EDB" in commercial food products and that "government scientists say that long-term exposure to even small amounts of EDB in any food can cause cancer and other diseases." Ellen Haas, executive director of an organization called Public Voice, then tells us that "the situation in baby food is really too sad to imagine," a well is identified as having "very high levels of EDB," the piece returns to Bob Kauther and another worker injured on the job, and it ends with a blast at EPA and the Occupational Safety and Health Administration. Interspersed throughout are brief comments by public officials ineffectually trying to explain the government's actions.

The discovery of EDB in nationally sold food products provided what Harold Sharlin has called the "microrisk" news peg It allowed reporters to personalize the story for the public at large, suggesting, as in the "First Camera" segment but for a far larger audience, that everyone was at risk. If "First Camera" did not reach a mass audience, it did reach an important audience of one. Robert Hager, who covered the environment for NBC, saw the segment on EDB and said later, "I thought to myself that Nykanen's piece was a little overdone, but nonetheless, I thought that he was on the right track there."[36]

Hager's first piece on the nightly news drew heavily on Nykanen's "First Camera" segment. It aired four days later on September 29, opening with Nykanen's footage of James Harris (misidentifying him as Robert Harris) being hosed down in his underwear and Bob Kauther shaking, then citing a House subcommittee charge of "inordinate delay" in banning EDB, and finally getting to the news, which was that "Tomorrow, Environmental Protection Agency administrator William Ruckelshaus will announce an immediate suspension of the most widespread use of the pesticide, and start proceedings that could lead to a ban of other uses." The same evening, Bettina Gregory on ABC focused her piece on EPA's long delay in banning EDB.

During October, November, and the first three weeks of December, EDB dropped out of network news coverage. But Between December 21 and December 23, all three networks carried pieces on EDB in food on their nightly news broadcasts. On the 21st, NBC anchorman Tom Brokaw posed the portentous question, "How dangerous is it?" The question was left dangling in the air, unanswered, because in the most relevant sense it was unanswerable. No one could tell viewers for certain whether or not they should avoid eating the Duncan Hines muffins or the Pillsbury cakes that contained X parts per billion of EDB.

The network news broadcasts of December 21 to December 23 established EDB as a national story of the first magnitude. These were the broadcasts that showed food being removed from the supermarket shelves. Hager's report featured the Florida state health officer, Dr. Stephen King, who stressed the national implications of the EDB story: "This problem is not a Florida specific problem. Most of the grain and flour and cornmeal products have found their way into the state from outside the state."[37]

On ABC the same night, Mark Potter said that according to Florida officials one part per billion of EDB is unsafe, and Hager quoted Richard Johnson of EPA saying, "There are no studies that indicate that ethylene dibromide is safe at any level."

At the same time, Doyle Conner, whose actions were pivotal in turning EDB into a national news story, wrote to Ruckelshaus "to formally bring to your attention the problems that we in Florida have found regarding ethylene dibromide." Conner noted that on December 9, Florida had "announced a stop-sale on grain products containing more than one part per billion of EDB" and said, "Our representatives are ready to meet with you to discuss this issue at your earliest convenience."[38] That meeting was held exactly a week after the date of Conner's letter to Ruckelshaus. According to King: "The State of Florida visited with the Office of Pesticides and their staff on the 29th of

December [and] we went over our concerns here in Washington. They were very receptive and we discussed at length our findings and our concerns and the need, the almost desperate need, for the cessation of its use at the source, and I think that the response is self-evident."[39]

The Florida delegation did not arrive alone for the December 29 meeting with EPA's EDB team in an eleventh-floor conference room at the agency's Crystal City, Virginia, facility. They were accompanied by "a couple of TV cameramen," according to Edwin Johnson. "We originally thought this was just going to be a meeting between state regulatory officials and us. . . . They took some shots at the beginning of the meeting. And then they hung around. And then they set up their cameras and interviewed a couple of people at the end of the meeting."[40]

EPA began concentrating on EDB at the highest level as soon as Ruckelshaus and Angell returned from their Christmas holidays According to Angell:

> . . . the first day back we convened one of those sort of task-force meetings in the administrator's office. And that became a ritual for the month of January. That's when the urgency really set in, where we'd have these almost interminable meetings where we began reviewing the risk information, reviewing the amount of data we had, realizing that we needed more data very quickly, realizing that we needed to reach out to a lot of different people very quickly. And at that point realizing the impact the press was having on this situation. . . . The risks from EDB are chronic risks.
>
> They're not acute risks. . . . That is an almost impossible message to get across if at the same time what you are seeing on television is somebody pulling cake mix off the shelf as if it contained rat poison which would cause you to keel over if you ingested it.[41]

Under Pressure

Under this kind of pressure, EPA issued a press release on January 5 saying that it was taking new steps to deal with the reported contamination of raw and processed agricultural products. The release said that the agency would decide "as soon as possible" whether to issue an emergency suspension of EDB as a fumigant for grain and milling machinery, as it had in September for soil fumigation; that the agency was "initiating the process of revoking" the 1956 FDA exemption that prevented EPA from setting tolerance levels for EDB; and that EPA would continue "on an accelerated basis" to determine appropriate guidelines for EDB residue levels in food.

Ruckelshaus recalls that on January 10, "I went over to the Agriculture Department without fully appreciating who was going to be there or the public visibility that was going to be given to the meeting."[42] As he went into the meeting, Ruckelshaus saw that reporters flanked Jack Moore, the EPA's assistant administrator in charge of pesticides, and his colleagues. Cass Peterson and Paul Taylor covered the meeting for *The Washington Post*. Their lead paragraph said: "Senior administration and food-industry officials held an emergency meeting yesterday on ethylene dibromide (EDB), a cancer-causing pesticide that has been found in more than 100 products on grocery shelves and may have tainted nearly all the nation's 7.7-billion-bushel grain stockpile."[43]

Ruckelshaus had expected to meet with grocery industry and farm representatives in front of whom he would have to defend the restrictiveness of his September 30 action on EDB. Instead, he was confronted as well by "a group of state agriculture and health officials saying, 'Don't just sit there, do something.' " Ruckelshaus continued: "The action that had already been taken by Florida, Texas, and Massachusetts . . . was triggering a wave of panic that was liable to sweep the country . . . and if we didn't preempt the field from these guys by taking very strong, forceful action, they wouldn't be able to resist the public pressure to do something themselves."[44]

At the time of the meeting at the Agriculture Department, Florida had set a standard of 1ppb of EDB, Massachusetts had set a level of 10 ppb that was scheduled to drop to 1 ppb in a month, and Texas agriculture commissioner Jim Hightower was locked in a battle with the state's health officer, Dr. Robert Bernstein, over where the level should be set. Unlike his counterpart in Florida, however, Bernstein said he did not believe 1 ppb, the detectable level, made sense. He was arguing for a higher level than Hightower. Bernstein said he did not believe that the health risk posed by somewhat higher levels that would persist in the food chain for a couple of years warranted the economic costs of setting the limit for EDB residues at the lowest detectable level.[45]

There was substantial pressure on Ruckelshaus to set federal guidelines so that there would be an orderly system that food producers could deal with and the burden on state health and agriculture officials would be eased, but he was also facing other kinds of pressure. The Soviet Union was beginning to inquire about the safety of U.S. grain.

Moscow had agreed to buy 7.1 million tons of U.S. wheat and corn in fiscal year 1984, of which 3.7 million tons had already been shipped. Efforts to provide economic aid by importing tropical fruit from several Caribbean nations could have been compromised by an EDB ban because Department of Agriculture import regulations could not be met without use of the pesticide by these countries. OMB and the White House both called Governor Robert Graham on the same day and urged him to stop Florida from setting 1 ppb limits on EDB for fear that it would lead to a similar federal standard and ruin President Reagan's Caribbean initiative. Most of all, however, the economic cost of a broadly based ban on the pesticide could be high. *The Washington Post* reported: "If the EPA finds that any detectable trace of EDB in food is unacceptable, according to a memorandum from a National Governors Association official, 'The economic consequences would be enormous; 7.7 billion bushels of grain and massive amounts of processed foods could possibly be destroyed.' "[46]

Meanwhile, newspapers around the country were giving EDB what is known in the trade as "a major ride." The lead story in *The Chicago Tribune* of Sunday, January 15, was written by its respected environmental writer Casey Bukro. It ran under a four-column headline that said "U.S. targets 'super-cancerous' EDB." Aside from the provocative headline, Bukro's lengthy wrap-up of the EDB situation was for the most part straightforward and accurate. There is an exception, however, toward the end of the article: "Dr. Samuel Epstein, a University of Illinois toxic chemical specialist, says EDB is in the same league as dioxin as a menace.... He described as 'an extraordinary potent cancer-causing chemical.' One study showed that if 1,000 persons were exposed to high levels of EDB 999 of them would get cancer."[47]

Although the article does not say so, Epstein's views on the risks of toxic chemicals are considered extreme by a great many of his colleagues. Bukro did not balance Epstein's assessment with that of a mainstream toxicologist. Instead, he quoted industry spokespersons, who by definition are interested parties and therefore less reliable than a "pure" academic like Epstein. But Epstein, of course, is not disinterested either. He is committed to a particular view of toxic chemicals.

During this same stretch, the networks were intensifying their coverage as food continued to be pulled off the shelves. Dan Rather called EDB the "newest three letters of chemical anxiety," adding imprecisely that although the chemical had been around for more than thirty five years, possibly dangerous amounts were showing up in food for the first time.[48] The fact was that EDB had been in the food all along, but new techniques such as gas chromatography that could detect parts per billion made it possible to find it. EPA's two Johnsons were making the rounds of the TV news and public affairs programs with what was, for them, numbing regularity. Richard Johnson said the pressure from the press "made me a mess." He explained:

> I went from having a couple of conversations over a two- or three-week period with the [*Washington*] *Post* and *New York Times* to having one or two a week, several major environmental newsletters and stuff, frequently local, regional, national television, and ultimately, at the end, in February at the peak, I spent about fifty or sixty hours in front of TV cameras and on the radio besides my regular work and stuff.... I worked [one] 150-hour week. That included the Sunday evenings on "Nightwatch," the all-day Monday in front of Cable News and Satellite News, and blah, blah, blah, and the "Today" show on Monday morning. I was just literally a tired buckaroo.[49]

Finally, or hastily, depending on one's perspective, EPA acted. In a February 3, 1984, press conference, Ruckelshaus announced the immediate emergency suspension of EDB as a grain fumigant and recommended residue levels in grain products of 900 ppb for raw grain, 150 ppb for processed grain that required cooking, and 30 ppb for ready-to-eat grain products. He also set in motion a process to revoke the 1956 exemption that prevents EPA from setting enforceable tolerance levels. Above all, he urged the public to "stay calm." Ruckelshaus used charts and graphs, emphasized that EDB posed a chronic as opposed to an acute risk to individuals, and generally succeeded in reducing the pressure. The press showed little interest in how EPA had come up with the levels of 900, 150, and 30 ppb, although economic concerns may have weighed more heavily in selecting those particular numbers than health considerations. According to King, Ruckelshaus told him in a House of Representatives office building bathroom that "he got his numbers by assuming an upper bound 10 percent financial loss. I mean, he was very straightforward about that. It was derived from an economic impact basis, not any other kind of basis."[50]

By mid-February, the national news magazines had all written about EDB, too, but the story was beginning to fade. On March 3, Ruckelshaus announced EPA's last major action on EDB, an interim tolerance of 30 ppb in the edible portions of fresh citrus and papayas, which would be reduced to zero by September 1. That action was followed by a couple of days of congressional hearings, the introduction of substitutes for EDB such as methyl bromide, whose carcinogenic effects are uncertain, the destruction of existing stocks of the pesticide, at public expense, and some lawsuits. But for the most part EPA's involvement with EDB was over, as was the nation's, except for the remaining residues that would be consumed by the American public or ingested by workers applying the chemical to fruit destined for Japan.

Conclusion

EDB had received intense press coverage by any standard. It appeared on the front pages of national newspapers and as the lead story on three network newscasts.[51] According to a Roper Poll taken between March 17 and March 24, 1984, 60 percent of Americans had heard that EDB could cause cancer. What people knew about EDB, their impressions of the threat it represented to their health, and their opinions about what should be done, were all generated through radio, television, and newspaper reports. At the same time the media were among the handful of forces dominating the lives of the public officials charged with making policy relating to EDB. At both the federal and state levels the media kept the pesticide on the public's agenda and therefore on the policymakers' agendas. And at the same time, the media provided policymakers with their most effective means of influencing the public for political or policy purposes.

Moreover, "the EDB case illustrates the problems regulatory agencies have when they must take regulatory actions and assure the public that the risks in question are being dealt with adequately."[52] And it illustrates the problem the media have in trying to report health-risk information while balancing two internal imperatives: giving the public the information it needs, which is often unclear or uncertain, while catering to the public's interests, which can translate into pandering to its fears or its taste for the sensational. The independence of the media in determining what the public needs to know beyond what government chooses to tell is one of the glories of American press freedom. But it can also be a highly problematic exercise because journalists sometimes lack the competence to make such judgments and the skill to convey nuanced information to a public that has relatively little knowledge of the risk at issue.

The media, of course, rarely if ever act alone in influencing public policy. Politicians, industry, public-interest groups, lobbyists, lawyers, and professional associations also influence decisions. Nor do the media influence policy in a way that is quantifiable. As a result, analyses such as the ones offered in this volume are qualitative and represent a series of judgments based on an apparent preponderance of evidence from varied sources.

For practical purposes, EDB was not even a blip on the media's screen until the summer of 1983 when it was discovered in Florida drinking water. Yet it had already been discovered in groundwater in Hawaii, California, and Georgia, in the last case more than a year earlier. EDB in drinking water became a story for the Florida media for several reasons: the state depends on groundwater to an unusual degree for its drinking water; EDB was being used in relatively large quantities to protect citrus groves from destructive pests; citrus is a major industry in the state; and the issue became political. The Florida press, unlike some newspapers in Hawaii and Minnesota, did not respond as a booster for the state's $1.4-billion citrus industry.[53] It also protrayed the problem as being more dangerous than the evidence warranted. In this way the press exerted pressure on the politician who was responsible for the application of EDB as a soil fumigant, commissioner of Agriculture Doyle Conner. It is not clear how Conner would have responded if the Florida press had treated EDB contamination of drinking water as a proper subject for long-term study rather than a cause for immediate action. Given the coverage as it was and the pressure from politicians, advocates for farm workers, and other groups, Conner took the initiative and set a detection-level standard for EDB contamination in his state. He also took action that shifted the media focus from water to grain-based food products.

This last shift quickly converted EDB from a local story to a major national media event. By chance, the administrator of the EPA was in Florida when local and national television news broadcasts were featuring the clearing from supermarket shelves of EDB-tainted products. He suspected that there was a potential for national panic. Four and a half years later, on reflection, Ruckelshaus questioned whether such a potential really existed, but he said there was no doubt in his mind that the press had contributed to the perception that it did.[54] He felt compelled to act as quickly as possible to eliminate a threat that he knew was minimal in the short term, without disrupting the nation's food supply, causing substantial economic losses to food producers, or eliminating an important pesticide for which there might not be acceptable substitutes.

Once the decision was forced on him, Ruckelshaus recognized that he was going to have to eliminate the press as part of the problem by making it part of the solution. His first major opportunity to do this was the February 3 press conference, of which he said years later:

> I also knew that whatever I did, when I announced the decision, I was going to have to announce it with as much confidence as I could muster that this was the appropriate thing to do and that everybody had to calm down and that this was going to contain the panic, contain the problem, and therefore the media became important in the last analysis in that they were the ones that were going to convey the conviction of the person in charge.... So that the media may have participated in generating the panic, but they were also a key part of my ability to contain people's emotions and reassure them that what I was doing was appropriate. So I think the media cut both ways. It may have helped to generate the emotions surrounding the decision, but also, if appropriately used—*used* may be the wrong word, but—[they] would help in containing [those emotions] and calming [them] down in support of the action that was taken.[55]

Ruckelshaus went on to say that "whatever goodwill I had been able to bank with the media that was there present and arrayed, I was going to call on it at this time and spend a little of it."[56] And indeed he did benefit from the media's goodwill. Robert Hager of NBC News said "we all regarded him [Ruckelshaus] as Mr. Clean and Mr. Honesty by contrast with Burford."[57] Even four and a half years later, Hager was willing to give Ruckelshaus credit for exercising the "art of the practical" in reaching his decision about EDB levels in grain and grain products by using principally economic rather than health-related criteria.[58]

Did the media influence the outcome? Certainly. At the very least, EDB was banned months or possibly years sooner than it would have been otherwise. The economic costs of that were in the tens of millions of dollars or higher as a result of product recalls, destruction of EDB stocks, and other actions. It is even possible that had the media not treated EDB as hot news, more testing would have indicated that EDB was preferable to its alternatives such as methyl bromide for some uses.

Was the media influence malign or beneficial? That depends on what you think of EDB. A more useful question is whether the media adequately served the public's need for information about EDB. The answer depends on which media one is talking about. If one relied mainly on television for news about EDB, unwarranted fear would have been a predictable reaction. Those who relied on *The New York Times*, on the other hand, had access to a generally sufficient amount of reliable information. Given the media habits of Americans, it seems reasonable to conclude that in this instance there was a great deal more unwarranted fear at large than well-informed opinion.

NOTES

1. Philip Angell, aide to William Ruckelshaus, interview, Washington, D.C., February 1, 1988.
2. Environmental Protection Agency, "Environmental News," September 30, 1983, p. 1.
3. Ibid., pp. 8–16.
4. Committee on Government Operations, hearing before the Intergovernmental Relations and Human Resources Subcommittee and the Environment, Energy and Natural Resources Subcommittee, U.S. House of Representatives, March 6, 1984.
5. Ibid., p. 839.
6. Marjorie Sun, "EDB Contamination Kindles Federal Action," *Science*, February 3, 1984, p. 466.
7. United Press International, "Inaction on a Pesticide Is Laid to E.P.A. Ex-Official," *New York Times*, September 26, 1983, section II, p. 11.
8. Sheila Jasanoff, *The Fifth Branch: Science Advisers as Policymakers* (Cambridge, Mass.: Harvard University Press, 1990), p. 132.
9. Environmental Protection Agency, *EDB Facts*, February 3, 1984, p. 2.
10. Angell interview.
11. William D. Ruckelshaus, interview, Washington, D.C., May 9, 1988.
12. George Fong, inspector, Florida Department of Agriculture, interview, Washington, D.C., March 2, 1988.
13. Stephen H. King, M.D., former health officer for the State of Florida, interview, Washington, D.C., February 26, 1988.
14. Doyle Conner, Florida commissioner of Agriculture, interview, Tallahassee, March 1, 1988.
15. Letter from Dr. Stephen H. King to Doyle Conner, in response to a letter from Conner to King asking King to recommend a guideline for an acceptable amount of EDB in drinking water.
16. William J. Bigler and Thomas D. Atkeson, "Chronology of Events Related to EDB," internal document, Florida Department of Health and Rehabilitative Services, August 31, 1983.
17. Victoria Churchville, "U.S. Probes Whether Florida Used EDB in Groves Illegally," *Orlando Sentinel*, September 27, 1983, p. 1.

18. Victoria Churchville, "EDB Threat to Drinking Water Grows Daily," *Orlando Sentinel*, November 6, 1983, p. 1.

19. Ibid.

20. Ibid.

21. Conner interview.

22. Ibid.

23. King interview.

24. John Harwood, "Agriculture Chief Faces Loud Critics of EDB Use," *St. Petersburg Times*, November 14, 1983, p. B1.

25. Letter from Roy G. Davis, second vice president of the Florida Nurserymen and Growers Association, to Lee Moffitt, speaker of the House of Representatives, December 21, 1983.

26. Vincent Giglio, former director, Division of Inspection, Florida Department of Agriculture and Consumer Services, interview, Tallahassee, March 2, 1988.

27. George Fong, paper presented to the Committee on Environmental Improvement of the American Chemical Society, Philadelphia, August 29, 1984.

28. King interview.

29. Ibid.

30. "Finally the Public's Interest Is Served," *St. Petersburg Times*, September 19, 1983, p. A14.

31. "Pesticide Inaction Prompts Inquiry," *New York Times*, September 26, 1983, p. B11.

32. Neil Skene and Christopher Smart, "Corn Products Are Recalled after Traces of EDB Detected," *St. Petersburg Times*, December 10, 1983, p. B1.

33. Richard Johnson, EPA's EDB task force leader, interview, Washington, D.C., February 2, 1988.

34. The apparent cause-and-effect relationship between the television newscast and the FDA testing program was made clear in an exchange between Rep. Ted Weiss (D-N.Y.) and John Wessel of the FDA during the hearings cited above. It went like this: Wessel: "It was not until 1983, this past fall, that we actually tested grain-based products on store shelves." Weiss: "It began after a local Washington, D.C., TV station had reported the presence of EDB residues in on-the-shelf grain products which had been detected by a private laboratory; is that right?" Wessel: "That is correct."

35. Harold Sharlin, "EDB: A Case Study in the Communication of Health Risk," unpublished study commissioned by EPA, January 9, 1985, p. 36. Sharlin's "typhoid Mary" quote applies specifically to press coverage beginning in December 1983, but its relevance to the September "First Camera" segment is clear from the context of the report.

36. Robert Hager, science reporter, NBC News, interview, Washington, D.C., March 2, 1988.

37. Stephen H. King, M.D., as quoted in a report by Robert Hager, "NBC Nightly News," December 21, 1983.

38. Letter from Doyle Conner to William D. Ruckelshaus, December 22, 1983.

39. Committee on Government Operations, hearing before the Intergovernmental Relations and Human Resources Subcommittee and the Environment, Energy, and Natural Resources Subcommittee, U.S. House of Representatives, March 5, 1984.

40. Edwin L. Johnson, director, Office of Pesticide Programs, EPA, interview, Washington, D.C., April 5, 1988.

41. Angell interview.

42. Ruckelshaus interview.

43. Cass Peterson and Paul Taylor, "EDB-Pollution Reports Grow," *Washington Post*, January 11, 1984, p. A1.

44. Ruckelshaus interview.

45. Dr. Robert Bernstein, Texas health officer, telephone interview, January 1988.

46. Peterson and Taylor, "EDB-Pollution Reports Grow."

47. Casey Bukro, "U.S. Targets 'Super-cancerous' EDB," *Chicago Tribune*, January 15, 1984, p. 1.

48. Dan Rather, "CBS Evening News with Dan Rather," January 13, 1988.

49. Richard Johnson interview.

50. King interview.

51. All three networks led with EDB in early February 1984: CBS gave the pesticide 5:20 on February 2; NBC devoted 2:40 to the topic the same night; and ABC followed on February 3, running a five-minute piece.

52. Sharlin, "EDB: A Case Summary," p. 1 of executive summary.

53. See ibid., pp. 23–28, 46–47.

54. Ruckelshaus interview.

55. Ibid.

56. Ibid.

57. Hager interview.

58. Ibid.

3

Radon: A Tale of
Two Towns

U NTIL the beginning of 1985, with very few exceptions, the
press and the public knew nothing about radon. The federal
Environmental Protection Agency had no money and no encourage-
ment to tell the public about the problem. The Reagan administration trimmed all radon money out of the fiscal 1982 budget.[1]
Moreover, within the technical community an often-cited estimate
of 5,000 to 20,000 radon-caused lung cancers a year was viewed as
a very soft set of numbers. Also, there was no solid news peg with
which to tempt the press; that is, not until December 1984, when
radiation alarms at the Limerick, Pennsylvania, nuclear power plant
started going off in the presence of an engineer named Stanley Watras for no discernible reason. After two weeks of puzzlement, during which Watras had to sit in a decontamination room for four to
six hours at a stretch, he decided to go straight from his home to a
radiation detector at the plant, which is owned by the Philadelphia
Electric Company. He immediately triggered the alarm, which suggested that he might be bringing the radiation from home rather
than picking it up at the work site. Watras asked technicians employed by the plant's owner to test his home in Boyertown, Pennsylvania, for radiation. What they found seemed almost unbelievable:
the radon reading in Watras's house was roughly sixteen times the
level permitted by the federal government in uranium mines.[2] Phil-

adelphia Electric notified the Pennsylvania Department of Environmental Resources, which confirmed the extraordinary reading and recommended to the Watras family that they move out of their house until something was done to reduce the radon to a safe level. They did so on January 6, 1985, settling into a Holiday Inn in Pottstown and wondering whether they would ever live in their house again. They were eventually able to move back, but not until July, when a $16,000 remediation effort funded by Philadelphia Electric was completed—and not until after more than 800 other houses in the Boyertown area were found to have radon concentrations higher than the level that is generally considered acceptable for a residence.[3]

Radon was now news. It was also mysterious, and the name was vaguely threatening. The fact that it was invisible and odorless and could cause cancer was frightening. It might also be ubiquitous, appearing at dangerous levels in millions of homes. No one seemed sure about its distribution, and there was considerable uncertainty and debate about the level of exposure at which it constituted a health hazard.

Exactly what radon is and how it causes cancer, however, was well known to radiation physicists. It is an inert, radioactive gas, which is produced when radium decays. (Radium is a decay product of uranium, which is fairly widespread, and is especially likely to be found in certain types of bedrock, such as granite and sandstone.) The radon gas itself does not do the damage. It in turn decays to solid isotopes of polonium, bismuth, and lead, which are called radon progeny or, in the days when we were less sensitive to sexist designations, radon daughters. Some of these isotopes, which enter the lungs either directly or on bits of dust, emit subatomic alpha particles that can damage cells and promote cancer. Most radon is naturally occurring, but as the account below will illustrate, not all is. And radon concentrations are most commonly expressed in picocuries (a measure of radiation) per liter of air. The EPA has settled on 4 picocuries per liter as the level above which home owners should consider taking some remedial action. Most of what is known about the health effects of radon, however, comes from studies done on uranium miners. Much less is known about the health effects of the generally lower levels that have been detected in homes.

The first local press account of the Watras situation provided a base around which future press coverage crystallized. Allan Mazur described the situation in this way:

At a 7 January township commissioners meeting, a DER [Department of Environmental Resources] spokeswoman told the story of the radon discovery, including the Limerick alarms, and she blamed the contamination on the Reading Prong [a granite formation underlying parts of Pennsylvania, New Jersey, and New York], known from the DER's 1979 survey as a source of uranium....

The first press account, a report of that meeting by Mary Jane Schneider, appeared January 10 in the township's weekly newspaper, the *Boyertown Area Times*. It repeated the DER's assumption that the Reading Prong was the source of the problem, a claim that would persist even as evidence accumulated that radon levels were not closely associated with whether or not a home was situated on the prong.[4]

The national media picked up the Reading Prong as the source of radon, as, of course, did the media in the affected tri-state area. But when a survey of 2,000 houses turned up no others with levels as frightening as that in the Watras residence, even though "about 7 percent had radon levels above the maximum recommended exposure for uranium miners, according to the CDC [Centers for Disease Control],"[5] the story faded quickly. It did not emerge again in the national media until Sunday, May 19, when Philip Shabecoff published a report on the front page of *The New York Times*. Shabecoff was alerted to the story by Robert Yuhnke, the Denver-based regional counsel of the Environmental Defense Fund. *The New York Times* article brought radon to the attention of numerous public officials, including several in New Jersey, where two dramatically different radon-related situations were about to emerge as major statewide news stories. With respect to one of these stories, John H. Dorsey, assistant minority leader of the state Senate in New Jersey, said: "There's absolutely no question that if it hadn't been for the [Shabecoff] article . . . I suspect the whole issue of naturally occurring radon would probably have never reached the halls of the legislature."[6] The two New Jersey stories, one concerning naturally occurring radon and the other radon from industrial waste, led to some but, again, relatively little national coverage. Nevertheless, these two stories, which played out side by side in northern New Jersey, demonstrate how news is made and how a group of determined small-town citizens, using the press as its principal weapon, manipulated the political establishment and confounded the bureaucracy to accomplish its goals. They also illustrate the importance of controversy in raising an event to the level of "news," irrespective of its inherent importance.

Vernon

"[Edith] Ryan [a pseudonym] believes she worked at U.S. Radium at least two years, though she can't pinpoint exactly when she started or quit. She does recall being there on Armistice Day of 1918, when she and her friends ran out of the factory and banged garbage can covers to celebrate the end of World War I."[7] So wrote *The Newark Star-Ledger*. It is with Edith Ryan and her colleagues at U.S. Radium's West Orange watch-dial plant that the Montclair–Glen Ridge–West Orange–Kearny–Vernon radon story begins. Watch-dial painting was delicate work, and at the behest of their employers, the young girls who did it pointed their camel's-hair brushes with their mouths or lips every time they used them. Mary Jo Patterson wrote in the *Star-Ledger* that "The dial painters from Orange became famous in the annals of occupational disease in the same way that the survivors of Hiroshima became textbook examples of how much radiation a human being could stand." Patterson quoted Ryan as saying, "It's a terrible thing to say, but it was the hungry ones who died." The point, of course, was that the more they painted, the more they earned, and the more radium they ingested. The last friend Edith Ryan remembers dying of radium poisoning was Lucy Sullivan, whose obituary in 1958 bore the headline "44th radium victim." The workers suffered from anemia, their jaw-bones decayed, they contracted bone cancer and other bone ailments. In 1925, the Essex County medical examiner, Dr. Harrison J. Mart-land, "concluded that radium poisoning was an occupational disease," and in the 1930s, five ill U.S. Radium workers sued the company. The U.S. Radium plant had closed in 1926, and it was razed in 1929.

In the 1970s, the U.S. Department of Energy started a program to identify sites at which radioactive materials were produced or processed. As a result of those studies, New Jersey's Department of Environmental Protection launched a similar search in 1979. An obvious source of concern was the site of the former U.S. Radium plant. It was strongly suspected, although no records have been turned up to prove it, that the plant's radioactive waste was blended with soil and used as landfill on top of which houses were built in the early 1930s. At the request of the New Jersey agency, the EPA conducted an aerial survey in 1981 that identified hot spots in areas of Montclair, Glen Ridge, and West Orange, which in February 1985 led to the designation of parts of Montclair and Glen Ridge as federal Superfund cleanup sites. In July 1983, a state survey had found several areas of high gamma radiation and radon gas, which indicated the presence of radium. "The study concluded that more than 200 homes on 50 acres in Glen Ridge and 45 acres in Montclair had unacceptably high levels of radon gas. A nine-acre area of West Orange was also affected."[8] But this was only the tip of the iceberg. The tainted area turned out to be more than 200 acres, and the soil was contaminated to depths of 15 feet or more. As many as 400 houses may have been contaminated.

For several months after the July survey, while the state was trying to figure out what to do, the public was not advised of the radiation problem. But on November 30, the story broke in a television news report.[9] Department of Environmental Protection commissioner Robert E. Hughey disclosed that at least nineteen houses in Montclair and Glen Ridge were contaminated by radium. The towns were immediately besieged by the local media. According to an account by Peter Overby and Jan Barry in the *Record* (Hackensack):

> residents and local officials were furious because... they learned of the radioactivity through news reports, not official channels. "You read the papers, you know as much as we know," said Stephen Berry, borough clerk of Glen Ridge.
>
> Epidemiologist William E. Parkin of the state Department of Health last night told several Montclair residents, "We're trying to get answers to the same questions that you have, so that we can answer you."
>
> In tests conducted by the state Department of Environmental Protection (DEP), 19 houses were found to have radon gas exceeding the limits recommended by the federal Environmental Protection Agency (EPA) for a dwelling....
>
> Seven of those homes had radiation levels above the federal standard for workers in uranium mines, which is 10 times the level recommended for residential areas. DEP Commissioner Robert E. Hughey and other state officials yesterday would not disclose the exact levels of radon found in any of the houses.[10]

The DEP's failure to inform the public and the public's angry response when the press disclosed the apparently dangerous concentration of radiation within about a mile of the old radium-dial plant foreshadowed a case of media and public information mismanagement of catastrophic proportions that almost all of the involved officials now acknowledge. DEP staff not only failed to enlist the press as an ally in an effort to let people know about the problem, but they appeared to view it as an obstacle. In the end, a group of citizens who understood the importance of the press in civic confrontations used mass media to vanquish the state agency in the final battle of a five-year campaign to rid three Essex County towns of what in the public mind had become 15,000 square yards of radioactive menace that the state was trying to pass off as "just dirt."

On December 5, ten public health officers began making the rounds of the affected area to collect brief medical histories. Five of the identified houses, thirteen of which were on Nishuane Road and Virginia Avenue on the south side of Montclair and six of which were on Carteret Street in Glen Ridge, had radon readings in excess of 100 picocuries per liter of air. Just a day later, the federal Centers for Disease Control issued a public health advisory that reached the following conclusion: "Based on current EPA standards and current risk estimates, CDC, with the concurrence of the New Jersey Department of Health, has concluded that elevated radon levels in some of these homes constitute a significant health risk."[11]

The CDC report set a two-year deadline for reducing radon concentrations to acceptable levels in twenty-two homes. A few days earlier, however, Governor Thomas Kean took an action that was to have more significant consequences. On December 2, he signed Executive Order 56, which directed the DEP commissioner "to take such measures as might be determined to be necessary to protect the health, safety, and welfare of the citizens of the state from the danger due to the radium and radon contamination." More importantly, the order allowed DEP to select a storage or burial site for the contaminated dirt without public participation. This was contrary to established procedures and was destined to cause substantial problems for Kean, DEP commissioner Richard T. Dewling, and other state officials. In the meantime, state and federal officials continued to identify affected houses, ultimately testing 471 in the three towns, and to seek ways to eliminate the health risk without unduly alarming the public or running up unnecessary costs. By early January, "temporary venting systems" paid for by EPA's Superfund had been installed "in the four most contaminated houses in Montclair, West Orange, and Glen Ridge," and other sites around the state were being examined.[12]

Soon thereafter, a decision was made by the state and federal governments to try to remove the contaminated earth under the affected houses and dispose of it. EPA and DEP agreed to work together on a pilot project involving twelve houses. According to Christopher Daggett, regional administrator for EPA, "Essentially what happened was people took a look at this and said it's of sufficient concern to people that we need to essentially remove the people from the soil or the soil from the people.... And to do that we want[ed] to make sure... that we could do it physically."[13] The choice to take the people away from the soil would have meant the buyout of between 44 and 200 homes, which would have had a devastating impact on the community. As a result, it was decided to try the alternative, for which the state appropriated $8 million.

One of the obvious requirements of the project was access to a disposal site for radioactive waste. New Jersey apparently believed it had received permission to permanently dispose of the soil at a privately owned dump in Beatty, Nevada. But that hope proved false. The plan was to truck the roughly 15,000 square yards of tainted soil, packed in 55-gallon drums, to Kearny, from where it would be shipped by train to Las Vegas, switched to trucks, and hauled to Beatty 110 miles to the northwest. But there was a hitch, described in a contemporary newspaper account: "The Las Vegas rail yard—where the shipment of soil could sit for days while the cars are being unloaded—is in the heart of casino land, and officials there are worried about what would happen if something went wrong.... Said City Manager Ashley Hall, ... 'In the minds of people around the country, if we had a spill here, that would be disastrous. And we're not willing to gamble.' "[14]

The Las Vegas city manager's comment, of course, was rich in unintended irony. If Las Vegas wouldn't gamble on serving as a brief transit site for the radioactive dirt, what city would? And could it also have been that Hall was thinking, what better place for the dirt than where it is? After all, the chief competition for the casinos of Las Vegas were in Atlantic City on the New Jersey seashore. As it turned out, even citizens of one of the affected towns, West Orange, would not permit their own town's armory to serve as a temporary storage facility. As Hall said, the problem was in "the minds of people." According to Peter Sandman, a professor of environmental journalism at Rutgers University, "the soil became tainted not by the radium but by the attention."[15] Before the New Jersey DEP was done, it had been turned down by radioactive waste facilities at Richland, Washington, and Barnwell, South Carolina. In another small irony, it was turned down at these sites partly because the waste was not sufficiently radioactive to qualify for burial. The site of a 1960 nuclear missile accident at McGuire Air Force Base in central New Jersey was also rejected as a dump for the dirt. Over the next couple of years, several lawsuits were filed, including an action in the Supreme Court of the United States, to try to get someone to take the tainted soil, but none was successful.

The Department of Environmental Protection even offered a number of New Jersey towns several million dollars to take the soil, but none accepted.

Amidst all these failures, however, there was one small success. New Jersey Transit and the owner of a private lot agreed to store about 10,000 barrels of excavated dirt at a facility in Kearny for several months until it could be moved to a permanent storage or burial site. The dirt in Kearny, all 9,500 drums and 53 boxes of it, came from four houses on Carteret Street and Lorraine Street in Glen Ridge. The Glen Ridge work was carried out expeditiously. The families were moved out, their properties were excavated by crews wearing white disposable coveralls, windows and doors were covered with plastic sheeting, as were the piles of dirt before they were hauled away, and by October the families were all back in their houses. Meanwhile, excavation also began in Montclair. But there things did not go quite so smoothly. Indeed, by the summer of 1988, four elderly couples who lived near the corners of Virginia Avenue and Franklin Street were still not back in their homes. And their lawns and yards had been turned into the storage facility for 5,000 drums of dirt dug up from under the foundations of their houses. Donald Deieso, an assistant commissioner in the Department of Environmental Protection, said:

> as you know each of these stories, your heart breaks. Two or three of these families who had moved out were appealing to us on a daily basis, "Please move us back into our home. We want to die there." They were 78 and 79 years old. Another couple in one of the rental accommodations we had for them were robbed two or three times. They had their TVs and personal belongings, treasured family things, stolen.... The assurance that we gave them that they would be out of their homes for three months turned into a nightmare.[16]

No out-of-state facility would take the dirt, and the state environmental agency told Sam Pinkard, chairman of the Montclair Radon Task Force, a citizens' group, that "there was no more room at Kearny."[17] Moreover, by September 1985, Kearny residents were already up in arms over storage of the Glen Ridge soil in their town. There had been a demonstration, and getting rid of the waste had become politically important for longtime mayor Henry J. Hill, who said, "We don't want any radioactive material in the town, period."[18] By the end of 1985, many Montclair residents were fed up, and the township in the name of two affected residents sued the Department of Environmental Protection in Superior Court to force resumption of the cleanup, which had stopped for lack of a disposal site. At the same time, the DEP came up with a plan to blend the radioactive dirt with clean dirt until it emitted radon at less than background levels and then to bury it or use it as fill somewhere in the state. The DEP's five-member Science Advisory Board gave its blessing to the soil-blending solution. Numerous sites in the state were considered, and by June 1986, the board made its choice. It was to be an inactive quarry in Vernon, in Sussex County, a bucolic but fast-growing community on the New York State border near the Appalachian Trial. This was a decision that Governor Kean, DEP commissioner Dewling, and many others in the state would come to regret.

Under Kean's Executive Order 56, which did not require public participation, the method of disposal and the disposal site for the Montclair–Glen Ridge–West Orange soil were selected on June 16. State Assemblyman Robert Littell was advised of the choice at about 10:00 P.M. on June 17, and he was told that Dewling would visit Vernon the following morning at 10:30 with official notification. Littell phoned the appropriate public officials.[19]

When Dewling and his aides arrived at the Vernon municipal building at about 11:00 A.M. on June 18, they were met not only by the town officials and their state representatives but also by a representative from the office of U.S. Representative Marge Roukema. More important, although it was not evident at the time, was the presence of several reporters from *The New Jersey Herald*, *The Newark Star-Ledger*, and WSUS Radio. Dewling, already wary because of traditional North Jersey resentment of the state government in Trenton, was expecting a closed meeting with state and township officials. He felt that he had been ambushed. Unprepared to deal with the press, he made a curt announcement of the siting recommendation to the officials and left. His behavior outraged the officials and the community, a fact that was to have major repercussions in the weeks to come. So the press played an important role from the start in Vernon. And it would continue to do so at every step along the way, often as the instrument of a well-organized group of citizens who understood that without it they could not accomplish their sole goal, which was to "keep the dirt out of Vernon." *The Record* (Hackensack) published an editorial six weeks later suggesting that the people and politicians of Vernon had manipulated the press unconscionably:

> Platoons of attorneys, local politicians and homeowners in Vernon Township have shown a genius for political and media promotion that is

matched only by their selfish parochialism.... When television stations said they did not want to come to the quarry way out in Sussex County, the protestors arranged to picket Governor Kean's home in Livingston. ... They picketed Kean in Rye, N.Y., while he was attending a meeting of the Coalition of Northeast Governors.... These people are no more friends of the environment than a junkyard dog is a friend of the junkyard.[20]

This, though, was not the only media perspective on the tactics of the Vernon activists. For the most part, area newspapers and radio and television stations relished the story as a classic confrontation between aggrieved citizens and an insensitive bureaucracy. Donald Deieso, assistant commissioner of the state Department of Environmental Protection, put it this way:

I would [argue] that the media enjoyed the controversy, sought out the legislators and elected officials and community-group leaders and opposition and made it possible... to inflame the situation.... It's one thing for a legislator to sit in opposition, quite another for every newspaper and television [station] in the state to create the forum for them to say the things that they were saying.[21]

Deieso had a point, as did the *Record*. The Vernonites did manipulate the press, and the press did thrive on the controversy. But it is also true that New Jersey officials were insensitive in failing to grasp that a community such as Vernon, which had already organized against a trio of local microwave towers, would rise up to challenge the bureaucracy. State officials should have recognized the political wisdom of consulting with the community.

In any event, after several failed attempts to ship the dirt out of state and under a court order to get it out of Montclair, the state found the Vernon quarry solution eminently reasonable. The plan was to blend the radium-contaminated soil with clean soil available at the quarry, which would be used to reclaim the quarry itself, adding about 100 acres to Waywayanda State Park and improving a segment of the nearby Appalachian Trail. Donald Deieso still finds it a bit hard to understand why the state's creative solution met such fierce resistance:

We were convinced of... our ability to communicate that the soil itself had little if any public health consequence.... We had all of the logic that this was a thimble of radium... in the soil; there's more in X-rays; there's more in your diet.... All the facts... support[ed] what we thought was an absolutely trivial public health concern [but] it became... the question of this is a public health threat, it's terrible, statewide opposition in [media] coverage—how can we possibly do this thing. . . . We thought we would dispose of it just by the sheer facts.[22]

Nothing could have been more wrong. After the June 18 meeting in the Vernon Township Hall, Deputy Mayor John Warren telephoned Mayor Victor Marotta, who was out of town when DEP commissioner Richard Dewling traveled to Vernon to deliver the news about the dirt. "That afternoon I got a call from the deputy mayor in Florida," Marotta recalled. "He said, 'I think you're probably going to be reading about us in the paper down there. Today we were told that the state wants to move the dirt from Montclair and Glen Ridge and West Orange, and we had quite a confrontation here at Town Hall and basically all the elected officials from the senator down to our committeemen said, "No, you're not going to do that." ' " Vernon resident Eileen Opfer recollected a call from Warren on June 17 or 18 in which he asked, "Are you willing to lie in the streets to stop this?" The Opfers and many of their neighbors said they were prepared to do exactly that. Marianne Reilly, another Vernon activist, said, "Many, many people in Vernon came here because of the clean air, the clean soil, and so forth. . . . And we were being told that something that was not wanted by another area, that was 'contaminated,' was going to be brought here without any input from us."

Mayor Marotta, the Opfers (Jim and Eileen), Marianne Reilly, and Maureen Sweeney acknowledge that they did not know at the time whether the blended soil represented a health threat or not. Reilly said, "I think you didn't need to know at that point anything else except that someone was making a decision like this without us knowing whether or not it was dangerous. It wasn't that we had determined that it was." The fact is that even now the Vernon activists are not sure that the blended dirt would pose a threat to their community. But they also contend that they are not sure that it wouldn't, and they do not know how much contaminated soil ultimately would have been dumped in the quarry. They point to a study indicating that radium had leached into the aquifer beneath Montclair,[23] and to the view held by some radiation scientists that there is no level above zero at which radiation does not increase one's risk of getting cancer. They also hired the engineering firm of Gerraghty and Miller to carry out a study of the quarry, which is directly above the main aquifer supplying water to Vernon. The study concluded that radioactive material could leach into the water supply, but the precise amount and health effects of such leaching are unknown.

This was obviously not a community over which the state was going to run roughshod, no matter how airtight its case or how good its intentions. Vernon was a closely knit community of fewer than 20,000 fairly homogeneous middle-class persons who had banded together before—among other things, to raise $100,000 for a liver transplant for a local resident—and clearly had the capacity and the will to do so again. The state turned out to be no match for them in good measure because the Vernonites understood that the battle would be won in the press, and they were determined to win it. State Senator Dorsey, who has sponsored radon legislation, said:

> Basically, the battle was fought in the press. . . . It was . . . the typical small community rising up to . . . fight city hall. So it was portrayed in the newspapers in that fashion. . . . The coverage of it, I suppose, was relatively factual, but always targeted at looking for controversy and writing about the controversy rather than any in-depth assessment of health risks. . . . Had the press taken a position that this is all a matter of absurdity, I think that it certainly would have dampened the kind of attention by the legislators who led the battle. . . . The citizens of Vernon . . . were pretty skillful, it seems to me. . . . They manipulated . . . they used the press as essentially the press offers itself to be used.[24]

Whether or not the health-risk question was absurd, as Dorsey seems to suggest, the scientific evidence is reasonably persuasive that the threat represented by the dirt in the quarry would have been significantly less, for example, than the risk from naturally occurring radon in some Vernon homes. Radon outdoors rarely represents a significant health risk, and although the matter of radium leaching into the aquifer has not been definitively answered, the overall risk seems low. Nevertheless, radioactive materials frighten people, and it should have come as no surprise to the state that one community would not want to accept another community's radioactive waste, even if it could be shown—almost beyond doubt—to be relatively harmless. The risk attached to burying the blended dirt in the Vernon quarry and the desire not to have someone else's problem imposed upon them were not the only issues for the people of Vernon. They also felt strongly about their right to be consulted on a matter of importance to their community. The state had failed to assess the situation correctly on all three counts.

Within ten days of the meeting with Dewling, twenty-six Vernon-

ites met on a farm to develop a press strategy. They discussed whether
to pursue the governor or not, what kinds of demonstrations and events
to stage, and how to organize media contacts. They assigned separate
individuals to handle radio, television, newspapers, and wire services
(plus two New York City television stations). By this time (June 23)
the township had already been granted a sixteen-day temporary restraining order to prevent the dirt from being shipped to Vernon. The
issue was being pressed in the state legislature by assemblymen Littell and Garabed (Chuck) Haytaian and Senator Wayne Dumont. And
the first T-shirts saying "Hell No—We Won't Glow" were ready for
distribution.

So far, only the local press had bitten. As for the media outside the
immediate area, Maureen Sweeney said, "they weren't interested initially. We really had to romance them." The Vernon group's concept
of "romance" consisted of a mix of making information available, stag-
ing events, providing creative "visuals" for the TV cameras, calling the
wire services in the middle of the night when nothing was going on,
constantly harping on the possibility of bloodshed and violence, and
grossly exaggerating the number of people expected at demonstrations.
According to Eileen Opfer: "If we said there were going to be 100
people at a demonstration, they wouldn't nibble at that one. But if we
said, there's going to be a thousand people in the streets or something,
we would inflate it purposefully . . . and they bit."

As a measure of their success, Jim Opfer, Eileen's Georgetown-
educated lawyer husband, cited this remark by a New York City television journalist: "I gotta tell you something. This is really historical.
This is middle-class America. We're not talking about hippies or cuckoo
birds. We're talking about a family-oriented, middle-class American
town that's about to participate in civil disobedience to protect their
homes. This is important stuff."[25]

The first big event staged by the No-Name Committee, as the
Vernonites called themselves, was a motorcade of buses to Trenton to
picket the statehouse. *The Newark Star-Ledger* carried the following
news on page 1:

About 1,000 people from Sussex County rallied on the steps of the
Statehouse yesterday against a state plan to dispose of tons of radon-
contaminated soil from Essex County at a quarry site in Vernon
Township.
    Nineteen busloads of residents, many wearing shirts emblazoned,
"Hell no, we won't glow," peacefully marched outside the Statehouse

for about 90 minutes in what was one of the largest and noisiest Trenton rallies in the past few years.

The residents and officials, who already are challenging the decision in court, vowed to lie down in the streets if necessary, to block the proposal. "Civil disobedience is always an alternative," said Richard Errico, a Vernon resident. "We'll do anything we can to stop it."

Some of the demonstrators wore surgical masks, many of the children carried signs that said, "Radium is bad for kids." Most who attended were Vernon Township residents, but they were joined by residents of neighboring Warwick, N.Y., and nearby Sparta, according to organizers.[26]

Although Governor Kean was not in his office when the demonstrators arrived, the battle between two counties in his state, as the news story posed it, had been dumped on his doorstep. The story went on to "balance" a contention by state scientists that the blended soil constituted no health hazard against a statement by Senator Dumont, who said, "We have other scientists who will say just the opposite." Dumont's scientists, however, were not identified. A fair-minded reader with no special knowledge about radon or radium would have been likely to sympathize with the Vernon demonstrators on better-safe-than-sorry grounds as well as the intuitive notion that it is unfair to export one community's troubles to another. All in all, the Vernonites had done well their first time out, taking their dispute to the doorstep of the governor, who was at that time angling to be Bob Dole's vice-presidential running mate if Dole were to get the Republican Presidential Nomination.

The next major media effort came only eight days later and again was aimed at the governor. This time a motorcade of private cars—estimated at 200 by the *Vernon News* in its special issue of November 28, 1986, but only 100 by the *Record* (Hackensack) of July 17—drove past Governor Kean's Livingston home at night blaring their horns and then demonstrated across the street on the Shrewsbury Drive sidewalk. Again, the governor was not there to meet the protesters, but again, they got the publicity they were seeking. Jim Opfer, as the No-Name Committee's designated heavy, shouted things like "If nothing else, it tells him if he attempts to move the trucks [of dirt] into Vernon, he better be prepared to call out the National Guard," and "If he doesn't clean up this state in preparation for his vice-presidential run . . . " to which the crowd responded, "He loses!" And "How many people here are prepared to stop a truck?" To which the crowd roared,

"We are!"[27] The *Record*'s Peter Overby wrote the following in a page 1 story on July 27:

> Governor Kean wasn't home when 600 or so Vernon residents descended on his neighborhood in a well-organized protest 11 days ago.
>
> But the demostrators won the audience they really wanted: the television cameras that wouldn't go to Vernon, a rural township in the Sussex County Hills.
>
> TV news editors "said 'that's too far,' so we said, 'we'll come to you,' " said Richard Errico.... "And we went to Livingston."
>
> A key strategy [of the Vernon protesters] is to sway Kean by threatening his future in national politics.[28]

On July 22, about 200 area citizens protested outside the Parsippany Hilton, where Kean was scheduled to speak. Since this was a relatively small turnout, the Vernonites had to be creative. According to Marianne Reilly:

> They [TV crews] were focusing their cameras on the Governor and his people who were talking to township officials, and we got all of the children out of the crowd. And we lined all of the children up in the center and gave them... signs [that] said, "Please don't bring radium into our valley."
>
> And the press—it was almost simultaneous—they turned around and focused on the children.... The last thing any politician wants is that type of attention.

Meanwhile, the courts were going back and forth on the dirt disposal, but on July 24 the New Jersey Supreme Court lifted a restraining order permitting transfer of the Montclair soil to Vernon with the provision that the DEP give Vernon forty eight hours' notice before moving the material and that the drums not be opened when they got there. During this time Assemblyman Haytaian had declared publicly that he was holding a $36-million "Green Acres" funding bill "hostage" in an effort to keep the Montclair–Glen Ridge dirt out of Vernon, although he later said it was because the Green Acres program already had enough land in the two counties that would have benefited from the funds.

At this point the Vernonites took two actions that some members of the group regard as the turning point in the battle against the state, because they elevated the attention Vernon was getting to the national level. The activists brought in an expert from Warwick to give them lessons in civil disobedience. "The kicker that made it go national," Eileen Opfer said, "was the fact that there [were] civil disobedience classes. That was printed in *The New York Times*,[29] and that was one of the articles that was picked up nationally as far as NBC, and so on." And they staged by far their largest rally at a local amusement area known as Action Park. Estimates of attendance ranged from 5,000 to 10,000, with Patty Paugh in the Sunday (July 28) *Star-Ledger* citing the lower number as a police estimate. Paugh's lead paragraph said: "Vernon's effort to keep radium-contaminated soil outside its borders reached a fever pitch yesterday as protestors called for the impeachment of Gov. Thomas Kean and vowed to form a massive human blockade to stop trucks bearing the drums."

Daniel Boorstin has called such media-oriented events "pseudo-events," and Vernon residents staged others such as the dedication of a fort built of railroad ties (and intended as a television visual). Other events drew media attention: New York Governor Mario Cuomo sent a message of support; Vernon's scientific advisory group, known as the Yellow Ribbon Panel, was permitted to review DEP documents; and the actor Tony Randall was host of a "Save the Valley Evening."

On November 26, the state announced that Vernon was no longer under consideration as a site for the dirt. Commissioner Dewling, in consultation with the governor's office, buckled under the political pressure and a perceived threat of violence. Christopher Daggett, the regional administrator for EPA, rued the outcome, for good reasons:

> this was probably the worst precedent... one that will haunt people for some time to come and already has in other siting decisions. Because when they decided to go to Vernon Township with this material and Vernon Township said no, the question came down to whether you force the issue. They had a Supreme Court decision from the state of New Jersey saying it was legally acceptable to do it. They had some Nobel Prize-winning physicists saying it is technically okay to do it. And in the face of strong community opposition, they backed down. Now what that's done is create a precedent in the state that says no matter what anybody says and what decisions are made, if you get enough people in the street, you can stop them.[30]

According to Daggett, "There were very real threats of violence. There was some undercover police work that verified that. So you have to ask the question, is the site worth a gunshot through a truck window?"[31] And Dewling said he received anonymous threats to himself and his family during the period of the dispute.[32] Whether or not the threats of violence were real, the Vernonites understood the value of injecting the threat of violence into the atmosphere. They managed to do so while playing the classic American role of a small, family-oriented community protecting its rights agains the incursions of big government.

Vernon's success, however, left Montclair with its unplaced drums of dirt until December 1987, when, in an ironic bureaucratic twist, the dirt was mixed with more intensely radioactive soil so that it could qualify for disposal in Richland, Washington. But over time, it was discovered that far more contaminated soil needed to be excavated in Montclair, Glen Ridge, and West Orange. The estimate in mid-1990 was 350,000 cubic yards, and the cost was put at $250 million. EPA will do the job over ten years if four conditions are met: (1) Congress pays the bill, (2) a disposal site can be found, (3) the communities cooperate, and (4) transportation of the soil to the disposal site does not present insurmountable problems.

The drums of radioactive soil stored in Kearny were trucked to a site in Utah. And four-term incumbent Mayor Henry Hill was ousted over the issue by Daniel Sansone, only the second Democrat the town had ever elected mayor.

Clinton

At about 7:00 in the evening on Friday, March 13, 1986, Gerald Nicholls, assistant director for radiation protection programs of the New Jersey Department of Environmental Protection, was in his office cleaning up some paperwork when the phone rang. It was a resident of Clinton, a mostly upscale northern New Jersey town of fewer than 2,000 residents that retains much of its rural charm despite the fact that its predominantly nineteenth-century downtown has been slightly tarted up. The man from Clinton told Nicholls that he had just spoken to Bernard Cohen, a radiation physicist at the University of Pittsburgh, who had given him the result of a radon test in his house. Cohen told him, Nicholls said, "that he had a result that was on the order of 1,200 picocuries per liter."[33] Nicholls, who has a doctorate in physics, takes radon seriously. He contends that extrapolations of radon risk in homes based on data from exposure in mines are very conservative. He was startled by the Clinton result and immediately called Cohen, who was also still in his office. Nicholls asked:

Do you think this thing is real? And [Cohen] said: "I've looked at the information on the screen myself. And not only that, we have two canisters from the guy's house. And they both are within 100 picocuries per liter of each other."

So while we sent some people up there to look at the house the next day we also started looking at the data we had from that area. We came up with two other houses that were in the hundreds of picocuries per liter. . . . One was over 1,000. And lo and behold, they were within sight of each other. If you stood on the roof of the middle one, you could see the other two. And that's when we, that afternoon, Friday afternoon, said we may have a bad problem here.[34]

Gerald Nicholls began paying attention to naturally occurring radon in January 1985, when the State of Pennsylvania notified his office about the Watras house. Before that, he had associated the radioactive gas mainly with the radium problem in Montclair, Glen Ridge, and West Orange, which had been nettlesome for his agency for three years and would become even worse in the wake of the June 1986 decision to ship Essex County's radioactive dirt to Sussex County. Nicholls's department had begun to study the problem of natural radon in New Jersey when Philip Shabecoff's lengthy article on radon appeared in the Sunday, May 19, 1985, issue of *The New York Times*. He said that the Shabecoff article alarmed people because it linked the radon in Pennsylvania to a rock formation that also runs through northern New Jersey. He knew people were alarmed because they called his department. "We began to receive hundreds of phone calls a day on it," Nicholls said.[35] Although not the first to mention the Reading Prong, the *Times* was instrumental in fixing it in the consciousness of New Jerseyites.

Nicholls recalled this anecdote, which he said reflected the public's response:

That first few weeks, when the phone was ringing off the hook and things were so hectic, one person called and insisted on coming in and looking at a map [to see] where the Reading Prong was. So finally they let them come in and look at a map downtown. We'll mail you a map. No, we want to come in, you know. So they came in. They looked at it. He looked at the Reading Prong, which had been penciled onto the map just for reference purposes. And he said, "Okay, I'm two miles below it, I'm safe." And there was no way to convince that gentleman that he was at any risk at all.[36]

The white, rose, and soft-yellow frame houses of Clinton, New Jersey, straddle Route 173 about halfway between New York City and Philadelphia. This picturesque little community, with its mill stream and mill pond, its gourmet delicatessen and Fine Crafts Collection, and it's brick Victorian municipal building, has a trouble-free look.

Clinton's public officials were aware of the extraordinary radon levels found in the Watras house in nearby Pennsylvania, and, according to Mayor Robert Nulman, they "investigated to see if we were indeed on the Reading Prong and to our delight we found that we were just outside of the geologic formation [and] we decided that we were protected."[37] But unlike the man who wanted to see the Reading Prong on a map, they had some nagging doubt in Clinton, which was also two miles from the prong.

Mayor Nulman started a program, perhaps the first of its kind in the country, to mass purchase radon detectors. About eighty-five families participated. By chance, however, the call Gerald Nicholls received on March 13, 1986, came from a man who did not take part in the program. He had purchased a faster-acting test on his own. After receiving the call, Nicholls immediately sent technicians to Clinton to confirm the reading and to determine whether the town's case involved an isolated house, as in the Watras situation, or a more widespread problem. The result the next day, Friday, March 14, confirmed the high reading, and tests shortly afterward showed that of forty-nine houses evaluated, thirty-seven had readings greater than the EPA action level of 4 picocuries per liter. (Subsequent tests of all of the houses in Clinton Knolls, a contemporary development of about 100 houses built on a limestone bluff west of the mill pond, showed levels above 4 picocuries a liter in every house; forty measured above 200, and five of those were in excess of 1,000.[38] Clinton Knolls was the neighborhood in which the first house with elevated radon levels was discovered.) State officials notified Nulman of the problem on Saturday, and they set up a meeting in Clinton for the following Monday, March 17, 1986. Nulman recalls that meeting as follows:

I was the only municipal official there. Everybody else came from [the state Department of Health and Department of Environmental Protection]. They proceeded to try to educate me on the fundamentals . . . it was Radon 101, I guess. They did a very good job. . . . At that point they didn't appreciate how extensive the problem might be. They tried to deal in the generalities of saying this is what radon is . . . here are the general dangers . . . there's not a heck of a lot of experience out there . . . everything is an extrapolation... we're not really sure, but we feel that we have to go after this thing as if it were a problem.... We proceeded to put together a strategy of how we would let the public know of this problem.[39]

The state officials offered to deal with the local press waiting outside the town hall, but Nulman decided that under the circumstances, even though he had no media experience, it would be better if he handled the press himself. He said, "I felt that if I made myself available and if I was the person, I felt I could do more, I had more at stake... in protecting the town."[40] That, according to EPA's Christopher Daggett, made a "large difference."[41] Nulman, a bearded, open-faced man, was an easy communicator who is widely credited with having contained a situation that could have degenerated into panic. Instead, the single largest concern that developed in Clinton was that the radon problem would depress real estate values. There is no real evidence that it did so, except possibly in the very short term.

"From the very start," Nulman said, "the television reporting was our biggest problem.... I don't think there was one report in those early stages that didn't entail filming in front of houses that were for sale, making it appear that houses had been put on the market because of the radon problem or intimating that these houses may never sell because they were so tainted by radon. That was never the case."[42] J. J. Drautman, a physicist who wrote about radon for *The Hunterdon Review*, a local weekly, said:

Channel 6 from Philadelphia called me.... They said... we want to see a house with radon in it. I said nobody knew where the house with radon was. Well, just point us in the right direction, and of course they were one of the ones that were on that night with three for-sale signs implying that everybody's abandoning Clinton. That's kind of typical of the coverage, I think.... One New York channel—I can't remember which one it was, so I can't get sued—ran a picture of the house that had the first high reading. Of course, they didn't know it. They were just going down the street, and to me that's irresponsible journalism. They just took pictures of the house and said, "Here's the house in the area with all the radon. Here's the for-sale sign. Isn't this exciting?" I didn't think it was that exciting. We [*The Hunterdon Review*] never ran a picture of the house.[43]

By early April, however, it was clear that what was happening in Clinton had little to do with the ongoing Montclair-Vernon affair.

There was clear evidence of a unified community, like the one in Vernon, but there was no conflict between the town and the state; the radon was not being shipped in from another community, so there was no outrage and no villain to blame; and even though the radon levels were extremely high and apparently much more dangerous than the radium threat to Vernon, the problem was remediable at a relatively small cost. The print press coverage reflected the difference. For instance, a (Hackensack) *Record* article on a Clinton town meeting April 5 noted:

> Reports of the highest radon levels found in New Jersey may disturb residents of this cozy town of 1,900, but the large crowd at a town meeting yesterday took a can-do attitude toward the problem posed by the radon gas.
>
> Questioning federal and state radon experts, many of the 350 area residents showed a knowledge of the problem—and a determination to solve it—that was not always evident at similar meetings held around North Jersey last year.[44]

By way of explanation two years later, Mayor Nulman said: "We have a rather sophisticated citizenry in this town, and it's an upscale community. The questions were excellent. The reaction was reasonable and appropriate. I think the newspapers were impressed."[45]

Donald Deieso, of New Jersey's Department of Environmental Protection, was quoted at the end of the *Record* article as saying, "Let's hope there's as much media attention when this [Clinton radon] problem has been controlled." In fact, however, the print press coverage of the radon in Clinton, the largest concentration of high levels in the country up to that time, was modest and accurate. The article on the town meeting appeared on page A49 of *The Record*. And indeed that coverage was noticed within Deieso's department, where, he said later, "we called one the good radon and the other the bad radon," reflecting the relatively smaller public information problem the naturally occurring radon in Clinton was causing the state.[46] State Senator Richard Zimmer, who has cosponsored radon legislation, said: "The residents of Clinton did not rely on TV for their information; they relied on their elected officials, on the DEP, and to a lesser extent on their local newspapers." Moreover, Zimmer said, "the coverage of Vernon was ... entirely on the political story, ... whereas in Clinton, it was much more focused on the objective of environmental health problems and what could be done about it." In comparing the two situations, he added, "A relatively trivial health risk [in Vernon] got all the news and all the attention, while the most serious single environmental health hazard in the state was overshadowed. And obviously, a lot more money was being spent on these damn drums [of radium-tainted soil] than on our . . . natural radon program."[47]

All four of Zimmer's points are correct. The flow of information in Clinton was different and less inflammatory; the Vernon story was one of political controversy, while in Clinton the focus was on health risks; the Vernon story, though less important in the long run, overshadowed the Clinton story in the press; and it cost far more to cope with the Montclair–Glen Ridge–West Orange dirt than it did to eliminate the problem caused by radon in Clinton, where the EPA remediated ten houses by sealing cracks and venting basements for a total cost of about $10,000, and other individuals paid from a few hundred to a couple of thousand dollars to have their basements vented, cracks sealed, drains covered, or whatever it took to reduce the radon levels in their houses to below 4 picocuries per liter of air. Mayor Nulman more or less summed up the situation:

> At least radon is something you can do something about. You can be the master of your own destiny as far as radon is concerned. I went out and bought a house. . . . I found a house that met my needs and I said, "Gee, I wonder if it has any radon in it?" It was just on the perimeter of [Clinton Knolls], and I said, well, there's one way to find out. . . . I made an offer on the house, and the offer was acceptable, and I proceeded to hire somebody to come in and test for radon, and lo and behold it had a 130 [reading], so I went to the . . . seller and I said, "Here are the results. I have talked to an expert in remediating these kinds of problems. He tells me that for $900 he can put in a ventilating system. . . . Will you pay for it?" The guy says, "Yep." So I had this guy . . . come in, do the work, had the testers come back, and lo and behold my level was below 2. . . . It did the job.[48]

Conclusion

Radon, although it may be as old as the earth, is relatively new as a public health hazard. Before studies in the late 1970s began to indicate that it was a significant cause of lung cancer, almost no radiation scientist worried about it except as a risk for uranium miners. And no one effectively alerted the public to the possibility

that it could pose a domestic risk until January 1985, when the results of the tests on Stanley Watras's Boyertown, Pennsylvania,
house began to be publicized. But even after the Watras discovery
and the two New Jersey radon cases discussed above, coverage was
spotty and sporadic.

The failure of the press to show more interest in radon would
appear to result from what is nearly always a fatal combination: scientific uncertainty, which in this case is about what level of radon
in a house is dangerous, not whether radon poses a cancer threat at
all, a distinction the press has frequently blurred; and lack of political controversy (the Vernon case is atypical) deriving from the fact
that there is no villain, industrial or otherwise, to blame for the
problem and that, once identified, radon can be eliminated relatively
inexpensively, which seems to diminish perceptions of the magnitude of the problem. Nevertheless, if Richard Guimond, former
head of EPA's Radon Action Program, and Nicholls are right, or
even close to right, insufficient attention is being paid to a significant cause of lung cancer.

Guimond said the most powerful tool he had was the news media
and that for the most part the quality of national press coverage of
radon has been reasonably good. But he added that he was unhappy
with the quantity of coverage.

Guimond believes in the power of the press, at least about matters
like radon, to influence both the public and senior policymakers, who,
he contends, continue to be concerned that a major federal attack on
radon would be a budget buster. The implication of his argument is
that if the press had covered the bureaucratic battling over the federal
government's failure to fund EPA's radon program, it could have made
a lifesaving difference by creating enough public pressure to force
either the administration or Congress to act.

From another perspective, New Jersey state Senator Zimmer, when
asked whether press coverage stirred him to legislative action on radon,
said, "Yes, I mean that's what stirs my awareness of virtually everything."[49] Zimmer is hardly alone among public officials in holding this
view. As in the case of radon, press coverage often brings issues that
they are unaware of to the attention of government officials, but more
often it gives a new reality to issues they are dimly aware of. This is
the well-know agenda-setting function of the press. The quantity and
tone of press coverage are sometimes the only measures officials have
of public opinion, and there are policymakers who regard the two as
functionally equivalent.

The media, of course, are most responsive to events. This is why the Watras house got coverage. It is also the most likely explanation why failure to adequately fund EPA's radon program got little or no coverage. Federal bureaucrats are always fighting over funding for programs. What makes this one worth writing about? It certainly isn't the fact that some scientists say radon cause lung cancer while others say we don't know whether it does or not at the levels at which people are exposed to it in their houses. The press abhors scientific uncertainty of this kind only slightly less than nature abhors a vacuum. As a result, print and especially electronic media have difficulty with stories like radon and cholesterol that reflect widespread disagreement among respected scientists. It would probably take an event of the magnitude of a surgeon general's report on radon, similar to the 1964 report on smoking, to capture the national media's attention for more than a fleeting moment. In the smoking case, which is discussed in Chapter 8, the weight of thirty-five years of accumulated data forced government action, without much help from the media. If it takes that long for radon, and the minimum EPA estimate for excess lung cancers is correct, there will be 175,000 early deaths that might have been prevented.

That would be a heavy burden to place on the shoulders of the media, and an unfair one because even with blanket coverage of radon, some people will choose to ignore the health message and not have their houses tested. Indeed, during a period when Senator Bill Bradley (D-N.J.) was talking around the state about the importance of testing for radon, his own house had not been tested. An interesting question is whether the media's ability to make some difference, both by informing the public directly and by creating pressure on public officials to act, gives them any responsibility to do so. Traditionally, editors have taken the view that news media have no obligation to educate, they have an obligation to inform. But this is often a distinction without a difference, one to which lip service is paid but which remains essentially unexamined, although AIDS, the subject of Chapter 6 in this book, may be changing that.

What the media should not do, of course, is indoctrinate. Most editors and reporters agree that the news media's role is to inform in ways that are adequate to convey information to readers or viewers, and to attempt to persuade by reasoned argument on editorial and op-ed pages, and in public affairs programs. They become somewhat uncomfortable, however, when anyone outside the profession couches this role in the language of duty or obligation.

NOTES

1. Peter Overby, *Record* (Hackensack), May 20, 1986, p. A8.

2. V. Elaine Smay, "Radon Exclusive," *Popular Science*, November 1985, p. 77.

3. Ibid.

4. Allan Mazur, "Putting Radon on the Public's Risk Agenda," *Science, Technology and Human Values*, Summer–Fall 1987, p. 89, citing William Makofske and Michael Edelstein, eds., *Radon and the Environment* (Mahwah, N.J.: Ramapo College, 1987), pp. 376–78.

5. Peter Overby, "A Grim Report on Radon," *Record* (Hackensack), November 1, 1985, p. A1.

6. John H. Dorsey, New Jersey state senator, interview, Trenton, May 16, 1988.

7. Mary Jo Patterson, "Cancer Watch: Surviving Radium Workers Face a Time Bomb," *Star-Ledger* (Newark), January 11, 1978, p. 12. The following account of the role played by the U.S. Radium plant has been compiled principally from Patterson's story in the *Star-Ledger*, but some of the details come from stories by Peter Overby ("Few Cancers Found at Radon Sites," December 22, 1983, p. C1) and Bettina Boxall, ("Radiation Cleanup Begins Tomorrow," December 4, 1983, p. A1) in the *Record* (Hackensack). Quotations, unless otherwise identified, are from the Patterson article.

8. "It's Just Dirt," Eagleton Institute of Politics, Rutgers University, May 1988, p. 3. Quoted by permission.

9. New Jersey Network News, November 30, 1983.

10. Peter Overby and Jan Barry, "Radiation Report Greeted Angrily," *Record* (Hackensack), December 2, 1983, p. A1.

11. Centers for Disease Control, Public Health Advisory for Glen Ridge and Montclair, December 6, 1983.

12. Peter Overby, "50 Houses Added to Radon Search," *Record* (Hackensack), January 6, 1984, p. C1.

13. Christopher Daggett, administrator, Region II, EPA, interview, Princeton, N.J., May 18, 1988.

14. Peter Overby, "Las Vegas Balks at Essex Radium." *Record* (Hackensack), July 11, 1985, p. A1.

15. Peter Sandman, interview, New Brunswick, N.J., April 28, 1988.

16. Donald Deieso, assistant commissioner, N.J. Department of Environmental Protection, interview, Trenton, May 16, 1988.

17. "It's Just Dirt," Eagleton Institute of Politics, Rutgers University, May, 1988, p. 10. Quoted by permission.

18. Peter Overby, "Kearny Angry over Radioactive Soil," *Record* (Hackensack), September 22, 1985, p. A47.

19. The chronology of events relating to Vernon that follows has been

compiled from interviews with Vernon Mayor Victor Marotta and town activists James Opfer, Eileen Opfer, Maureen Sweeney, and Marianne Reilly; also from accounts in the *Vernon News* (November 28, 1986) and the *Sussex County Voice* (August 1986). Other sources are individually identified.

20. "The Nimbies in Vernon," *Record* (Hackensack), July 31, 1986, p. A20.

21. Deieso interview.

22. Ibid.

23. Draft Final Feasibility Study for the Montclair, West Orange, and Glen Ridge, New Jersey, Radium Sites, U.S. Environmental Protection Agency, September 13, 1985.

24. Dorsey interview.

25. The quotation reflects Jim Opfer's recollection of what was said by Larry Mendel of Channel 7, New York.

26. Tom Johnson, "1,000 Radon Foes Rally at Statehouse," *Star-Ledger* (Newark), July 9, 1986, p. 1.

27. Peter Overby, "Vernon Protests Hit Home," *Record* (Hackensack), July 17, 1986, p. E1.

28. Peter Overby, "Vernon's Network of Protest," *Record.* (Hackensack), July 27, 1986, p. A1.

29. The *New York Times* published a story on July 26, 1986, on page 30, by Alfonso A. Narvaez, under the headline "Town Protests Plan by Jersey to Store Radon." The story did not specifically mention disobedience classes, but it did convey the sense that the citizens of Vernon were remarkably well organized and prepared.

30. Daggett interview.

31. Ibid.

32. Richard T. Dewling, telephone interview, June 25, 1990.

33. Gerald Nicholls, assistant director for radiation protection programs, N.J. Department of Environmental Protection, interview, Trenton, May 16, 1988.

34. Ibid.

35. Ibid.

36. Ibid.

37. Robert Nulman, mayor of Clinton, N.J., interview, Clinton, N.J., May 17, 1988.

38. J. J. Drautman, "Federal, State and Local Officials Say Radon Project Results Prove Problem Can Be Fixed Economically," *Hunterdon Review*, November 19, 1986, p. 1.

39. Nulman interview.

40. Ibid.

41. Daggett interview.

42. Nulman interview.

43. J. J. Drautman, physicist and writer for the *Hunterdon Review*, interview, Clinton, N.J., May 17, 1988.

44. Peter Overby, "Clinton Ready to Tackle Radon," *Record* (Hackensack), April 6, 1986, p. A49.

45. Nulman interview.

46. Deieso interview.

47. Richard Zimmer, New Jersey state senator, interview, Trenton, May 16, 1988.

48. Nulman interview.

49. Zimmer interview.

4

Nuclear Power:
How Safe Is
Safe Enough?

O N Thursday, March 1, 1990, the Nuclear Regulatory Commission voted to give a full-power operating license to a nuclear reactor in Seabrook, New Hampshire, a beach town near the Massachusetts state line. The plant received its license more than a decade behind schedule, and its cost overrun was $5.5 billion. The dispute surrounding the Seabrook reactor, ostensibly about its evacuation plan, cost one governor (Meldrim Thompson Jr., R-N.H.) his job and helped earn another (Michael S. Dukakis, D-Mass.) a presidential nomination. Still another New Hampshire governor, John H. Sununu, eventually witnessed the licensing of Seabrook from the West Wing of the White House, where he dominates environmental policy as chief of staff in the administration of President George Bush.

During the eleven years bounded by America's closest nuclear call at Three Mile Island in Pennsylvania and the issuing of the Seabrook license, the nation's nuclear industry was turned on its head. An industry in which everything once seemed possible, at least to its boosters in government and industry, and to the media, which in the 1940s and 1950s often reported uncritically on promising scientific and technological developments, was down to its last gasp. There had been no new orders for plants since 1978, and a hundred orders dating from between 1974 and 1978 had been canceled. The safety scare resulting from the accident at Three Mile Island and a surprisingly plentiful energy supply in the wake of the 1974 oil shock dealt the nuclear power industry a severe blow. Largely because of the public notice given to global warming in the late 1980s, however, the industry has been struggling to rise from its decade of dormancy. It has been trying both to address the safety concerns raised by plant operation and waste disposal and to contain costs. The safety-related problems are as much political as technical, reflecting the public's conditioning to fear anything nuclear and a legacy of the mistrust created by a secretive industry and regulatory agency. Keeping costs down depends on technical factors like standardization of plants and speeding up the licensing process, and political ones like avoiding lawsuits by groups opposed to nuclear power.

Critical reporting of these issues was inevitable, given the nature of nuclear power. This coverage played an important although not necessarily decisive role in the decline of the nuclear industry, which was already under way by the mid–1970s. For a decade, from the time of the accident at Three Mile Island until the burgeoning of global warming as a major environmental policy issue, the press repeatedly focused on minor mishaps at nuclear plants, demonstrations by opponents of nuclear power, the history of secrecy and foul-ups by the government's administrative bureaucracy, and the ever-rising costs of construction. This media spotlight has had the salutary effect of focusing the industry's attention on the right kinds of safety issues and on cost reduction. But it may also have contributed to billions of dollars in extra energy costs. To illustrate this point, consider news coverage of the central event in the American nuclear debate, at least until the Chernobyl disaster in the Soviet Union in 1986: the accident at Metropolitan Edison's Three Mile Island plant near Middletown, Pennsylvania. For years after the accident, Three Mile Island kept turning up in the news in ways that stoked the public's fear.

On Sunday, June 2, 1985, for example, *The Washington Post* ran an Associated Press story under the headline "TMI Reactor Decision Rekindles Scare of '79." The news that stimulated the article was a 4–1 decision by the Nuclear Regulatory Commission to authorize the restart of the undamaged twin of the nuclear reactor at Three Mile Island that was shut down because of the March 28, 1979, accident.[1] The article did not report on that decision, however, until its nineteenth paragraph. Before getting to the news, it reported colorfully on the original "scare" at Three Mile Island. It said, among other things: "In the early hours, Metropolitan Edison Company, operator of the plant, played down the seriousness of the accident. But those who had seen the Jack Lemmon-Jane Fonda film 'The China Syndrome' didn't have to be told. . . . The meltdown in that movie—all the way to China, maybe—might have been a script for TMI, with minor changes."[2]

But there was no containment-breaching meltdown in the movie or at Three Mile Island. Fuel melted at TMI, perhaps half of the core—a not insignificant event but a very significant difference for the health and safety of those living in the surrounding Pennsylvania countryside.

The word *meltdown* in the AP article implied molten fuel burning through the reactor containment into the ground below with the attendant release of massive amounts of radiation. At Three Mile Island, as far as anyone can tell, the amount of radiation released posed little danger to human health.

Why characterize the accident at Three Mile Island more than six years after it occurred by using an analogy to a movie that depicts an event of a kind that to this day has never happened? More than eight years ago, the President's Commission on the Accident at TMI (Kemeny Commission) determined that the air the local citizens were breathing at the time was no more dangerous than the air residents of Denver breathe every day.[3] The article did not mention the Kemeny Commission report or any of the health studies carried out by state and private groups. It set out to recreate the atmosphere of fear and confusion surrounding the events at Three Mile Island on March 28, 1979, and the following days, an atmosphere never entirely dissipated by findings such as the Kemeny Commission's.

Although this particular article was more extreme than most, the fact that *The Washington Post* published it, as did many other papers around the country, is emblematic of an approach toward coverage of nuclear power in general since Three Mile Island. The use of dramatic but largely irrelevant imagery and the misuse of risk assessments have distorted the public's perception of the risks associated with nuclear power generation.

Until the disaster at Chernobyl on April 26, 1986, which happened thousands of miles away in the Soviet Union at a reactor lacking a radiation containment dome—the thick protective cap that all U.S. reactors have—no accident in the history of nuclear power generation received anything like the press coverage given to the accident at Three Mile Island (although a 1968 accident led to the publication of a book titled *We Almost Lost Detroit*).[4] The Three Mile Island accident was judged to be extraordinary by news organizations in large measure because it was a "unique" event that threatened catastrophe.[5] According to David Salisbury of *The Christian Science Monitor*: "There was the perceived possibility of an extremely large catastrophe, which plays to people's morbid curiosity. The larger and rarer a catastrophe, the more interest it seems to evoke."[6] As events were unfolding, news sources used the highly charged word *meltdown* to describe the catastrophic potential of the accident. Other sources said that a hydrogen bubble in the reactor vessel might explode, suggesting incorrectly that the plant could blow up like a giant atomic bomb. Confusion and uncertainty led to inaccurate reports of dangerous levels of radiation in the air, which would require emergency evacuations.

As many as 500 reporters were at the scene trying to make sense of the chaos for their readers, viewers, and listeners. But most of them were not adequately equipped to do the job because nuclear power was not their beat. They did not know how reactors worked, they were unfamiliar with the technical language, and they knew little or nothing about the health risks of radiation. These inadequacies made them highly vulnerable to manipulation by industry or government sources, but not as vulnerable as they would have been if their sources hadn't been so confused themselves about what was happening. Taking into account the disadvantages under which most journalists at Three Mile Island were working, they performed relatively well. And, for what it is worth, most of them reported more often in a reassuring than in an alarming tone, at least to the extent that this can be determined by content analysis, a technique to examine news coverage quantitatively.[7]

On balance, national media coverage of nuclear power has become negative since the mid-1970s.[8] This coverage is consistent with polling data on the attitudes toward nuclear power held by journalists employed by the national media.[9] These attitudes cannot fairly be treated as proof of biased coverage because there is no evidence that reporters' or editors' personal views have been reflected in their stories, but it would be naive to think that journalists' opinions and values never influence what they write or broadcast.

Most relevant surveys show a small but statistically significant link between the accident at Three Mile Island and a decline in public support for nuclear power generation. Similarly, interviews with policymakers, executives of power companies and reactor manufacturers, and representatives of public-interest and nuclear-industry lobbies reveal a belief bordering on religious faith that the way in which the press portrayed the accident, and nuclear safety generally after the accident, influenced energy policy and investment decisions. The sociologist Allan Mazur, on the other hand, has argued that in a technical controversy, irrespective of the quality or bias of media coverage, the more of it there is, the more opposition to the controversial technology there will be. The sheer intensity of the press coverage of the Three Mile Island accident, Mazur contends, turned the public against nuclear power, at least in the short run. He wrote:

> Fluctuations in public opinion throughout 1979 are precisely what would be predicted from the coverage-opinion hypothesis. The proportion of the public opposing the building of more nuclear power plants rose sharply after the first burst of coverage. This is hardly surprising since the specter of the accident would be expected to increase opposition regardless of any independent effect of the quantity of coverage. However, one would not expect, on this basis alone, that support for nuclear power would rebound within two months, as soon as the media coverage had fallen away, yet that is what happened, in accord with the coverage-opinion hypothesis.[10]

It seems far from conclusive that media coverage is ever sufficiently sustained on a particular controversy for the coverage-opinion hypothesis to have much significance in a relatively long-term process such as policy formation. Moreover, trying to parse out the precise impact of media coverage from that of other influences such as congressional pressure, economic factors, advocacy groups, and local politicians is a fool's errand. Nevertheless, it has been possible to correlate news coverage with the results of public-opinion polls and more subjective analyses to reach some rough conclusions about the influence of media coverage on the nuclear power industry and the role played by safety and health considerations.

The accident at Three Mile Island was a kind of epiphany of the nuclear age. It brought home to everyone the obvious, which at the same time was unthinkable: that a catastrophic accident could happen. If ever there was going to be a turning point in public opinion, short of a catastrophe, Three Mile Island was it. Attitudes measured by random surveys showed a statistically significant swing away from nuclear power almost immediately after the accident at Three Mile Island.[11] Before the accident, the public was in favor of building new nuclear plants by a 2-1 margin. After the accident, a majority of Americans was opposed to new construction. But when asked if they would favor new plants "if the federal government supervises their construction more strictly than has been the case up to now," public support returns to the pre-TMI levels.[12] Factors other than press coverage of TMI, however, such as the increasing costs of plant construction and a lack of perceived need for additional electrical capacity, could easily have been responsible for sustaining that shift in public opinion. But even by the late 1980s, about half of all Americans expressed some degree of support for the continued generation of nuclear power in the United States. In fact, some erosion of support for nuclear power was discernible before the accident. A 1984 study by the Office of Technology Assessment noted:

> From Earth Day in 1970 through the mid-1970s, opposition levels [to nuclear power] averaged 25 to 30 percent, indicating that substantial majorities of the public favored further nuclear development. However, by 1976, anti-nuclear referenda appeared on ballots in eight states.
>
> Polls taken between 1976 and 1979 indicated that slightly over half of the American public favored continued construction of nuclear plants in the United States.[13]

The OTA study displayed a chart based on surveys by the polling firm Cambridge Reports, which indicated that by 1983, 60 percent of Americans opposed the construction of new nuclear power plants. The precise question asked was "Do you favor or oppose the construction of more nuclear power plants?" In July, September, and November 1983, however, Cambridge Reports asked this question: "Do you strongly favor, somewhat favor, somewhat oppose, or strongly oppose the use of nuclear energy as one of the ways to provide electricity for the United States?" Combining the "strongly" and "somewhat" results, the totals for the three polls were, respectively: for nuclear energy, 53 percent, 45 percent, and 50 percent; against nuclear energy, 45 percent, 45 percent, and 48 percent. "Don't knows" accounted for the missing percentage points. More revealingly, from May 1984 through August 1987, Cambridge Reports asked this question thirteen times: "If additional supplies of electricity are needed in the years ahead, would you strongly favor, somewhat favor, somewhat oppose, or strongly oppose using more nuclear energy to generate electricity?" The pronuclear totals went as high as 58 percent and fell below 50 percent only once, in May 1986, after the Chernobyl accident in the Soviet Union. By August 1986, it was up to 50 percent again.[14]

The Accident

Although the event at Three Mile Island, widely referred to in the press as "the nation's worst commercial nuclear accident,"[15] was surrounded from beginning to end by confusion, there is now little disagreement about the essentials of what happened beginning at 4:00 A.M. on Wednesday, March 28. Cooling-system pumps malfunctioned; backup pumps went on, but operators failed to notice that valves for those pumps were closed; a relief valve opened properly but then stuck open; because of a faulty control panel warning signal, operators were unable to tell that it was open; as a result, the operators took a series of incorrect actions that removed water, exposing part of the reactor core, causing fuel to melt and some radiation to be released, mainly inside the containment dome. In other words, operator error (resulting at least in part from poor training and poor control-room design) combined with technical failures (the malfunctioning pumps, the stuck valve, and the broken signal) to put one reactor out of commission permanently and to shut down the other for more than six years.

By just past 9:00 the morning of March 28, a news story about the problem at Three Mile Island was moving on the Associated Press wire. At 6:30 P.M. on the "CBS Evening News," Walter Cronkite called it "the first step in a nuclear nightmare." On Thursday, Nuclear Regulatory Commission officials said the danger was minimal, but on Friday, Pennsylvania Governor Richard Thornburgh advised local residents that radioactive gases were still escaping from the plant and that they should stay indoors with the windows closed. The NRC also announced that there were gas bubbles in the reactor's cooling system. Also on Friday, an NRC official in Bethesda, Maryland, used the phrase "ultimate risk of meltdown," which was picked up by the networks and other major media. Over the next couple of days, one of the two gas bubbles, which was composed of hydrogen and erroneously believed to be explosive, and the perceived threat of meltdown were the focus of news coverage. On Sunday, April 1, President Jimmy Carter visited Three Mile Island with Governor Thornburgh to try to calm the public. And on April 2, Harold Denton of the NRC announced that the hydrogen bubble was subsiding. This marked the end of the event itself.

No one has died to date from radiation or other causes linked to the accident, but the possibility cannot be ruled out since the health effects of low-level radiation have not been definitely determined. The most comprehensive and reliable studies available suggest that the likely toll will be somewhere between zero and thirteen deaths.[16] (A study released in December 1989 by the National Research Council suggests that mortality associated with low-level radiation could be two to eight times greater than previously estimated.)[17]

There is widespread consensus on how poor the preparation for nuclear accidents was before Three Mile Island. Despite plenty of warnings that an accident of this kind could occur, no one was prepared for it—not the power company, not the federal government, not the state of Pennsylvania, and not the press. Nobody heeded the warning signs of earlier accidents such as those at the Brown's Ferry plant in Decatur, Alabama, in 1975, or the one at the Davis-Besse plant near Toledo, Ohio, in 1977, which was so similar to the accident at Three Mile Island that it could have been a rehearsal for it. (The plant managers at TMI had never been shown the postaccident report from Davis-Besse.) A study done by the American Physical Society in 1977 was also ignored, despite the fact that in it nuclear power advocate Edward Teller added his voice to those supporting increased precautions in plant operation and siting.

As a result, confusion reigned at Three Mile Island, and communications, both internally and externally, were chaotic. There was disagreement about what was happening and about what isolated bits of data meant; different sources were putting a different spin on information that was already mainly characterized by its uncertainty. For example, when asked during a press conference about the status of a hydrogen bubble in the reactor core, John Herbein, a vice president of Metropolitan Edison, the reactor's operator, said that it posed no danger to the core. Meanwhile, two NRC officials in Bethesda offered a worst-case scenario during a briefing in which they said the bubble could lead to a "meltdown."[18] The hundreds of reporters at the scene and in Washington were unable to get reliable information about the condition of the reactor and, to an even greater degree, about what the risks of a disaster were. Often no one at the site knew. Reliable data were being gathered on radiation releases by the Department of Energy, but it was not only the press that was not getting this information. According to John Kemeny, chairman of the commission that wrote the government's postaccident report, "four weeks after the accident, the other three major branches of the executive that participated still had not discovered that DOE had this crucial information."[19]

The Struggle for Public Opinion

How much did press coverage influence this concern? What about the broader issue of how the press covered the whole nuclear power industry between 1976 and 1986? For example, did television news, as psychiatrist Robert DuPont suggested after reviewing ten years' coverage from August 5, 1968, to April 20, 1979, focus on fear in its reporting on nuclear power?[20] How is the public influenced by the fact that roughly seven of ten sources cited in nuclear stories on television oppose the technology?[21] Do the media's questions about nuclear power frame the issue in a way that shapes the public's answers about the technology? Does the fact that the media frequently focus on controversy surrounding nuclear safety create undue public concern?

The news media objectify issues or events; in a certain sense, being reported on makes them "real," especially for legislators. Rep. Edward Markey (D-Mass.) said that news reports of issues and events represented a "legitimization of concern by Congress,"[22] which justifies spending time on them. From a different viewpoint, Carl Goldstein, who is in charge of media relations for the nuclear industry's main lobby, the U.S. Council on Energy Awareness, said the right news clipping was "an idiot's delight. A congressional staffer can show it to a member and say, 'This is all you need to know on this subject.' "[23] Goldstein's comment means that press coverage gives legislators a handle on the issue, something they can use to discuss it on the floor of the House, or in communications with constituents. Rep. Tom Bevill (D-Ala.) said he read the local papers carefully to anticipate questions at town meetings in his district.[24] Inevitably, the news coverage and opinion pieces Bevill reads on his way to the rural Alabama communities he represents help shape his answers to questions and, depending on how persuasive he is, the thinking of his constituents.

With that in mind, Goldstein and his staff do what they can to stimulate news articles and especially op-ed pieces that are favorable to their cause. They seek out writers, provide them with expense money and research and writing help if they need it, and advise them on how to place the articles. Groups opposed to nuclear power such as the Union of Concerned Scientists also use the op-ed pages as a vehicle for their views, but they generally write the pieces in-house. Even frustrated regulators resort to the press to get the attention of legislators and the public. They do so through standard techniques such as leaking information to reporters, but sometimes they try more direct routes. James K. Asselstine, who was appointed to the NRC by Ronald Reagan in 1982 and served until he resigned in 1987, frequently went public with dissents to NRC decisions in letters to Congress and on other platforms and regularly criticized the nuclear industry and the commission itself. When Asselstine's dissents were no longer allowed to be sent along with the opinions of the other commissioners, this action got some media attention, but neither his speeches nor his dissents were reported on, which suggests that although they might have had some direct influence on Congress, they had no impact on public opinion.

The two words that turn up most often in academic discussions of press influence on policy are *framing* and *agenda*. The conventional wisdom is that through a framing effect that characterizes an issue, the press shapes further discussion of that issue. In the nuclear weapons arena, *Washington Post* reporter Walter Pincus's characterization of the so-called neutron bomb as a weapon that kills people and preserves property is a classic example of framing a policy issue. President Carter prevailed upon West German chancellor Helmut Schmidt to take on the thankless task of persuading the NATO allies to deploy neutron artillery shells in Western Europe. Schmidt expended substantial political capital in getting the job done. But when the Carter administration's explanation that the weapon was designed to neutralize Soviet armored forces while doing minimal damage to West German civilians and buildings failed to catch up with the Pincus characterization, the weapon was never deployed. As a result, relations between the United States and West Germany were soured for the rest of Carter's term in office.

There is no equally clear-cut example of the press influencing policy on nuclear power by a framing effect, but post-TMI coverage of the industry was almost uniformly bleak (the exception was the newsweeklies, which concentrated more on economics and politics than science or safety). Broadly speaking, the entire issue can be said to have been negatively framed during the 1980s. Moreover, the fear of nuclear power, because of its identification with atomic weapons, was a source of either conscious or unconscious dread for many people. By the end of the decade, however, questions about reactor safety, waste disposal, the economics of nuclear power, and the need for the technology were being revisited by the news media in a more positive light. With global warming on the front burner, *The New York Times* and *The Washington Post* both wrote lead editorials urging a return to nuclear power. The *Times* editorial's headline was "Revive the Atom," and it said: "The United States cannot afford to wash its hands of an energy option that could prove both competitive and environmentally benign. The nuclear industry is worth reviving."[25] The *Post*, bemoaning the global inability to reduce carbon dioxide emissions, wrote: "One obvious solution is nuclear energy."[26] The *Times* also accused Massachusetts Governor Michael Dukakis of costing the owners of the Seabrook nuclear plant $2 billion by refusing to help develop an evacuation plan for the surrounding area.[27]

In Asselstine's view, the nuclear safety debate is "too polarized," and the press has contributed to that polarization, which in turn "places too big a roadblock in front of a fundamentally good technology."[28] Harold W. Lewis, a physicist at the University of California, Santa Barbara, who directed a study that cast doubt on the degree of certainty of previous NRC safety assessments, also said that "somewhere along the line things polarized around the safety issues" and that the press played a role in that polarization. Lewis, who is plainspoken and accessible to reporters, amplified his remarks by saying that the press, although in a secondary way, "contributed to the slowdown in the development of the nuclear industry."[29]

Although Lewis is vocally though not uncritically pronuclear, he was characterized in a *Washington Post* headline shortly after his study appeared as an "Anti-Nuclear Cult Hero."[30] The full headline said: "Anti-Nuclear Cult Hero Backs Atomic Power Safety." Indeed, Lewis does back "atomic power safety," along with coal power safety, highway safety, freedom of speech, and motherhood. But that's not what the *Post* story was about. The story, strikingly, was about Lewis saying that he considered nuclear power to be safer than suggested by the Rasmussen report, the study he criticized for improperly calculating the uncertainty surrounding the likelihood of a core melt. Somehow the headline writer and the head of the copy desk, who is responsible for checking the headline against the copy, allowed the misleading headline to appear. Lewis says he believes there is a mind-set about nuclear safety in the press, and perhaps in society at large, that provides a favorable environment for errors of that kind.

According to politically conservative social scientists S. Robert Lichter and Stanley Rothman,[31] science journalists are three times more likely (40 percent to 12 percent) to agree than to disagree with the statement about nuclear power that "Present risks are unacceptable." Also, when asked which sources they deemed reliable, a majority trusted antinuclear groups (55 percent) while only one in three would rely on industry sources for information.[32]

In the *Post* story, written four weeks after the release of the report, Lewis was paraphrased as saying that he should have offered his view about reactor safety before, "but nobody asked him." After reading Lewis's report titled "Risk Assessment Review Group Report to the U.S. Nuclear Regulatory Commission,"[33] one wonders why nobody asked him. The Lewis report says repeatedly that "the Group could not judge whether the central value [for the likelihood of a catastrophic accident] given [in the reactor safety study] is high or low." In other words, Lewis's report nowhere says that nuclear power is less safe than the Rasmussen report says it is.

Even when the initial story on the NRC's actions in response to the Lewis report was carefully and responsibly written, as was the case with David Burnham's account in *The New York Times*,[34] the most penetrating message delivered was that nuclear power might not be as safe as you think. The headline on the *Times* story, which appeared at the top of page 1, said, "Nuclear Agency Revokes Support for Safety Study," and the "bank," or subheadline, said, "Risk Estimate on Reactors Now Called Unreliable." The headline is about as accurate as possible given the constraints of fitting it into a single column. But who would draw the conclusion from reading it that nuclear power might be safer than previously thought?

Properly, Burnham's story in the fourth paragraph said: "The [Nuclear Regulatory] commission's statement [on release of the report] did not say that it had now decided that nuclear power reactors were more hazardous than it estimated in 1975 [in the Rasmussen report]." But the story went on to say that "the commission's decision to disown the major conclusion of the [Rasmussen] study . . . was considered a serious blow to nuclear energy. The nuclear industry and its supporters in government, Congress and academic circles, in their efforts to undermine the critics of nuclear energy, have strongly relied on the study's assertion of the relative safety of atomic reactors."

What seems lacking most of all at this point in the story is Harold Lewis's perspective. Since the report treats the safety question without resolving it, it seems reasonable to wonder why Lewis was not asked to comment. If Lewis were quoted here as saying that he believed, as he now says he does, that the Rasmussen report overstated the risk of a nuclear accident, rather than understating it, the whole thrust of the story would have been different. Rather, Burnham quoted an NRC spokesman who said that "the chances of an accident could be greater or could be less than was stated in the report." This is both accurate and fair. But it is not as authoritative as a quote from the author of the study, and it could be viewed as self-serving coming from a government spokesman. In his January 20 story and in follow-up stories on January 21 and March 19,[35] Burnham and the *Times* failed to provide Lewis's view, which, polls have consistently shown, represents the mainstream view of nuclear physicists and engineers in this country.[36] Instead, they quoted Rep. Morris K. Udall (D-Ariz.), an anti-nuclear member of Congress, as saying that "nuclear proponents have for years used the study to assure the public that nuclear power is safe"; Daniel Ford, an economist with the antinuclear Union of Concerned Scientists, who saw Lewis's report as a "signal" that nuclear policy would be reevaluated; Peter Bradford, at the time perhaps the most antinuclear member of the NRC, who said "time had run out on the self-delusions of the [nuclear] boosters"; and two industry spokesmen whose views tend to be discounted by the public because of self-interest, real or perceived.

As noted above, the national newsweeklies represented something of an exception to the rule that the media gave undue emphasis to safety problems at nuclear power plants. A review of all nuclear-safety-related articles in *Time, Newsweek*, and *U.S. News & World Report* from January 1977 through December 1986, a total of 146 articles,[37] reveals an approach that is generally thoughtful and fair to both sides and to the facts. There is no obvious explanation for the contrast between weekly magazine coverage and what appeared in daily newspapers or on television, except that on balance at the time newsmagazines tended to be a bit more conservative than newspapers and television.

The bias for news, however, dictates that stories about safety are written only when something has gone awry, not when all systems are working well. No matter how carefully the stories are written, and no matter how evident it is that the problems being recounted are remediable, and that no one was killed, was injured, or suffered any adverse physical effect from the accident, such stories can hardly help but reinforce the view that a catastrophic accident at a nuclear power plant is, if not imminent, inevitable.

An important logical consequence of framing the debate in terms of the possibility of a catastrophic accident is that it tends to make nuclear power seem unacceptable. The syllogism is simple: catastrophes are unacceptable; nuclear power generation may lead to a catastrophe; therefore, nuclear power is unacceptable. But what is the real likelihood of a catastrophe, what is its potential magnitude, and what are the trade-offs for taking the risk? Philip Handler, a former president of the National Academy of Sciences, answered the question this way:

> If we deny ourselves nuclear energy, we are heading for a real catastrophe down the road, a day when we will simply not have enough energy

to meet the nation's needs. I have suggested that that would be a much greater catastrophe than the kind the critics are talking about, even though I agree that there is a small but finite possibility of a truly major accident in a nuclear reactor somewhere down the road.

There are risks associated with every technology. They should be identified and minimized by reasonable means at reasonable costs— reasonable in relation to the benefits involved. Large benefits warrant significant risks; trivial benefits warrant little or none.[38]

Should news stories simply reflect Handler's view of nuclear safety along with that of a Ralph Nader or Daniel Ford every time the safety issue arises? Or should news media try go beyond an uncritical presentation of both sides in an effort to help readers and viewers better assess the policy debate? The answer to this question depends on the relative weight of opinion supporting contending positions. Journalists who cover science and technology for elite media are often well enough trained to be able to tell when a preponderance of scientific opinion favors one view over another, even if they cannot evaluate the underlying science. If one view is prevalent, and it is not unduly tainted by political or other forms of bias, it should be presented as such, not as the equivalent of a less authoritative view. There can be little disagreement that the press should provide its audience with accurate, understandable, thoughtfully balanced, and substantially complete information. But technically complex public policy debates cannot be resolved in the press. The best the press can usually do, because of inherent uncertainty and lack of time and expertise, is to provide a sense of the parameters of the controversy and some clues to the relative strengths of the forces arrayed on either side of it.

Although the press is fairly good at portraying what the various interests think is at stake in the nuclear debate, it rarely reports that scientists, engineers, and energy specialists consider the technology to be acceptably safe.[39] This group of nuclear specialists has strong interests in promoting nuclear power, but its members are also more familiar than the general public with technology, probability calculations, and risk assessment, and less susceptible to the emotional anecdotes, imagery, and mythmaking that have fed public fear of anything nuclear.[40] As a result, they are more receptive to the trade-offs involved and less fixated on the potential human and financial costs of an accident. They are aware, for example, that the more familiar hazards of burning coal—respiratory disease; cancer from arsenic, lead, and mercury inhalation; mining accidents; acid rain—are more certain and could well be more deleterious than those encountered in operating nuclear plants.

Does this mean that society should accept the judgment of the technical community that nuclear power generation constitutes an acceptable risk? Not at all. It simply means that scientists and engineers have a more systematic way of getting to the bottom line than most of the public, who do not understand or much like considerations of probability or uncertainty. Society's judgment about which risks are acceptable may not be wholly rational, but emotional, religious, moral, ideological, psychological, and other factors have a legitimate social role to play in these determinations.

Sometimes, legislators and regulators agree, the press can make an immediate difference in nuclear-related bureaucratic or administrative matters by calling the attention of Congress and the public to inappropriate government action. Asselstine, for example, is persuaded that press coverage of a 1985 effort on the part of the NRC to evade the federal Sunshine Act, which seeks to ensure that most government activity is open to public scrutiny, prevented the NRC from doing it. Rep. Markey criticized what he called the agency's "sunset regulations" at a hearing of the House Subcommittee on Energy Conservation and Power that was covered by both *The New York Times* and *The Washington Post*.[41] He was referring to a 3-2 vote by the commission to hold closed meetings. This vote followed the public disclosure of the transcript of an earlier secret meeting about reactor problems. The *Post* subsequently wrote an editorial criticizing the NRC's attempt to bypass the law by creating "a new kind of nonmeeting called a 'gathering.' A gathering can be closed and does not require a transcript," as do closed meetings under the Sunshine Act.[42] The NRC has not repealed its regulation authorizing "gatherings," but neither has it met under its provisions.

On the Road in Vermont

The news media's influence on nuclear power development was not always played out on the national scene. Plants must meet state regulatory requirements, as the Seabrook situation in New Hampshire illustrated. In nearby Vermont, extensive press coverage of a nuclear issue in 1982 probably forced Governor Richard Snelling to cancel shipments of high-level radioactive waste through the state. The waste originated at the Chalk River nuclear plant in Ontario and was being

shipped to the Savannah River reprocessing plant in Barnwell, South
Carolina. New York and Michigan had already refused permission for
the waste to be transported on their highways. Snelling gave his approval for the radioactive cargoes to be hauled along I–91 without
public notice and without even notifying the appropriate members of
the legislature. But on August 24, three environmental groups held a
news conference to announce that "At least one and possibly more
shipments of high-level and highly dangerous radioactive waste was
trucked through Vermont in July with the blessing of state officials."[43]

The 24th was a Tuesday, and by Thursday the issue was hot politics
in Vermont. Democratic Lieutenant Governor Madeline Kunin, who
was challenging Snelling in the upcoming November election, called
that day for suspension of the shipments until the relevant safety and
insurance questions could be answered. *The Burlington Free Press*
reported that Kunin charged Snelling with too lightly dismissing "serious issues surrounding the transportation of highly radioactive
wastes." According to the *Free Press*, Kunin also said that keeping the
shipments secret from the public was unacceptable.[44] For the next
week, the battle was fought in the Vermont press and on evening news
programs. Snelling was clearly on the defensive. Even aging Yippie
Abbie Hoffman entered the fray, speaking out against the shipments.
The next day Snelling's secretary of transportation did his best to link
Kunin and Hoffman in a scenario involving a terrorist takeover of a
radioactive waste truck on I–91. A story by UPI's Rod Clarke assessed
the episode as follows: "Friday, the administration rolled in the
medium-range artillery and proceeded to shoot itself in the foot."[45]

The nuclear waste dispute was shaping up as a prime example of
the role the press plays in an acute political controversy with technical
dimensions. First, advocacy groups that oppose the technology found
a legitimate issue—the public and its appropriate representatives were
not advised that Canadian nuclear waste was being transported
through the state—the same kind of issue that moved the people of
Vernon, New Jersey, to vigorously contest the burial of radioactive dirt
in their community. They then disclosed it to the press with a spin of
their own choosing: that the shipments were inherently unsafe. Within
twenty-four hours the waste shipments had become a gubernatorial
campaign issue. All the press had to do at that point was to hang
around Kunin and Snelling and report on the missiles they were firing
at each other. This coverage in turn stoked up the dormant fires in
thirty-one Vermont towns that had previously passed ordinances banning shipments of nuclear wastes within their jurisdictions. There

were virtually no assessments in the press of the possible health effects of an accident or the likelihood of an accident, but there was this headline in the *Times Argus*: " 'Nightmare' seen in Nuke Wastes."[46] According to the story, based on an interview with the chief of medicine at Copely Hospital in Morrisville, Vermont, "hospitals in the state have neither the facilities nor the experience to respond to an accident involving nuclear materials." The story did not speculate on the likelihood of an accident, but its tone was panicky.

On September 3, Governor Snelling suspended the shipments, saying that their security had been breached by aides to Kunin, who passed along the dates of completed shipments to the media. Snelling subsequently asked the NRC to investigate the release of the dates. Kunin, denying any security breach, said she was delighted that the shipments were being stopped. She added that she thought the governor was responding to mounting public protests, not a security breach.[47] On September 4, the *Rutland Daily Herald* reported that Snelling said he had "directed officials to begin drafting revisions to state regulations so Vermont highways will not receive a 'disproportionate share' of nuclear waste shipments." By September 8, the Thousand Islands Bridge Authority had said it would ban shipments of the Canadian nuclear materials until the federal government guaranteed that it would pay for any accidents. And by mid-September, a number of Vermont communities, including Burlington and Brattleboro, had asked the state to stop the shipments. By the beginning of October, the debate had escalated to the federal level on the question of whether Vermont could have legally put into practice tough regulations limiting the use of its highways by nuclear waste trucks. The Department of Transportation, supporting Snelling, said no, while Senator Patrick J. Leahy (D) said yes.

Toward the end of October, press coverage was focusing on charges by the Vermont Public Interest Research Group, which opposed the shipments, that the casks in which the waste was shipped were unsafe and a complaint against Vermont filed with the federal Department of Transportation by Nuclear Assurance Corporation, the waste shipping company. Nuclear Assurance sought relief from the federal government because it was prohibited by Vermont from resuming shipments. The Nuclear Assurance complaint resulted in a small chain reaction with the potential to alter national policy on nuclear waste shipments.[48] As a result of Snelling's ban on shipments, Nuclear Assurance challenged regulations in New York and Michigan as well. Then, on October 30, *The Burlington Free Press* reported that "The Orleans County town of Glover has become the first community in Vermont to regulate radioactive waste transportation. Townspeople voted to require prior notice [of shipments] and proof of container quality."[49] When the Vermont Agency of Transportation issued "Proposed Regulations Regarding the Transportation of Hazardous Materials" on January 18, 1983, policy decisions were being made at the local, state, and federal levels. And on May 27, 1983, the state transportation agency issued a press release on new rules governing the shipment of hazardous materials that said: "Shipments of high level radioactive hazardous materials could not be routed through Vermont for the purpose of avoiding more direct routes through other states." The new rules went into effect on June 24, 1983.

The Vermont waste shipment story shows the role the press can play in setting the policy agenda. Three environmental groups uncovered the issue and used the press to amplify it. Without the press, it probably would not have existed as a political reality. The fact that the nuclear waste issue emerged during a gubernatorial campaign, and therefore was immediately politicized, added to the controversy, and thus to the news coverage. Policy in this case was driven by a mix of citizens' groups, industry, and local, state, and federal officials, all using the press as an instrument, and often the main instrument, of their ambitions. The print press (I did not examine television in this case) by and large did a respectable job of balancing the political interests—that is, neither Kunin nor Snelling was treated unfairly. To put it another way, the press generally avoided being manipulated by the politicians.

The safety issue, however, the putative focus of the debate, was never seriously addressed. Reading through months of clippings from the major Vermont newspapers provides almost no help in deciding whether to be for or against the shipments. There is no real discussion of the risks or benefits of permitting the shipments to go through the state.

Sins of Omission

The agenda-setting effect may be most profoundly felt when journalists fail to put an item on the agenda. For example, since 1967, technology has existed to build nuclear reactors in which a meltdown of the fuel in the core is substantially less likely than in conventional reactors, which is why these reactors are termed inherently safe. Lawrence M.

Lidsky, a professor of nuclear engineering at the Massachusetts Institute of Technology, is an advocate of these inherently safe reactors. He wrote the following in the *New Republic*:

> Reactors can be built today that are able to survive the failure of any single component or any combination of components without fear, indeed without even the possibility of fuel damage. Without fuel damage, there can be no release of radiation. . . .
> We have known for a long time how to build such reactors—a prototype has been operating since 1967. It is only recently . . . that we realize how badly they are needed. The key to the new reactors is a radically different fuel form that is capable of withstanding very high temperatures. The reactors are small to ensure that it is physically impossible for such temperatures ever to be achieved.[50]

For twenty years, the press ignored this technology. Lidsky said he could remember no coverage in the media, which was "one of the main reasons why [he] wrote the article." There were two basic reasons why he thought nothing was getting into the press. No one outside the industry, he said, really knows about or understands this technology, and no one inside the industry wants to publicize it because to do so would be an implicit statement that the reactors we are currently employing are not as safe as they could be. Lidsky emphatically noted that the prototype that has run continuously since 1967 in Julich, Germany, is an "inherently safe reactor."

The nuclear industry and the federal government largely ignored so-called inherently safe technology, Lidsky said, not only because any suggestion that reactors might be made safer indicated that they were not currently safe enough, but because a major economic and technical commitment had been made to existing reactor technology, and because the political climate was perceived as inimical to expansion of U.S. nuclear energy capacity.

By the end of the 1980s, however, Westinghouse, General Electric, and a small company called General Atomic were moving ahead with new designs for reactors that are safer than those now operating because they reduce or eliminate weak points in design of control rooms and in the plumbing systems of nuclear plants such as valves, pumps, welds in pipes, and gauges. These new designs also dilute the concentration of fuel in the core, which prevents meltdown by containing the amount of heat that can be accidentally generated as a result of loss of coolant. The *New York Times* carried a lengthy and well-informed story on these developments.[51] How well these safer reactors will work and how cost-efficient they will be remain uncertain. And it will probably take another couple of hot summers before a serious effort is made to find out.

Conclusion

The press has played a significant role in shaping the public policy debate on nuclear power. Overall, at least since the mid–1970s, press coverage has been more critical than favorable toward the technology. This is manifested in a variety of ways. For example, more than half the expert sources called on by the media are opponents of nuclear power despite the fact that more than 80 percent of the academic experts in nuclear physics, engineering, and related fields support it.[52] Polls indicate that when the need for nuclear power is strongly perceived, a substantial majority of Americans finds it acceptable, but when the need is not so evident, concerns about safety reduce public acceptance of nuclear power well below 50 percent. After the accident at Three Mile Island, media coverage was overwhelmingly about safety, and most of it was negative. The general tenor of the coverage gives the impression that nuclear power is not safe enough to be acceptable. As it turns out, however, that is not what most Americans believe. Some have concluded that nuclear power is unacceptable on the ground of safety, some that it is too expensive, some that we don't need it now, and some (34 to 52 percent, depending on when the survey was taken) have concluded that it is the best way to add to our electricity supply. In other words, the impact of press coverage of nuclear power is hard to calculate.

Media coverage influences policy not only through public opinion. It also affects who gets elected, how public officials prepare for hearings, what issue legislators pay most attention to, how legislators and regulators frame their responses to problems, and what the public gets to know that officials would rather keep secret. What it cannot do, in areas as complex as nuclear technology, is to resolve technical controversies. It can, however, present controversies in ways that illuminate (and separate) the technical and political issues rather than obscuring them. In the Vermont waste shipment stories, for example, the press should not have downplayed the political story, but ideally it should have devoted enough space to both sides of the technical controversy to enable Vermonters to decide in an informed way whether or not the shipments should continue.

Finally, although one can't be sure that press coverage has retarded the development of nuclear power in the United States, it could easily be that if the press had given more coverage to the "inherently safe reactor" twenty years ago, this country's energy grid would look different from the way it looks today.

NOTES

1. The restart took place on October 3, 1985.

2. AP, "TMI Reactor Decision Rekindles Scare of '79," *Washington Post*, June 2, 1985, p. A9.

3. President's Commission on the Accident at Three Mile Island, "Report to the President," October 30, 1979, pp. 34–35.

4. John G. Fuller, *We Almost Lost Detroit* (New York: Readers' Digest Press, 1975).

5. President's Commission, pp. 235–36.

6. Ibid.

7. Ibid., pp. 267–76.

8. Stanley Rothman, S. Robert Lichter, and Linda Lichter, *The Media Elite* (Washington, D.C.: Adler and Adler, 1987), pp. 216–19.

9. Ibid.

10. Allan Mazur, *The Dynamics of Technical Controversy* (Washington, D.C.: Communications Press, 1981), p. 108.

11. Rothman, Lichter, and Lichter, *The Media Elite*, p. 161.

12. *Public Opinion*, June–July 1979, p. 7.

13. Office of Technology Assessment, *Nuclear Power in an Age of Uncertainty* (Washington, D.C.: U.S. Congress, OTA-E–216, February 1984), p. 211.

14. Cambridge Reports, Appendix A, The Questionnaire, CR 2434, August 1987, pp. A–5, A–8.

15. Lindsey Gruson, "After 6 Years, Undamaged Reactor at 3 Mile Island Is Restarted," *New York Times* October 4, 1985, p. A16. That phrase or one that has approximately the same meaning, appears in almost all the articles reviewed for this chapter.

16. President's Commission, p. 34; and Jan Beyea, "A Review of Dose Assessments at Three Mile Island and Recommendations for Future Research," Three Mile Island Public Health Fund, 1984, p. 34.

17. Philip J. Hilts, "Higher Cancer Risk Found in Radiation," *New York Times*, December 19, 1989, p. A22.

18. Daniel Martin, *Three Mile Island: Prologue or Epilogue* (Cambridge, Mass. Ballinger, 1980), p. 164.

19. John G. Kemeny, "Saving American Democracy: The Lessons of Three Mile Island," *Technology Review*, June–July 1980, p. 73.

20. DuPont Robert, *Nuclear Phobia - Public Thinking about Nuclear Power*, Media Institute, March 1980.

21. Rothman, Lichter, and Lichter, *The Media Elite*. Page 213 contends that 62 percent have an antinuclear bias.

22. Edward Markey, U.S. congressman., D-Mass., interview, Washington, D.C., November 23, 1987.

23. Carl Goldstein, U.S. Council on Energy Awareness, interview, Washington, D.C., November 23, 1987.

24. Tom Bevill, U.S. congressman, D-Ala., interview, Washington, D.C., November 17, 1987.

25. "Reviving the Atom," *New York Times*, December 8, 1989, p. A8.

26. "Keeping Cool," *Washington Post*, February 10, 1990, p. A22.

27. "Clean Power's Strange Enemies," *New York Times*, March 12, 1990, p. A16.

28. James K. Asselstine, former member, Nuclear Regulatory Commission, interview, Washington, D.C., November 27, 1987.

29. Harold W. Lewis, physicist, University of California at Santa Barbara, interview, Santa Barbara, Calif., December 15, 1987.

30. Joanne Omang, "Anti-Nuclear Cult Hero Backs Atomic Power Safety," *Washington Post*, February 17, 1979, p. A1.

31. Rothman, Lichter, and Lichter, *The Media Elite*, p. 179.

32. Ibid., p. 61.

33. U.S. Nuclear Regulatory Commission, Washington, D.C., September 1978.

34. David Burnham, "Nuclear Agency Revokes Support for Safety Study," *New York Times*, January 20, 1979, p. 1.

35. David Burnham, "Panel Plans Study on Nuclear Safety," *New York Times*, January 21, 1979, p. A1; and "Federal Actions Renew Questions on Nuclear Power's Future in U.S.," *New York Times*, March 19, 1979, p. A16.

36. Rothman, Lichter, and Lichter, *The Media Elite*, pp. 177–83.

37. *Newsweek*, 61; *Time*, 53; *U.S. News & World Report*, 32.

38. "In Science, No Advances Without Risks," *U.S. News & World Report*, September 15, 1980, pp. 60–61.

39. Rothman, Lichter, and Lichter, *The Media Elite*.

40. Spencer Weart, *Nuclear Fear* (Cambridge, Mass. Harvard University Press, 1988). See Chapter 18.

41. Ben Franklin, "Nuclear Agency Defends Change," *New York Times*, May 22, 1985, p. 19; and Stephen Labaton, "House Democrats Hit NRC Decision to Close More of Its Deliberations," *Washington Post*, May 22, 1985, p. 19. A review of several newspaper, including the *Washington Post*, *New York Times*, *Wall Street Journal*, *Arizona Daily Star*, *Des Moines Register*, *Los Angeles Times*, *San Francisco Chronicle*, *St. Louis Post-Dispatch*, *Houston*

Post, and *Chicago Tribune,* showed virtual unanimity in framing and tone among the papers that ran the story. The stories are best exemplified by an Associated Press story as it ran in the St. Louis paper. This article referred to the NRC as "relying on an obscure Supreme Court rule" and quotes Asselstine as saying the change "shows disdain for the public." The *Post-Dispatch* then ran an editorial five days later condemning the NRC. Half the papers surveyed carried similar stories to that of the *Post-Dispatch.* The *Wall Street Journal* ran a facetious fourteen-word story explaining that the NRC had just redefined the word *meeting.* Three months later, the *Journal* ran an article on page 64 that was sympathetic to the NRC.

42. "When a Meeting Isn't," *Washington Post,* July 13, 1985, p. 16.

43. Rod Clarke and Kevin Goddard (UPI), "Atomic Waste Shipped Through State," *Times Argus* (Barre-Montpelier, Vt.), August 25, 1982, p. 1.

44. Neil Davis, "Kunin Calls for Suspension of Nuclear Waste Shipments," *Burlington Free Press,* August 27, 1982, p. A1.

45. Rod Clarke (UPI), "Snelling Administration Response to Kunin a Misguided Missile," *Times Argus,* August 28, 1982.

46. UPI, September 3, 1982.

47. Candace Page, "Snelling Halts Nuclear Waste Shipments in State," *Burlington Free Press,* September 4, 1982, p. 1A.

48. "Vermont Sets Off a Chain Reaction," *Rutland Daily Herald,* October 28, 1982, p. 14.

49. William J. Donovan, "Glover Regulates N-Waste Shipments," *Burlington Free Press,* October 30, 1982, p. A1.

50. Lawrence M. Lidsky, "Safe Nuclear Power," *New Republic,* December 28, 1987.

51. Matthew L. Wald, "The Nuclear Industry Tries Again," *New York Times,* November 26, 1989, section 3, p. 1.

52. This is from a questionnaire sent to journalists and scientists in 1980. See Rothman, Lichter, and Lichter, *The Media Elite,* pp. 177–84.

5

The Greenhouse Issue Heats Up

S ENATOR Timothy E. Wirth knows a lot about the news media. He made a reputation in the House of Representatives for his mastery of communication issues. It comes as no surprise, therefore, that he takes imaginative approaches to publicizing matters he cares about. Even so, the liberal Colorado Democrat's attempt to enlist conservative former president Richard Nixon to deliver his message on global warming in the heart of the New York financial district was unusually creative. Wirth positively glowed when he talked about the press attention Nixon would get if he warned Wall Street about the perils of the greenhouse effect "in that media center."[1]

Nixon, who has achieved elder statesman status since being driven from office, never even responded to Wirth's entreaties, but that didn't stop the senator. He reverted to a more traditional strategy to get the media interested. He held hearings calculated to yield nationwide press coverage. Some of these hearings were duds, but one in the hot summer of 1988 succeeded beyond, if not Wirth's wildest dreams, then at least his reasonable expectations. It got front-page and network news coverage for the projected "catastrophic" social and economic consequences of the greenhouse effect.

Wirth became interested in global warming in the mid-1970s, but he was not the first member of Congress to seize the greenhouse effect as a policy issue. His Democratic colleague from Tennessee, Albert

Gore Jr., learned about the problem of excess carbon dioxide in the atmosphere in a Harvard classroom in the early 1960s. His professor was Roger Revelle, the first scientist to calculate how much carbon dioxide had been added to the air since the Industrial Revolution. Gore went on to hold congressional hearings on global warming in the early 1980s, and by 1987 he made the issue a centerpiece of his campaign for the Democratic presidential nomination.

The History

Concern about the possible malign effects of global warming has a long history beginning in the nineteenth century. As early as 1863, British physicist John Tyndall measured carbon dioxide in the earth's atmosphere and recognized that it contributed significantly to the warmth that makes possible life as we know it. Even earlier, the widely learned Frenchman Jean-Baptiste-Joseph Fourier speculated that such an effect was likely. But it is Swedish chemist Svante Arrhenius who is most often cited as the godfather of greenhouse theory. Arrhenius actually calculated in 1896 that a doubling of carbon dioxide in the air, resulting largely from coal burning and other by-products of industrialization and agriculture, would cause a global temperature rise of up to 9 degrees Fahrenheit. That is still within the range considered reasonable by most climatologists, many of whom now use supercomputers to attack a problem Arrhenius confronted with a pad and pencil. What Arrhenius could not prove, however, was that the amount of carbon dioxide in the air was actually increasing. That proof would not come until the middle of the next century.

Although the ability to accurately measure trace gases in the atmosphere is relatively new, the basic mechanism of what has been dubbed the greenhouse effect has long been understood. Sunlight passes through the atmosphere and reaches the earth, which radiates it back in the form of infrared rays. Some of the heat radiated from the earth is absorbed by trace gases such as carbon dioxide, chlorofluorocarbons, or methane, which raises the temperature of the air. Since it is now possible to measure the increase in carbon dioxide and other greenhouse gases, not only in the present, but by analyzing ice cores from thousands of years in the past, projections can be made about the future. There is now about 25 percent more carbon dioxide in the air than there was in the late 1800s, and a doubling from that time has been predicted by the middle of the next century. There is disagreement among respected climatologists about whether this roughly 25 percent increase in carbon dioxide is responsible for the roughly 1 percent increase in temperature worldwide over this time period.

Many poorly understood factors influence the magnitude of the greenhouse effect, and others unrelated to the greenhouse effect may also cause atmospheric warming. Some of the confounding forces that act on climate are sunspots, ocean circulation patterns, cloud cover, rates of plant respiration, and cutting and burning of forests. Computer models designed to predict the effects of these elements on climate are still primitive. As a result, there is considerable disagreement among scientists about the extent of the warming to be expected in the next fifty years. Moreover, it is not clear precisely what implications should be drawn from warming within the most often cited range of 1.5 to 4.5 degrees centigrade. There is also disagreement about whether warming attributable to greenhouse gases is already discernible amidst the "noise" of other factors that might be warming the planet.

The Politics and the Press

The complexity and uncertainty of the science, the inability to predict with precision the magnitude and impact of global warming, the uncertainty about what the health effects might be, and the long lead time before anything will actually happen make global warming a difficult issue for the handful of legislators such as Wirth, Gore, and John Chafee (R-R.I.), who think it is important. It is not by chance that these men are all senators, who run for office only every six years and therefore are somewhat freer than House members to focus on problems whose uncertain effects are unlikely to be felt for decades. Representatives, who must be reelected every other year, tend to focus on grass-roots issues that are more amenable to short-term solutions. Only one House member, Rep. Claudine Schneider (R-R.I.), has shown sustained interest in global warming. Another reason for political inaction, in Gore's words, is that, as a rule, "politicians like uncertainty because it is an excuse to do nothing,"[2] which makes passing legislation even harder for the few members who are trying to do something.

The issue is also difficult for scientists such as Stephen H. Schneider of the National Center for Atmospheric Research in Boulder, Colorado, who wrote this in a letter to *The Detroit News:*

> On the one hand, as scientists we are ethically bound to the scientific method, in effect promising to tell the truth, the whole truth and nothing but—which means that we must include all the doubts, the caveats, the ifs ands and buts. On the other hand we are not just scientists but human beings as well. And like most people we'd like to see the world a better place, which in this context translates into our working to reduce the risk of potentially disastrous climatic change. To do that we need to get some broad based support, to capture the public's imagination. That, of course, means getting loads of media coverage. So we have to offer up scary scenarios, make simplified, dramatic statements, and make little mention of any doubts we might have. This "double ethical bind" we frequently find ourselves in cannot be solved by any formula. Each of us has to decide what the right balance is between being effective and being honest. I hope that means being both.[3]

A pair of Roper polls done in December 1987 and January 1988 ranked global warning twenty-third in a tie with nonhazardous waste dumps as an environmental concern,[4] which would seem to confirm that as late as the beginning of 1988 it was not a very good horse to run for office on. But press coverage of global warming soared in 1988 and 1989, and, according to some accounts, so has public concern. A similar set of Roper polls released in March 1990 showed that 48 percent of the respondents considered global warming a "very serious" problem, up from only 33 percent in the earlier poll.[5] When he announced his candidacy for president in 1987, Senator Gore characterized the greenhouse effect, ozone depletion, and the global ecological crisis as the most serious issues facing the United States and the world, indicating that he hoped to ride them into the White House. Although he was wrong with respect to the 1988 race, Gore still believes global warming is an issue whose political time has come.

But Gore's view is a minority one. Global warming remains relatively tough to promote as a public issue. Indeed, when asked, even the Tennessee lawmaker will tick off a number of reasons why the issue is so hard to sell. His list includes "denial," the "unprecedented" nature of the phenomenon, the difficulty of remedying the situation, the degree of international cooperation required, the "illusion that there will be winners and losers," and the fact that "a lot of people just don't care what happens after they die."[6] At the same time, however, global warming is an especially appealing issue for environmentalists because it serves as an umbrella for so many of their concerns, including air pollution, the promotion of solar and other nonnuclear and non-fossil-fuel-burning energy alternatives, deforestation, and the continuing use of chlorofluorocarbons (although these are now beginning to be phased out).

Global warming is also problematic for the news media for the same old reasons—complexity, scientific uncertainty, and lack of immediacy are all antithetical to the ideal of a "good story." They conspire to sap drama from stories by requiring qualifications that interrupt narrative flow. If global warming is to be sustained as a running story, the drama has to be found somewhere. It is here that scenarios and "worst-case" projections come into play. These dramatic characterizations of possible futures are devised and circulated by policymakers and environmentalists, among others, to get their message out by exploiting the media's seemingly insatiable taste for drama. The technique often works. For example, one news story in late 1988, which offered a scenario of California in 2030, reported in the present tense:

> California's vast flood control and irrigation projects, designed for 20th-Century climatic conditions, are no longer able to stem the tide of winter floods or provide enough water in the summer.
>
> The sea level has risen at least 11/2 feet, creating a vast inland sea in the San Joaquin–Sacramento Delta, usurping unique ecosystems and causing the collapse of levees that protect rich agricultural lands as well as vital pumping plants that send fresh water to Southern California.[7]

Predictions made in the name of global warming are nothing if not dramatic—New York and Miami under water; Washington, D.C., over 90 degrees Fahrenheit almost one day in four; droughts and crop devastation throughout the Midwest; hurricanes of exceptional force; flooding in California's richest agricultural belt. These predictions are designed for front-page display, but they come from the back of an envelope. How accurate are they? When, if ever, will they come to pass? How seriously should they be taken? Should we be worrying about heat-related mortality, especially among the elderly, or the migration of disease-bearing insects into temperate zones?

Reporters can't be expected to provide definitive answers to questions like these. They can only use their journalistic skills to honestly evaluate and carefully convey information that they judge to be important and of interest to the public. They try to do this in ways that meet the "good story" criteria because this is how they ensure that their editors will respond favorably and their audience will read what they write. Generally speaking, and with varying degrees of success, they also try hard to get the facts right, put them in proper context, explain the science and the politics, and provide informed speculation by selected experts on the potential implications of the phenomena they are describing. In the case of global warming, the public's interest level was low, and so was journalism's collective evaluation of the issue's importance—that is, until the long, hot summer of 1988.

For more than half a century after Svante Arrhenius speculated brilliantly on global warming, relatively little of interest on the subject emerged from the scientific community, and the press ignored it altogether. For a long stretch during that period, from about 1940 to 1965, it even looked as if the earth might be cooling rather than warming, which further dampened interest. Then, in 1957, Roger Revelle, the scientist who was leading the International Geophysical Year, joined with a colleague named Hans Suess to publish a paper demonstrating that the oceans would not absorb nearly as much carbon dioxide as had previously been thought.[8] This meant that much of the carbon dioxide that was being pumped into the air by humans would stay there and absorb heat, eventually raising the temperature on earth. A year later, Charles David Keeling began making precise measurements of carbon dioxide in the air from a station on the slope of the Mauna Loa volcano in Hawaii. Keeling's annual measurements showed what Arrhenius couldn't—that the carbon dioxide content of the atmosphere was increasing rapidly.

The Revelle-Suess article and the Keeling measurements were important, but they did little to stir press, public, or political interest in global warming. As far as the public and the news media were concerned, the issue lay dormat until 1977, when a panel of the National Academy of Sciences (NAS), of which Revelle was chairman, issued a report titled "Energy and Climate," which contained some highly charged front-page language. *The Washington Post* took the bait, running a page 1 story on July 25.[9] The *Post* story began:

> If industrial nations continue to burn oil and coal for energy, the world's average temperature could increase more than 6 degrees centigrade in the next 200 years. . . .
> Such an increase could have "adverse, even catastrophic" effects around the world, including dramatic changes in agricultural areas and ocean fisheries and a rise in sea level that could flood coastal cities. . . .

The *Post* followed up with an editorial two days later, which said that "policy-makers should . . . start thinking very seriously about long-range, large-scale alternatives to fossil fuels. The NAS report is a timely reminder that every energy option has its costs, and that the policy decisions of the next several decades could affect the world in unintended ways for a millennium or more."[10]

The *Post* was out in front of its competition in recognizing global warming as an emerging issue. It ran a total of two articles and one editorial on the subject in 1977 and also distributed an issue of *Parade* magazine that carried an article on global warming. *The Wall Street Journal* carried one article on the greenhouse effect in 1977, but *The New York Times*, *The Los Angeles Times*, and the three major newsweeklies carried nothing. From 1978 through 1982, there was only a smattering of stories on global warming, all but two of them in *The New York Times* and *The Washington Post*. *Time* and *Newsweek* ran one article each. In 1979, the *Times* sent Walter Sullivan to Geneva to cover a World Climate Conference, which the *Post* did not cover at all. Sullivan filed three stories with the following revealing headlines: "Climatologists Are Warned North Pole Might Melt," "Scientists at World Parley Doubt Climate Variations Are Ominous," and "A Vast Interdisciplinary Effort to Predict Climate Trend Urged."[11] In the first article, Revelle was quoted as saying that the world faced a "Faustian bargain" between nuclear power with its attendant risks and the continued burning of fossil fuels. The message, though, for anyone who read all three headlines, or, for that matter, all three stories, was that not enough was known about whether global warming posed a threat to humanity to serve as a basis for making public policy. This would remain the overall media message almost until the end of the decade.

Another blip in press coverage occurred in January 1981, just before Ronald Reagan was inaugurated as president. Jimmy Carter's Council on Environmental Quality (CEQ) released a report urging that global warming be taken into account in the formulation of both U.S. and international energy policy.[12] This report, which received nine paragraphs in the *Times* on page A13 and six paragraphs in the *Post* on page A12 (both on January 14, 1981), not only made some prescient observations about dealing with the problem of global warming, but it also characterized well the difficulties the greenhouse effect poses for policymakers. It made these points:

The CO_2 issue may present the ultimate environmental dilemma. Collective judgments of historic and possibly unique importance must be made—by decision or default—largely on the basis of scientific models that have severe limitations and that few can understand. To some, the competing factors will be seen as whether to provide the energy needed for economic and military security or whether to protect humanity from a distant and uncertain threat that currently affects no one....

Clearly a deeper appreciation of the risks of a CO_2 buildup should spread to leaders of government and business and to the general public. The CO_2 problem should be taken seriously in new ways: it should become a factor in making energy policy and not simply be the subject of scientific investigation....

In this period of intense interaction between science and policy, the scientist will have a special role owing to the elusive nature of the CO_2 problem—to explain, to provide strong public leadership, and yet to remain a scientist.[13]

This brief excerpt from the CEQ report offered several important insights. To begin with, global warming represented a "distant and uncertain threat that currently affects no one," which made it unappealing as a political issue. Therefore, lawmakers and environmentalists had to find a way to raise the level of political concern. To do this, as Stephen Schneider indicated, scientists would have to explain this complex technical problem to the public in a way that would promote an appropriate level of concern without either oversimplifying or exaggerating the existing science.

Each of these themes bears directly on the use of the news media as an instrument of public policy. The goal is to get the word out to the public because, as Michael Oppenheimer of the Environmental Defense Fund has put it, "Congress responds to constituents."[14] Or, as Rafe Pomerance of the World Resources Institute notes, policy judgments aren't based on the seriousness of the problem; they are based on the depth of public concern, which to a large extent is fashioned by what people read in newspapers and magazines and watch on television.[15]

Senators Gore and Wirth have focused sharply on the media in their struggle to make global warming a heavyweight political issue. They both understand how hard it is to get the news media to pay attention to an issue that seems uncertain and in any event poses no immediate threat to anyone. Wirth once asked a witness at a hearing held in Santa Monica, California, "how do we go about globalizing public opinion ... in a democratic society? You know, how do we get 235 million Americans ... to understand the size and scope of this [global warming problem]?"[16] His interlocutor was the actor Robert

Redford, who was not, one might imagine, invited to the hearing because of his expertise in climatology or oceanography. Redford said he recognized a responsibility to "get the word out to the people," but offered no concrete advice about how to do it. The only newspaper coverage of the hearing appeared in *The Los Angeles Times*. It led with the predicted effect of global warming on a Southern California air-quality management plan and mentioned Redford in the twelfth paragraph of sixteen.[17] The story ran on the front page of the *Times*'s Metro section.

While the CEQ report advocated that scientists carry the message to the public, it ignored the fact that many scientists (not all) are uncomfortable about and not adept at publicizing their work. Sometimes, however, a scientist who does not seek the limelight is thrust into it and makes a difference. This happened in August 1981, when an article appeared in *Science* magazine[18] that stirred enough interest to make page 1 of *The New York Times*.[19] The newspaper article, by Walter Sullivan, began:

> A team of Federal scientists says it has detected an overall warming trend in the earth's atmosphere extending back to the year 1880. They regard this as evidence of the validity of the "greenhouse" effect, in which increasing amounts of carbon dioxide cause steady temperature increases.
>
> The seven atmospheric scientists predict a global warming of "almost unprecedented magnitude" in the next century. It might even be sufficient to melt and dislodge the ice cover of West Antarctica, they say, eventually leading to a worldwide rise of 15 to 20 feet in the sea level. In that case, they say, it would "flood 25 percent of Louisiana and Florida, 10 percent of New Jersey and many other lowlands throughout the world" within a century or less.

The lead author of this dramatically presented *Science* article was James Hansen, a young climatologist with the Goddard Space Flight Center in New York, who subsequently referred to the *Science* paper as his "original sin" because of the publicity it received.[20] Along with other climate researchers such as Schneider of the National Center for Atmospheric Research in Wirth's home state of Colorado, Hansen came to share the CEQ report's viewpoint that scientists would have to forgo their normal reticence and play an important role in alerting the public to the potential hazards of global warming. As Schneider put it, "no media, no message."[21]

Despite his clear recognition of what it takes to get media attention,

Schneider's willingness to draw conclusions from the available data usually lagged behind Hansen's. But both researchers appear to have understood early the inherent tension between informing the policy process in a timely fashion and adhering to the conservative practices of scientific disclosure. Soft-spoken, almost shy, Hansen has nonetheless become the point man in publicity about global warming. And the news media have been his instrument of choice.

Although it caused less controversy when the young government scientist gave his views on global warming in 1981 than it did in the late 1980s, Hansen recalled that even then, Fred Koomanoff, the new Reagan administration official who oversaw funding for Hansen's research, "didn't like publicity."[22] The Reagan administration, and subsequently the administration of President George Bush, came to regard the publicity Hansen generated for global warming through the news media as nettlesome, and more than once they tried to censor his congressional testimony.

Hansen was coauthor of another paper in 1981 that received no media attention at all. For one thing, it did not appear in a widely read journal like *Science*, which is a frequent source for news stories, but rather in the relatively obscure *Geophysical Research Letters*.[23] This paper asserted that trace gases other than carbon dioxide, such as chlorofluorocarbons, methane, and nitrous oxide, were also increasing in the atmosphere to the extent that they had apparently doubled greenhouse warming in the 1970s from what it would have been as a result of carbon dioxide alone. The implication was that as a result of the increase of these other trace gases, greenhouse warming was likely to become evident a lot sooner than was previously thought.

In all of 1982, despite the publication of a report on the greenhouse effect by the National Research Council,[24] the major print media in the United States carried only three news articles on global warming. Hansen was mentioned in two of them. *The New York Times* ran an editorial that was skeptical of the science underlying some of the dire predictions about global warming but which concluded by saying that "While research continues, skeptics with an itch to throw stones at the greenhouse effect should remember they may be living in a glass house."[25] The *Times* editorial was typical of the mixed messages the news media were continuing to deliver. Press coverage at the time reflected considerable scientific uncertainty, and its paucity reflected the facts, as far as the press was concerned, that the threat posed by the greenhouse effect was still distant and ill defined, if indeed it was correct to conclude that there was any significant threat at all. The news stories also implicitly reflected the unwillingness of many scientists to say on the record that they now thought the evidence for greenhouse warming was sufficient to warrant an immediate policy response. A few scientists and environmentalists were saying it, but they were not finding the right phrases or the right platforms to get media attention. For the first nine months of 1983, there was not a single story on global warming in the American press. But suddenly, in October, a total of nine global warming stories appeared in *The New York Times*, *The Washington Post*, *The Wall Street Journal*, and *The Christian Science Monitor*, along with two editorials, one in the *Times* and one in the *Post*, and a story each in *Time* and *Newsweek*.[26] There were also four network news stories and a commentary by John Chancellor. The reason for the awakening of interest was the controversy engendered by two reports on global warming, one issued by the Environmental Protection Agency and the other by the National Academy of Sciences. The two studies differed just enough in emphasis to stimulate press interest. The EPA report, which focused on policy options, and the slightly more cautious NAS study, which concentrated on the need for more research, came out within days of each other. One EPA official involved in overseeing his agency's report said the EPA was well aware of the NAS project and pushed to get its study out in time to benefit from the media coverge they knew even the relatively minor differences between the two reports would generate.

One of the apparent paradoxes of journalism is that although editors usually want stories to be written with as much certainty as the evidence can possibly sustain, the news media also thrive on the controversy stimulated by uncertainty. In fact, however, there is no paradox. If a "hard lead" (a first paragraph without significant qualifications) can be justified, or sometimes just rationalized, the story will usually be written that way. But if an unqualified lead cannot possibly be supported, emphasis—sometimes undue emphasis—will generally be put on whatever controversy surrounds the story. Alternatively, a provocative lead will be written, one that focuses on the most sensational aspect of the matter being reported on. Keeping this in mind, it seems noteworthy that all three networks covered the more provocative EPA report, but only CBS covered the relatively conservative NRC study, which appeared three days later. A good example of controversy-oriented coverage was provided by *Newsweek* magazine's article on the two studies:

The EPA predicted "catastrophic consequences" if contingency plans weren't made with "a sense of urgency."

Fortunately the news improved later in the week when the National Academy of Sciences said that although the greenhouse effect was very real, "caution, not panic" was in order.[27]

By contrast to *Newsweek*'s ironic tone, *Time* correctly labeled the controversy a media phenomenon and noted that in many ways the two studies were consistent with each other.[28] In 1983, however, the testimony of experts, constrained as it was by lack of scientific proof, made it premature for journalists to write in an unqualified fashion that global warming had arrived or that it posed a definite future hazard. As a result, controversy among experts became the story, and both the EPA and NAS reports got more attention than they might have received if only one of them had been issued.

In 1984, there were only five stories on global warming in the major print media, all of which appeared in the *The New York Times*. One of the five stories was a column by Russell Baker speculating, among other things, that global warming might lead to the growth of hundred-foot-tall tomato plants, which in turn would attract lightning, resulting in a rain of tomatoes twice the size of pumpkins.[29] One of the stories was just five paragraphs long, and another never specifically mentioned global warming, so all in all, 1984 wasn't much of a year for media coverage of the greenhouse effect.

A subcommittee hearing held by Senator Gore received no coverage at all, even though the lead-off witness was Carl Sagan. Like Wirth of Colorado, the Tennessee Democrat was obviously concerned that the public and other policymakers were paying too little attention to global warming. Presumably this is why he invited Sagan—a well-known "TV scientist" fresh from the campaign trail, where he had been promoting concern about "nuclear winter"—to testify, rather than a bona fide climate expert. At a similar hearing held by Rep. James Scheuer in 1982,[30] Hansen and a handful of climatologists testified and received no press coverage. Interestingly, of only two questions Gore asked Sagan, one was about public relations, not science. It harkened back to the 1981 CEQ report. "How would science communicate with public policymakers about the urgency of doing something?" the senator asked, adding that "the ability of political and economic institutions to respond to a challenge of this magnitude will depend in large part upon how clearly the challenge is perceived, which in turn will depend a great deal upon how the scientific community explains the problem, how much certainty it invests in that explanation, and how actively involved it becomes in spelling out what the clearly sensible choice might be."[31]

Sagan, like Robert Redford, had little advice to offer. He said he didn't see much of a problem with respect to informing laypersons about global warming and then went on to discuss his concern that international cooperation would not be easy to mobilize. He did not foresee that the United States would be the chief obstacle to mobilizing international cooperation, and he was wrong about the ease of informing laypersons.

In 1985, a major international conference in Villach, Austria, concluded that the greenhouse effect would cause rising sea levels in the first rather than the second half of the next century and that without significant government action, temperatures would increase to the highest levels ever recorded. *The New York Times* ran a short story on page 23 of its November 3 edition, and *The Christian Science Monitor* mentioned the conference in one paragraph on December 13. There were also a couple of stories in 1985 on how trace gases other than carbon dioxide were adding to global warming as well as a column in *The Boston Globe* by the respected writer and former ambassador to Ireland, William V. Shannon, who asked, "Is the greenhouse effect an impending reality or a science fiction fantasy?" Shannon answered, "No one knows."[32] And this from *The Chicago Tribune* by Pulitzer Prize-winning humor columnist Dave Barry:

> I watch these genial weather buffoons on the television news every night, and they can't reliably predict the weather for tomorrow. They can't predict with accuracy any greater than 50 percent what days the weekend will fall on. Why on Earth should I believe anybody who's predicting the weather for 100 years from now?[33]

And finally, this dismissive note from *The Wall Street Journal*:

> Pop science has put us through ozone scares, NOX scares, dioxin scares, snail darter scares—to name a few—only to discard these urgent dangers in favor of new ones. The one that really worried us, however, was the "greenhouse effect," which said all our earthbound activity was generating a carbon dioxide layer that would shut off the sun. Now a NASA scientist says don't worry, the greenhouse has in fact kept life on earth from being cooked by an ever-brightening sun. Next item.[34]

The fact that the greenhouse effect was ridiculed in major media as late as 1985 is enlightening, but less so than the fact that *The Wall Street Journal*, whose reports and judgments influence stock trades totaling in the trillions of dollars every year, could misunderstand the basic fact that, far from shutting off the sun, the greenhouse effect traps the sun's radiant energy, otherwise known as heat. Polling data are thin, but they suggest that this display of ignorance by America's largest-circulation serious newspaper was reflective of public knowledge at the time, although concern about the problem was beginning to increase.[35] Something else happened in 1985, however, that contributed significantly to interest in global warming. A vast hole in the ozone layer, which protects the earth from a kind of ultraviolet ray that can cause skin cancer, was discovered over Antarctica. The hole was apparently caused by the release of chlorofluorocarbons, chemicals used as coolants and propellants, which are also greenhouse gases. This put a media spotlight on an environmental problem closely linked to global warming.

On June 10, 1986, at a hearing before a subcommittee on environmental pollution, Hansen, who was usually half a step ahead of his scientific colleagues on global warming, called for more research, noting "I would like to understand the problem better before I order any dramatic actions."[36]

The hearing was covered by both *The New York Times* and *The Washington Post*,[37] but both papers led with another aspect of Hansen's testimony—that the greenhouse effect would cause temperatures to rise in the next century to "the warmest the earth has been in the last 100,000 years."[38] This was dramatic language, spoken with the authority of science, and it got front-page coverage in *The Washington Post*. Never mind that Hansen's basic plea was for better understanding of the problem; his testimony contained headline-grabbing language.

The fact that the *Times* and the *Post* covered this hearing at all indicated a new level of interest in global warming and therefore a new level of success for the lawmakers and environmentalists who were promoting it as a public issue. Although media coverage increased in 1986, the Reagan administration was still urging a slow approach (it edited out of Hansen's congressional testimony efforts to stimulate the hiring of more researchers to work on global warming), there were still some naysayers in the scientific community, and much of the media and public remained ignorant about the greenhouse effect. All of this was reflected in the year's news coverage, which remained relatively thin and continued to be almost exclusively print.[39]

An example of the continuing lack of understanding about global warming appeared in the *Atlanta Constitution* on June 11: "A dramatic loss of ozone over Antarctica proves that the greenhouse effect is real and presages a gradual warming of the Earth that threatens flood, drought, human misery in a few years and—if not checked— eventual extinction of the human species, scientists warned."[40] Although the article linked global warming and the ozone layer, it didn't quite get what the connection was. More typical, however, were stories that balanced proponents of immediate action on global warming with advocates of more study.[41] Op-ed and other opinion articles also began appearing. These were written by environmentalists such as Michael Oppenheimer and Gus Speth, former chairman of the Council on Environmental Quality, and skeptics like Patrick Michaels, a climatologist from the University of Virginia.[42] Two of the three newsweeklies also published articles on global warming, with *U.S. News & World Report* moving from a posture of ridiculing or ignoring the phenomenon to asserting that "Most scientists feel that the evidence for a greenhouse effect is strong enough to warrant corrective action now."[43] Despite the paucity of coverage, by late 1986, 45 percent of the American public said it had read a lot about the greenhouse effect.[44]

Time carried a balanced, science-oriented cover story on global warming and ozone depletion in 1987. The *Time* story ran a few weeks after a visit to *Time's* office from the campaigning Gore, who urged *Time* to publish such an article.[45] Still, global warming had not begun to take off in the policy arena. A number of congressional hearings were held in 1987, none of which attracted much attention. But one Senate hearing in November laid the groundwork for thrusting global warming into the Washington limelight. J. Bennett Johnston (D-La.), chairman of the Committee on Energy and Natural Resources, ceded the chairmanship for both hearings to Tim Wirth, the Colorado Democrat who had been following the issue since the mid–1970s. Wirth, a longtime friend of Schneider and some of his colleagues from the National Center for Atmospheric Research, was beginning to think about comprehensive legislation on global warming. Wirth's staff invited James Hansen to testify, asking him, among other things, to "address the question of how the greenhouse effect may modify the temperature in the Nation's city,"[46] a request calculated to provoke media coverage. Hansen complied, saying at the hearings:

for Washington, D.C., the number of days in which the temperature exceeds 100 degrees Fahrenheit has been one day per year on the average in the period 1950 to 1983. In the doubled CO_2 climate . . . there are about 12 days per year above 100 degrees Fahrenheit.
The number of days per year with temperatures exceeding 90 de-

grees Fahrenheit increases from about 35 to 85, and the number of nights in which the minimum does not drop below 80 degrees Fahrenheit increases from less than one per year to about 20 per year.

Hansen who was becoming wise to the ways of Washington, testified as a private citizen to prevent the Office of Management and Budget, a White House agency that, among other things, coordinates policy statements, from softening his testimony. He went on to say that "the greenhouse effect is real, it is coming soon, and it will have major effects on all peoples." But either the words or the music or both weren't appealing enough. Press coverage was nil, and Wirth was disappointed. The November 1987 hearing, he said later, "was like hearings we held in the House—no impact." Yet "the data seemed to me so startling," Wirth added, "that we had to get it out."[47]

Wirth asked the committee chairman, Bennett Johnston, for permission to start crafting a major piece of comprehensive legislation on global warming. Johnston assented, and Wirth immediately enlisted the interested environmental groups such as the World Resources Institute, the Environmental Defense Fund, and the Natural Resources Defense Council to begin providing guidance on the direction the legislation should take. He also called on an industry group, the Alliance to Save Energy, of which he is chairman. Wirth's staff, together with Senate Energy Committee staff, drafted the legislation, which was then widely circulated for comment. The bill sought to reduce emissions of carbon dioxide and other greenhouse gases, to increase energy efficiency, to encourage the development of affordable solar energy technologies, to reduce deforestation, and to increase reforestation.

At the same time, Wirth and his staff began thinking about how they could get the kind of high-profile media attention for global warming that they knew their legislative effort would require if it were to have any chance of succeeding. One thing they did was to check with the National Weather Service to find out which days tended to be the hottest each year. Based on these data, they picked June 23, 1988, to hold a hearing titled "Greenhouse Effect and Global Climate Change."

By early June, however, it was beginning to look like there would not be time to line up enough witnesses to hold the hearing. But when Hansen told a Wirth staffer that he would publicly announce that global warming had arrived, all doubt was removed. There would be a hearing, and it would succeed like none before it because the weather and James Hansen were doing what was required of them—the weather was producing heat and drought, and Hansen was about to become the first respected scientist to declare that the extra greenhouse gases man was pumping into the atmosphere were discernibly warming the earth. The press, too, did what was expected of it by providing above-the-fold front-page newspaper coverage, a spot on the NBC evening news, and extensive articles in the newsmagazines.

The temperature outside was 98 degrees Fahrenheit, and an ebullient Senator Dale Bumpers (D-Ark.) stated explicitly what the hearing was all about. In nine previous hearings, he said, "we couldn't get one [TV] camera—I see we have three cameras here today." Bumpers continued:

> And Dr. Hansen is going to testify today to... some... things that ought to be cause for headlines in every newspaper in America tomorrow morning because after all, we're going to have to have a lot of political support for this. Nobody wants to take on the automobile industry. Nobody wants to take on any of the industries that produce the things that we throw up into the atmosphere. They don't want that stopped and that's understandable. But what you have are all these competing economic interests pitted against our very survival.[48]

Bumpers posed the issue as an apocalyptic environmental conflict—big business against the survival of humanity. And he indicated with minimal ambiguity that the forces of light could not hope to triumph over the forces of darkness unless they mobilized the media under their banner.

It was clear even before the committee received Hansen's statement that he was going to say something provocative, because once again OMB was holding up his testimony. Twice before, in 1986 and 1987, OMB had held up or revised Hansen's written statement, but he managed to get around this bureaucratic obstacle in oral testimony or by speaking as a private citizen. Each time, however, he worried about the effect his testimony might have on his career. But this time, to his great surprise, he was allowed to submit written testimony that contained a media bombshell. Hansen ascribed "a high degree of confidence" to "a cause and effect relationship between the greenhouse effect and the observed warming." What this circumspect-sounding jargon meant in media terms was that there was now something immediate and dramatic to talk about. A respected scientist had said that global warming had arrived; it was no longer a phenomenon of the next decade or the next century. It was here.

Hansen was careful not to say that an increased concentration of greenhouse gases in the atmosphere had caused the 1988 heat wave— too many other factors might be responsible for a short-term phenomenon such as a single heat wave—but he did say that this accumulation of carbon dioxide and other gases made such heat waves more likely. It didn't take long for environmentalists to take this ball and run with it. Later that day, in the same hearing, Michael Oppenheimer of the Environmental Defense Fund capitalized on Hansen's testimony by mentioning the heat wave once and the drought twice in his brief oral testimony.[49] And the press ran with it, too. Reporters had been alerted that Hansen would have something startling to say, and they were in the hearing room waiting. Bob Hager of NBC News did a two-minute, twenty-second piece complete with graphics.

But the most influential news story to appear that day was written by Philip Shabecoff in *The New York Times*. The Shabecoff story ran in the top left-hand corner of the *Times*'s front page under a three-column headline. It said flatly that Hansen had attributed global warming with 99 percent certainty to the greenhouse effect. The phrase that stuck in people's minds, however, was not from Hansen's testimony. It was a casual remark he made to Shabecoff at the back of the hearing room that "it is time to stop waffling so much and say that the evidence is pretty strong that the greenhouse effect is here."[50] That quotable, offhand comment was picked up by media all over the country. It did not, however, stop the waffling. As late as July 1, 1989, *The New York Times* hedged in an editorial, "If the greenhouse warming is for real . . . "[51] But it did get Hansen on a number of national television programs where he propagated his views.

Many of the scientists, journalists, and policymakers interviewed for this chapter say they are convinced that global warming was about to take off anyway as a political issue in 1988 for various reasons, including the international attention it was beginning to get from foreign leaders such as Gro Bruntland of Norway, Margaret Thatcher of Great Britain, and Helmut Kohl of West Germany; the fact that the 1980s produced several of the warmest years on record; and the burgeoning interest in a range of other environmental issues, many of which are related to global warming. But all agree that no matter what might have otherwise happened, Hansen's decision to step out in front of his colleagues once again by making an assertion that journalists could get their teeth into was a turning point. The *New Yorker* magazine wrote that Hansen's testimony "conferred respectability" on some of the more extreme predictions of the effects of global warming such as "that the United States will have to import grain from the Soviet Union."[52] And *The New York Times*, not known for its avid support of nuclear power, used Hansen's testimony to assert in an editorial that the Reagan administration had "scandalously neglected" new nuclear technology.[53]

Hansen expressed satisfaction with the way Shabecoff handled the story, even though it was technically inaccurate. According to the Shabecoff story, Hansen said that "it was 99 percent certain that the warming trend . . . was caused by a buildup of carbon dioxide and other artificial gases in the atmosphere."[54] What Hansen actually said was that "with 99 percent confidence we can state that the warming during this time period is a real warming trend."[55] The difference, of course, was that Hansen did not say he was 99 percent certain that the greenhouse gases caused the warming. But he did say that he had "very high" confidence that the gases caused the warming, which was enough to cause consternation among his colleagues.

Richard Kerr, a reporter with a Ph.D. in chemical oceanography, chronicled the dispute between Hansen and the climatological community in *Science* magazine. Kerr wrote about a gathering of scientists in Amherst, Massachusetts, in May 1989, which was organized to "set the record straight with hard facts" about what could really be said with confidence about global warming.[56] Hansen was invited but didn't attend because once again he was in Washington giving congressional testimony. Kerr quoted Michael Schlesinger, who constructed global climate models at the University of Oregon before moving to the University of Illinois, who said, "Taken together [Hansen's] statements have given people the feeling the greenhouse effect has been detected with certitude. Our current understanding does not support that. Confidence of detection is now down near zero."

Kerr noted, however, that "had it not been for Hansen and his fame, few in public office, and certainly not the public itself, would have paid much attention to a problem that everyone at Amherst agrees threatens social and economic disruption around the globe." And in a letter to *Science*, Wallace Broecker, a climatologist at the Lamont-Doherty Geophysical Laboratory of Columbia University, said, "The fact that we cannot prove that the warming . . . was caused by . . . greenhouse gases is not the major issue. Rather, the issue is that, by adding [these] gases to the atmosphere, we are effectively playing Russian roulette with our climate."[57]

Most scientists are reluctant to do what policy-making usually requires: drawing a conclusion based on circumstantial evidence that is not overwhelming. Hansen was willing to do this. As a result, the national news media elevated global warming to the status of a major running story and gave substantial impetus to the comprehensive global warming legislation introduced in the 100th and 101st Congresses by Senator Wirth.[58] "Hansen's [1988] testimony marked an instantaneous shift in perceptions," Kerr said. "It was possibly the only way you could get from point A to point B with the media and the public."[59]

George Bush took office at the beginning of 1989 having said that he intended to be the "environmental president." His new secretary of State, James A. Baker III, at the urging of Frederick Bernthal, the Reagan administration's assistant secretary for environmental affairs, made global warming the subject of his first public talk. In his brief address on January 30, Baker said, "we can probably not afford to wait until all of the uncertainties have been resolved before we . . . act. Time will not make the problem go away."[60] White House chief of staff John Sununu and others in the new Bush administration were angered at Baker's call for action, which at least in part led to Bernthal not being reappointed.[61]

Just two weeks into the new administration, the global warming story was gaining momentum quickly. On February 4, 1989, *The New York Times* reported on page 1 that "The average temperature around the world in 1988 was the highest since reliable records began nearly a century ago."[62] Three days later, William K. Stevens wrote in the *Times* that "Spurred by the anxiety of a public suddenly alert to the potential dangers of global warming, a small fraternity of scientists is running a high-stakes race against the environmental clock, trying to predict the precise impact of the greenhouse effect in time to take effective countermeasures."[63]

In early May, just as the climatologists were gathering in Amherst, the global warming story was given an unintended boost by the Bush White House. And once again the incident involved several of the same key players—James Hansen, Senator Albert Gore, and Philip Shabecoff of *The New York Times*. The Office of Management and Budget, having slipped up in 1988, was not going to let Hansen's testimony get by again without close scrutiny. After telephone negotiations with Hansen, language was added to soften the scientist's judgment that buildup of greenhouse gases would cause, among other things, drought in the middle latitudes, a modeling result that Hansen had told Gore was "pretty reliable."[64] But OMB insisted that Hansen's projections be characterized as "estimates from evolving computer models and not as reliable predictions."[65] Hansen, however, had figured out how Washington worked in his years of appearing before Congress. He immediately phoned subcommittee chairman Gore and coached the senator on what questions to ask to elicit his uncensored views. Gore in turn called Shabecoff to let him know that Hansen's testimony had been tampered with. The *New York Times* reporter called Hansen for confirmation and details and then wrote a story that appeared on the front page of the *Times*. It began:

> The White House's Office of Management and Budget has changed the text of testimony scheduled to be delivered to Congress by a top Government scientist, over his protests, making his conclusions about the effects of global warming seem less serious and less certain than he intended.[66]

The next day, the White House confirmed that Hansen's testimony had been altered. By leaking to the *Times* early enough for a story to appear before the hearing opened, Gore made sure that there would be television cameras in the hearing room. The hearing made all three networks with pieces ranging in length from two minutes to two minutes and forty seconds, substantial coverage by evening news standards. Robert Hager's NBC story even included an interview with Jerry Mahlman, a scientist with the National Oceanographic and Atmospheric Administration who also had had testimony censored by OMB. The censorship story and a *New York Times* editorial titled "The White House and the Greenhouse"[67] spurred senators from both parties to press the administration to reverse its opposition to an international convention on global warming. Three days after the appearance of the *Times* editorial and five days after Shabecoff's story on the softening of Hansen's testimony, White House chief of staff Sununu sent new instructions to a U.S. delegation attending a U.N.-sponsored Intergovernmental Panel on Climate Change in Geneva. The revised instructions authorized the delegation to propose a workshop in the United States that would begin preparations for negotiating a treaty on global warming. It looked as if a major policy corner had been turned, but events in the fall proved otherwise.

On October 25, *The Washington Post* reported that the White House had turned down a bid by EPA administrator William K. Reilly "to invite representatives of other nations to the United States next year to begin negotiating an international convention on global warming."[68]

But in the press and on Capitol Hill, global warming's time had come. Using global warming as its principal news peg, *Time* magazine capped 1989 off by making Earth "Planet of the Year." And a global warming bill in the House of Representatives introduced by Rep. Claudine Schneider[69] attracted 105 cosponsors, indicating that the issue had reached critical mass politically.

Conclusion

Proving that press coverage has a cause-and-effect relationship to policy may not be as hard as proving that global warming is here, but often there is insufficient evidence to do the job. The circumstantial case, however, is a strong one. Politicians like Gore and Wirth worked for years to turn global warming into important news. They did so by using the news media to raise public awareness so that there would be a constituency for action on the issue. Polling data suggest that they have had some success, but polls also indicate that roughly half the population still knows little and cares less about the issue. Public knowledge is much greater, however, than just a few years ago, when most Americans had never heard of global warming or a greenhouse effect.

The press has been the primary means of getting the word out, although Gore, Wirth, and a handful of other legislators speak about the issue to small gatherings of their constituents, including one Wirth held in Meeker, Colorado, "a high plains cow town with 65 people," where, the senator said, "They wanted to know about global warming. I was amazed."[70] But Gore said that "on an issue like this you almost have to enhance public awareness" by using the press.[71]

The willingness of more than 100 members of the House to sponsor Schneider's global warming bill is a fair measure of the success Gore, Wirth, Senator John Heinz (R-Pa.), Senator John Chafee (R-R.I.), and a few others have had in publicizing the issue through the news media. Moreover, the media were the instruments of pressure brought to bear on the administration to reverse policy on an international convention on global warming. More importantly, no discussion of energy policy can take place any longer without consideration of the fact that fossil fuels deposit carbon dioxide and other pollutants in the atmosphere. Global warming concerns were influencing energy policy by the end of the 1980s, and to a considerable extent, global warming policy decisions were being driven by media coverage.

Although the evidence for dire effects from global warming remained inconclusive, political pressure had grown sufficiently to encourage the Bush administration to reverse its position and support international initiatives on reduction of carbon dioxide emissions, mainly by curtailing the use of fossil fuels. A *New York Times* report on September 24, 1989, said: "Members of Congress and interest groups viewed President Bush's clean-air proposals as 'a national energy policy in the making.' "[72] And *The Washington Post* quoted deputy Energy secretary W. Henson Moore as saying that energy conservation and the development of alternatives to nuclear and fossil fuels are "your good faith ante into the pot for people to start taking you seriously" on energy policy.[73]

NOTES

1. Timothy Wirth, U.S. senator, interview, Washington, D.C., October 20, 1989.

2. Albert Gore Jr., U.S. senator, interview, Washington D.C., November 20, 1989.

3. Stephen H. Schneider, "News Plays Fast and Loose with the Facts," *Detroit News*, December 5, 1989.

4. Adam Clymer, "Polls Show Contrasts in How Public and E.P.A. View the Environment," *New York Times*, May 22, 1989, p. B7. Although it only tied for twenty-third, 33 percent of those surveyed said they thought the greenhouse effect was "very serious" and 37 percent said they thought it was "somewhat serious." EPA called the risks of global warming "potentially very significant."

5. Roper Report, Vol. 90–2, March 1990.

6. Gore interview.

7. Larry B. Stammer, "California in 2030: A Greenhouse Vision," *Los Angeles Times*, December 13, 1988, p. 3.

8. Roger Revelle and Hans Suess, "CO_2 Exchange between the Atmosphere and the Ocean," *Tellus* 9, no. 1, 1957, pp. 18–27.

9. Margot Hornblower, "World Faces a Heating-Up, Study Warns," *Washington Post*, July 25, 1987, p. A1.

10. "Coal and the Global Greenhouse," *Washington Post*, July 27, 1977, p. A22.

11. The dates and page numbers for these stories were, respectively, February 14, p. A21; February 16, p. A13; and February 24, p. A44.

12. Council on Environmental Quality, "Global Energy Futures and the Carbon Dioxide Problem," January 1981.

13. Ibid., pp. v, vi.

14. Michael Oppenheimer, senior scientist, Environmental Defense Fund, interview, New York, October 13, 1989.

15. Rafe Pomerance, policy analyst, World Resources Institute, interview, Washington, D.C., October 17, 1989.

16. Sen. Timothy Wirth, "Global Warming and Its Implications for California," hearing before the Committee on Energy and Natural Resources, U.S. Senate, Santa Monica, Calif., May 20, 1989.

17. Larry B. Stammer, "Air Gains May Be Undone by Ozone Harm, Panel Is Told," *Los Angeles Times*, May 21, 1989, section II, p. 1.

18. James Hansen et al., "Climate Impact of Increasing Atmospheric Carbon Dioxide," *Science*, August 28, 1981, p. 957.

19. Walter Sullivan, "Study Finds Warming Trend That Could Raise Sea Levels," *New York Times*, August 22, 1981, p. 1.

20. James E. Hansen, "The Greenhouse, the White House and Our House," paper presented at award ceremony of the International Platform Association, Washington, D.C. August 3, 1989.

21. Stephen H. Schneider, *Global Warming* (San Francisco: Sierra Club Books, 1989), p. xii.

22. James E. Hansen, interview, Ridgewood, N.J., October 14, 1989.

23. A. Lacis et al., Greenhouse Effect of Trace Gases, 1970–1980," *Geophysical Research Letters* 8, no. 10, October 1981.

24. National Research Council, *Carbon Dioxide and Climate: A Second Assessment.* (Washington, D.C.: National Academy Press, 1982).

25. "Waiting for the Greenhouse Effect," *New York Times*, August 3, 1982, p. A20.

26. This list is not meant to include all newspaper and magazine coverage.

27. Eileen Keerdoja with Mary Hager and Jeff Copeland, "Is the Earth Getting Hotter?" *Newsweek*, October 31, 1983, p. 89.

28. Frederic Golden, reported by Jay Branegan, "Hot Times for the Old Orb," *Time*, October 31, 1983, p. 84.

29. Russell Baker, "Growing Pains," *New York Times Magazine*, September 2, 1984, p. 12.

30. Committee on Science and Technology, "Carbon Dioxide and Climate: The Greenhouse Effect," hearing before the Subcommittee on Natural Resources, Agriculture Research and Environment and the Subcommittee on Investigations and Oversight, U.S. House of Representatives, March 25, 1982.

31. Committee on Science and Technology, "Carbon Dioxide and the Greenhouse Effect," hearing before the Subcommittee on Investigations and Oversight, and the Subcommittee on Natural Resources, Agriculture Research and Environment. U.S. House of Representatives, February 28, 1984, pp. 18–19.

32. William V. Shannon, "It's Time to Take Action against This Dangerous 'Greenhouse,'" *Boston Globe*, January 2, 1985, p. 19. Despite the headline, the article does not advocate action on greenhouse warming.

33. Dave Barry, "A Weather Forecast to End All Other Weather Forecasts," *Chicago Tribune Sunday Magazine*, February 24, 1985, p. 6.

34. "Another False Alarm," *Wall Street Journal*, May 31, 1985, p. 22.

35. A Roper survey taken in February 1985 showed that only 37 percent of the population thought global warming would be "a serious problem" for their children or grandchildren. Polling data were supplied by the Roper Center.

36. Subcommittee on Environmental Pollution, "Ozone Depletion, the Greenhouse Effect and Climate Change," June 10, 1986, p. 29.

37. Philip Shabecoff, "Swifter Warming of the Globe Foreseen," *New York Times*, June 11, 1986, p. 17; and Cass Peterson, "A Dire Forecast for 'Greenhouse' Earth," *Washington Post*, June 11, 1986, p. 1.

38. Ibid., *Washington Post*, p. 21.

39. The only network news piece on the issue in 1986 was a fifty-second segment on ABC's "World News Tonight" on June 10. The piece looked at the implications of evidence of the effect.

40. "Ozone Loss Could Have Dire Effect, Experts Say," *Atlanta Constitution*, June 11, 1986, p. A2.

41. Examples of this kind of coverage include Cass Peterson, "'Greenhouse Effect' Needs More Study, U.S. Aide Says," *Washington Post*, June 12, 1986, p. A17; and Jeff Nesmith, "Scientist Calls Threat of Greenhouse Effect Exaggerated," *Atlanta Journal and Constitution*, November 23, 1986, p. 14.

42. Michael Oppenheimer, "Will the Planet Remain Habitable?" *New York Times*, June 30, 1986, p. A19; James Gustave Speth, "Sweltering in the Greenhouse," *Los Angeles Times*, August 1, 1986, section II, p. 5; and Patrick Michaels, "Greenhouse Effect? Then Why Is It Colder?" *Washington Post*, June 15, 1986, p. F2.

43. Stanley N. Wellborn, "Facing Life in a Greenhouse," *U.S. News & World Report*, September 29, 1986, pp. 73–74. *Newsweek* published an article titled "The Silent Summer" on June 23, 1986. It appeared on p. 64, and the authors were Sharon Begley and Bob Cohn.

44. Louis Harris and Associates, poll taken for the Office of Technology Assessment between October 30 and November 17, 1986. Data supplied by the Roper Center.

45. Gore said in an interview on November 20, 1989, that he had visited the offices of *Time* in September 1987 to urge the magazine to do a cover story on global warming. The *Time* cover story appeared on October 19, 1987. The international edition of *Newsweek* also ran a cover story on March 2, 1987.

46. Committee on Energy and Natural Resources, "Greenhouse Effect and Global Climate Change," hearings, U.S. Senate, November 9–10, 1987, p. 53.

47. Wirth interview.

48. Committee on Energy and Natural Resources, "Greenhouse Effect and Global Climate Change," hearing, U.S. Senate, June 23, 1988, p. 38.

49. Ibid., pp. 80–81.

50. Philip Shabecoff, "Global Warming Has Begun, Expert Tells Senate," *New York Times*, June 24, 1988, p. A1.

51. "The Global Bonfire," *New York Times*, July 1, 1989, p. 22.

52. "The Talk of the Town," *New Yorker*, August 29, 1988, p. 17.

53. "Heat and Light as Killers," *New York Times*, October 9, 1988, p. 22.

54. Shabecoff, "Global Warming Has Begun."

55. Committee on Energy and Natural Resources, hearing, June 23, 1988, p. 39.

56. Richard A. Kerr, "Hansen vs. the World on the Greenhouse Threat," *Science*, June 2, 1989, p. 1041.

57. W. S. Broecker, "Hansen and the Greenhouse Effect," letter to the editor, *Science*, August 4, 1989, p. 451.

58. S. 2667, a bill "To establish a national energy policy to reduce global warming, and for other purposes," 100th Congress, 2nd session; and S. 324, a bill "To establish a national energy policy to reduce global warming, and for other purposes," 101st Congress, 1st session.

59. Richard Kerr, reporter, *Science*, interview, Washington, D.C., September 15, 1989.

60. James A. Baker III, address to the Response Strategies Working Group of the Intergovernmental Panel on Climate Change, January 30, 1989.

61. Bernthal was appointed the deputy director of the National Science Foundation in March 1990.

62. Philip Shabecoff, "Global Warmth in 1988 Is Found to Set a Record," *New York Times*, February 4, 1989, p. 1.

63. William K. Stevens, "With Cloudy Crystal Balls, Scientists Race to Assess Global Warming," *New York Times*, February 7, 1989, p. C1.

64. Gore interview.

65. Subcommittee on Science, Technology and Space, Committee on Commerce, Science and Transportation, prepared statement by James Hansen, p. 4. Not printed in published version of May 9, 1989, hearing.

66. Philip Shabecoff, "Scientist Says Budget Office Altered His Testimony," *New York Times*, May 7, 1989, p. 1.

67. "The White House and the Greenhouse," *New York Times*, May 9, 1989, p. A30.

68. Michael Weisskopf, "White House Balks at Hosting Talks on Global Warming," *Washington Post*, October 25, 1989, p. A2.

69. H.R. 1078, Global Warming Prevention Act of 1989, introduced by Rep. Schneider, 101st Congress, 1st session.

70. Wirth interview.

71. Gore interview.

72. Allan R. Gold, "Bush Clean Air Plan Called Energy Policy in the Making," *New York Times*, September 24, 1989, p. 22.

73. Thomas W. Lippman, "Conservation, Renewable Fuel Stressed," *Washington Post*, November 26, 1989, p. A4.

6

AIDS: A Missed
Opportunity

O N June 5, 1981, a publication of the U.S. Centers for Disease Control (CDC) called *Morbidity and Mortality Weekly Report* (*MMWR*) published a brief article title "Pneumocystis Pneumonia— Los Angeles."[1] In the bland, stylized prose typical of scientific journals, it said: "In the period October 1980–May 1981, 5 young men, all active homosexuals, were treated for biopsy-confirmed Pneumocystis carinii pneumonia at three different hospitals in Los Angeles, California."

A month later, on July 4, *MMWR* published another article titled "Kaposi's Sarcoma and Pneumocystis Pneumonia among Homosexual Men—New York City and California."[2] It began: "During the past 30 months, Kaposi's Sarcoma (KS), an uncommonly reported malignancy in the United States, has been diagnosed in 26 homosexual men (20 in New York City, 6 in California). The 26 patients range in age from 26–51 years (mean 39 years). Eight of these patients died (7 in NYC, 1 in California)—all 8 within 24 months after KS was diagnosed."

Although unknown to the general public, the *MMWR* is carefully read by everyone seriously concerned with public health. It is the journal in which new outbreaks of disease are most frequently first reported. Its articles are short, factual accounts of what physicians have seen in their practices or their laboratories. They don't explain unusual medical occurrences but rather describe them and alert physicians and others concerned with public health to their existence. In this instance, we know with hindsight, *MMWR* was alerting its readers to a coming pandemic. By the end of 1982 the underlying condition on which it was reporting would be known to the world as AIDS. The disease is caused when a microorganism called the human immunodeficiency virus (HIV) enters white blood cells called T lymphocytes, which when functioning normally trigger the immune system's response to infection. The HIV virus takes over the T cells and reproduces itself. This prevents the T cells from stimulating the immune system to produce antibodies, which fight invading microbes. This in turn leaves the body vulnerable to infections that are usually easily fought off.

The principal authors, respectively, of the two articles, Michael Gottleib, an immunologist at UCLA, and Alvin Friedman-Kien, a dermatologist at NYU, each knew he was onto something interesting, but neither had any idea of the catastrophic implications of what he was reporting. Neither had any idea that he was dealing with a new disease whose death toll within twenty years would be counted in the hundreds of thousands in the United States alone.

Although at the time the two physicians reporting on patients a continent apart had no way of gauging the importance of what they were seeing, their publications took account of related factors that were to prove epidemiologically and medically significant. Friedman-Kien had noticed that the infected gay men were unusually active sexually and that their immune systems were suppressed. And Gottleib's article in *MMWR* was followed by an editorial note saying that pneumocystis carinii pneumonia in the United States occurred almost exclusively in severely immunosuppressed patients. The epidemiological investigations that got under way immediately at CDC would demonstrate the relevance of these observations. Moreover, within a year, *MMWR* would report that 63 percent of heterosexual men who contracted one of the infections associated with a suppressed immune system used intravenous drugs.[3] By the middle of 1982, therefore, the two routes by which the HIV is now known to be transmitted were strongly suspected, although not proved.

Meanwhile, on June 8, 1981, while attending a seminar in San Diego, Drs. James Curran and Harold Jaffe of CDC's Division of Sexually Transmitted Diseases learned about cases of Kaposi's sarcoma (KS), a rare cancer characterized by purple lesions on the skin, and pneumocystis carinii pneumonia in San Francisco. Ten days later a task force was set up at CDC to investigate the outbreak of Kaposi's sarcoma and this relatively rare form of pneumonia in previously healthy homosexual men. Curran was appointed to head it. Over the next month this group searched for cases of KS and other unusual infections in gay men between 15 and 60 years old in selected hospitals around the country. They discovered that a few cases had occurred in New York City as early as 1978 and 1979.

Although the implications were still unclear, even before the publication of his *MMWR* article Friedman-Kien thought he had seen enough to call Lawrence K. Altman, M.D., who covers medicine for *The New York Times*. The two men were acquainted through Ron Roberto, a physician at CDC. Altman also had been an attending physician at NYU's Bellevue Hospital in 1978 and 1979, and the *Times* reporter had been Friedman-Kien's patient for a minor skin disorder. Altman was sufficiently intrigued to interview Friedman-Kien and some of his patients and write an article in which he reported Friedman-Kien's observations about large numbers of sexual contacts and immunosuppression. Altman said in an interview almost eight years later that he remembers being struck by the "sexual boastfulness" of Friedman-Kien's patients.[4] He made no reference to Gottlieb's June 5 article, which had, however, been reported in *The Los Angeles Times* by Harry Nelson.[5] Nelson's story was the first on what was to become known as AIDS to appear in the mainstream press anywhere in the United States. It had been preceded by a story in *The New York Native*, a gay newspaper.[6] Altman said he had been aware of the "Kaposi's sarcoma cluster" reported by Friedman-Kien because of his work at Bellevue.[7] *The New York Times*'s next account of the mysterious outbreak appeared on August 29, 1981. It reported that more than 100 homosexual men had been stricken with either Kaposi's sarcoma, pneumocystis carinii pneumonia, or both, and that almost half of them had died.[8] The *Times* also noted that one woman had contracted pneumocystis carinii pneumonia and that 94 percent of the patients whose sexual preference was known were homosexual men.

For the rest of 1981, the *Times* carried nothing about the unusual outbreak of rare diseases among gay men. Altman indicated that this was at least partly because the period was exceptionally busy. He was assigned to cover the aftermath of the shootings of President Reagan and Pope John Paul II, as well as the implantation of an artificial heart in Barney Clark.[9] The *Times* was not atypical. *The San Francisco Chronicle*, which eventually became a leader for its AIDS coverage, also carried only two stories in 1981, despite the city's large gay population. The networks carried only one story, a feature on "Good Morning America" in December, the month in which *Time* and *Newsweek* had their first reports and in which Gottlieb published an article on the new disease in the *New England Journal of Medicine*.[10]

Meanwhile, however, CDC investigators were interviewing thirty surviving immunosuppressed men who were suffering from opportunistic infections, or those that took hold only because the immune system was weakened. The investigators discovered among other things that more than 90 percent of them used amyl or butyl nitrates, sexual stimulants known as poppers. This suggested to some epidemiologists that these chemicals, widely used in the gay community, might be linked to the new disease.

Early Coverage

There was nothing remarkable about the performance of the news media with respect to AIDS coverage in these early stages. News organizations in general behaved predictably. Relatively short but accurate reports were published about what appeared to be a serious condition affecting almost exclusively male homosexuals. Would there have been more coverage if those infected were all Roman Catholic nuns or black lawyers? There seems to be little reason to think this would have been the case in the first months of the still developing epidemic. Nevertheless, Rep. Henry Waxman (D-Calif.), whose district includes predominantly gay West Hollywood, said in the spring of 1982, "There is no doubt in my mind that if the same disease had appeared among Americans of Norwegian descent, or among tennis players, rather than among gay males, the response of both the government and the medical community would have been different."[11] Perhaps if more people had been sick and the entire population had appeared to be at risk, there would have been more stories and more interest from doctors and public officials from the outset. But that wasn't the case.

It is reasonable to expect a quicker response to early evidence of a potential epidemic from medical professionals and public officials than from journalists, partly because journalism is event-oriented and conservative, a theme that will be explored later in this chapter. It also appears true that television news and some publications avoided the story longer than could be justified by invoking traditional standards of news judgment because the afflicted were homosexuals. Comments both public and private by science correspondents, including George Strait of ABC, Bob Bazell of CBS, and Jerry Bishop of *The Wall Street*

Journal, suggest that this was so.[12] Does that mean that some television news producers and print editors are homophobic? Probably. But it also suggests that a disease of uncertain origin, which might result from life-style choices viewed by many as distasteful, and which seems confined to a limited community widely considered aberrational, cannot fight its way onto a twenty-two-minute network newscast beamed at tens of millions of people, or into conservative newspapers with traditionalist audiences, until the number of sick persons reaches some undefinable critical mass. J. Ronald Milavsky, in a paper delivered at the annual meeting of the American Psychological Association, supported this view when he said that "[news] professionals are guided a great deal more by evaluations of importance and of market interest than by their own personal tastes and values [when making news judgments about issues like AIDS]."[13]

No one was thinking at this point of comparing AIDS to the Black Death, as Otis Bowen, assistant secretary of the Department of Health and Human Services, would subsequently do,[14] however inappropriately. There is, however, a statistical correlation between concern that AIDS may be a serious threat to heterosexuals and volume of press coverage. In 1986, for example, NBC ran 204 stories on AIDS, and only 38 of them referred to homosexuals, compared to 1983 (the last year in which the disease was still widely believed to be confined mainly to homosexuals) in which the network carried about 50 stories.[15]

One of the great tensions in journalism is between the temptation to hype a story—for example, by projecting an outbreak of AIDS among heterosexuals that the exisiting epidemiological evidence won't sustain—and the fear of being wrong. It is a damned-if-you-do and damned-if-you-don't situation because the public is just as critical of journalists who are perceived as too conservative as it is of those who go too far too fast. Quality newspapers and the television networks hate to be beaten on stories, but they hate even more to be wrong. The striving in the media that may be more often overriding than any other is for accuracy. Those who do not believe this because they frequently find mistakes in news reports simply do not appreciate how difficult it is to fill a newspaper or newscast with accurate information. They should be exposed to the challenges of news gathering and the chaos of a newsroom on deadline to have their consciousness raised. As for those who do not believe it because they are convinced that journalists are animated by ideological biases and personal agendas, they are occasionally right. But my own experience has persuaded me that in the large majority of cases they are wrong.

Along with their dread of being wrong, the news media also display a pervasive desire to be in the center of the social spectrum. Milavsky, vice president for news and social research at NBC, said that "most mass media try to attract and maintain the broad middle of the social landscape by keeping a mainstream tone and avoiding things that might drive audiences away—like bad taste."[16] AIDS, unfortunately, does not fit the centrist profile. In the words of Anthony Fauci, director of the National Institute of Allergy and Infectious Diseases, AIDS mainly affects "people who have traditionally and historically been disenfranchised from the mainstream of society,"[17] and precise reporting on AIDS requires clear breaches of taste as the mass media have traditionally defined it. Taking into account both of these conservative biases, for accuracy and for the center, it is no surprise that journalists are slow off the mark on most stories that are not pegged to events in which quotations and easily verifiable observations can substitute for harder-to-get (and possibly distasteful) more relevant "facts." Similarly, it is not surprising that journalists rarely report on social trends until they are well entrenched, and are unwilling to break cultural taboos such as publishing sexually explicit material, even when the goal is to curtail an epidemic. It took a combination of the ever-mounting numbers of dead and the fear that the disease would break out of the gay and drug-using communities to get the press to use sexually explicit language.

Given these home truths about journalism, the early coverage of AIDS, by those who bothered to cover it, was as good as could reasonably have been expected. Although there were only two stories in 1981 in *The New York Times*, they were very good stories totaling twenty-five paragraphs, which seems a reasonable amount of space to devote to a new, if mysterious, illness with a relatively small number of sick persons. James Curran, who has headed AIDS activities at the Centers for Disease Control from the beginning, contends that the press should have grasped the magnitude of the story earlier, and Friedman-Kien agrees. But this view seems to reflect either wishful thinking or 20/20 hindsight. In 1981 researchers were not telling reporters that an epidemic was on the horizon. By May 1982, when *The Los Angeles Times* carried the first front-page story on AIDS by any major newspaper, it could be argued that matters were clarifying sufficiently to justify a substantial increase in coverage.[18] Such retrospective judgments, however, are not terribly illuminating. What seems more important is that these carefully written early stories by reporters like Altman and Nelson set the tone for much of the medical coverage to follow. With a handful of exceptions, science and health reporters wrote about each new development relating to AIDS with perspective, skepticism where appropriate, and occasionally insight.

The failure was not in the reporting of the medical science itself. It was that most journalists did not recognize, or at least were not reporting, two major nonscience stories about AIDS: the toll the disease was taking in human suffering and the thoroughly inadequate Reagan administration response, which began to be evident as early as the fall of 1982. The news media eventually caught up with the human story, but they never fully came to grips with the failure of the administration to give AIDS the priority it deserved. One CDC official said in 1988, "The thing that has always astounded me is that the media have not put this administration's feet to the fire as far as the fact that the funding that occurred occurred because of the Congress. . . . If truth be known the only reason we've spent anywhere near [the] amount [we have] was because it was added by the Congress."[19] The record is clear on that. Year after year Congress appropriated funds substantially in excess of administration requests so that epidemiology, biological research, and to a lesser extent education could be funded.

The story of why the news media covered AIDS the way they did is complex. According to David Shaw, the respected media reporter of *The Los Angeles Times*, "while many see the press as a monolithic institution, AIDS coverage was, in some ways, a classic instance of the individualized, even idiosyncratic, nature of the press." Shaw also noted that papers with good medical writers who were trusted by their editors "did a relatively good job covering the early stages of the AIDS epidemic."[20] Subsequently, reporters like Randy Shilts of *The San Francisco Chronicle*, Laura McLaughlin of *The Boston Globe*, Donald Drake of *The Philadelphia Inquirer*, Vincent Coppola of *Newsweek*, and Laurie Garrett of National Public Radio made significant contributions.

Just what difference it would have made if coverage of the politics surrounding AIDS at the federal level had been more intense and had come from *The New York Times* and the networks is not clear. After all, the money was forthcoming even though Congress had to provide it against the administration's wishes. But when the president's attention is engaged—and the *Times* and the evening newcasts are known to be relatively riveting to presidents—things happen faster and usually on a larger scale than they otherwise might. Therefore, it is worth exploring why the news media failed to tell an important part of a truly major story. This is in some ways an exploration of why six years and

20,800 deaths separated Michael Gottleib's article in *MMWR* in June 1981 and Ronald Reagan's only speech about AIDS on June 1, 1987.

AIDS was typed as a medical story, and most political reporters wanted nothing to do with it. At the same time, many medical reporters wanted nothing to do with the sex- and drug-related politics of AIDS. (Some science reporters argue that "If I deal with the politics of an issue, then I stop being a science writer.")[21] At the same time, most researchers failed to use the media, manipulatively or otherwise, in a situation where public health considerations cried out for the media. And dedicated congressional staffers, schooled in the use of news media, were unable to get the attention of journalists on an issue of national importance.

The Media, the Congress, and the Administration

In the first few months of 1981, while Michael Gottleib, Joel Weissman, Alvin Friedman-Kien, Linda Laubenstein, Marcus Conant, and a relatively small number of other physicians were treating the young men who would make medical history as the first patients identified with the disease now called AIDS, James Curran, Harold Jaffe, Mary Guinan, and Roy Eng formed a CDC task force to track the newly emerging condition. The research-oriented private physicians and the CDC merged their efforts almost immediately. Gottleib called his friend Wayne Shandera, a Los Angeles–based investigator for the CDC's Epidemiological Intelligence Service, to request that he study the unexplained outbreak of opportunistic infections. Curran said years later that

> although [the new syndrome] was not affecting large numbers of people
> and it was unclear what the cause was, there was sufficient concern
> and suspicion that it was due to a transmissible agent from day one. I
> mean one of the leading hypotheses was that it was caused by a virus
> and the fact that it was so fatal and so seemingly unsolvable in terms
> of therapy and cure and that it was mysteriously affecting homosexual
> men in cities where other STD's [sexually transmitted diseases] were
> present in very large excess, in the same populations, meant that it well
> could have been transmissible and gotten much worse. Secondly, that
> it was very unlikely to be restricted to any city or subgroup, that it would
> be present elsewhere.... There was a gap between interest in the sci-
> entific community, medical community, and the interest in the press.[22]

Curran, of course, is right about the gap in interest, if what he meant by the scientific and medical community was the small group of specialists who were interested in this deadly new disease. Even though AIDS was reported on almost instantaneously, it did not totally capture Nelson's or Altman's imagination, let alone the imagination of their editors, the way it did that of Gottleib, Friedman-Kien, or Curran himself. The core question implied in Curran's comment is whether journalists should have concluded from what they were being told by researchers like Gottleib, Curran, and Friedman-Kien that this mysterious set of symptoms showing up in homosexual men was the first sighting of a epidemic. If the answer is yes, clearly more should have been written sooner, and television should have covered the disease much sooner. If the answer is no, as numerous interviews with reporters and researchers suggest, then many newspapers performed about as well as one could reasonably expect them to perform.

It is true, of course, that the gay press took the disease seriously before the straight press did. But this does not mean the straight press should have been equally alert. Gay journalists were more sensitive to the implications of AIDS because at first it seemed confined to their community; they knew people who were infected or who had died after displaying the new syndrome; the likelihood of sexual transmission was threatening, especially among "fast-lane" gays with multiple partners; and hepatitis and other infectious diseases were prevalent among gays, which raised the level of fear about a new condition that appeared to be transmissible and was fatal. Gays were afraid; straights were not. If straights had been afraid, news coverage would have reflected their fear. Instead, reporters like Altman relied on a principle common to journalism and public health: "Don't create panic."[23] It is a conservative and generally sound principle that fosters skepticism toward speculative claims, even if they are well informed. When confronted by a story such as AIDS, which in the beginning was characterized by high levels of uncertainty, reporters and editors at papers like *The New York Times*, *The Los Angeles Times*, and *The San Francisco Chronicle* reported verifiable facts, relevant epidemiological data, and limited assessments by the reporting physicians. Their stories were not especially alarming—except to homosexual men, the only clearly identified risk group during the first six months of reporting on the disease. Overall, therefore, it is difficult to fault the reporting on AIDS done in America's best newspapers during the second half of 1981, even though there was not much of it. Later, when complicated questions arose about mortality rates, the incubation period of the virus, and, most of all, heterosexual spread of the disease, there were many examples of sloppy journalism, but not at the beginning.

It is also true that general-circulation newspapers did not cover, indeed may have been hostile to covering, gay life.[24] But these reasons by themselves are inadequate to explain why early AIDS coverage was sparse. Joe Lovett, who produced several programs on AIDS for ABC's "20/20" and became one of the best-informed journalists in the country on the disease, offered this evaluation:

> AIDS was different originally because it affected, for the most part, homosexual—or was being reported as affecting—homosexual men and IV drug users, most of whom were perceived as black. These were considered "disenfranchised" groups. What people didn't realize was that a lot of people that they knew were being affected. I think it was perceived as a disease of "other" people. In a sexually transmitted disease, there aren't "other" people; everyone is available to be infected. . . . I think the press and the executives involved in decision making have been no slower than anybody else; perhaps they've been faster than the general population to perceive what's been going on. But that's not fast enough.[25]

Even today the subject of heterosexual spread is controversial. The fact that the percentage of AIDS cases represented by non-drug-injecting heterosexuals is only 5 percent is viewed by some as undermining the thesis that heterosexuals who don't use drugs intravenously are at significant risk. But that 5 percent represents between 40,000 and 60,000 people, which lends weight to Lovett's argument. And until 1990, the CDC estimate was only 4 percent. Despite these significant statistics, it was reported at the 1990 International AIDS Conference in San Francisco that "Sexually active heterosexual high school and college students only rarely used condoms,"[26] still the best way short of abstention from sex to avoid infection. When should journalists have sensed the magnitude of the story, the true proportions of the epidemic? Robert Bazell, a journalist trained in immunology, wrote in the *New Republic* in August 1983:

> There are more than seventeen hundred cases now and there will be more than thirty-four hundred six month from now. But it is not likely there will be sixty-eight hundred a year from now. Almost certainly the number of cases is not going to double every six months as it has since the onset of the epidemic. At some point the disease will have swept through the susceptible populations and the number of new cases will level off.[27]

Bazell was correct. By August 20, 1984, a total of 5,699 cases had been reported to the CDC. And after that the number of reported cases did not come close to doubling every six months. But six years later AIDS was still epidemic and highly newsworthy. In early June 1986, at a meeting held at the Coolfont Conference Center in Berkeley Springs, West Virginia, a report was issued predicting that by 1991 there would be 270,000 AIDS cases in the United States and 179,000 deaths. In mid–1990 that report seemed to be just about on target. The current CDC estimate is that there are about a million infected persons in the United States, almost all of whom will develop symptoms and die, unless a cure is found.

On May 24, 1983, Dr. Edward N. Brandt Jr., the assistant secretary for health of the Department of Health and Human Services, told NIH and CDC officials that AIDS was the Reagan administration's number one health priority. He repeated this statement at congressional hearings in August, but the Reagan administration's minimal funding request for AIDS research and education belied Brandt's claim. Meanwhile, by mid-1983 it was known that the AIDS virus was in the blood supply, that women, hemophiliacs, and babies were infected, and the CDC listed "heterosexual contact" as a transmission route for AIDS. Still, there were only 1,700 cases nationwide. As for news stories, the networks were running about five a month, with upward blips for Brandt's announcement and a story in the *Journal of the American Medical Association* about the possibility of transmission of the virus to children through routine household contact.[28] *The New York Times* published 128 stories on AIDS in 1983, 52 of them between April and June, the time period of the Brandt announcement and the *JAMA* article.[29]

Another reason for the lack of sustained coverage might have been a failure to recognize that this was not just one more example of hard choices about allocation of scarce funds. There was nothing unusual, after all, about one branch of the government squabbling with another over money. Moreover, the Reagan administration had an electoral mandate to cut federal spending, and respected federal spokesmen like Edward Brandt were saying they were getting all the money that could be productively spent. Under these circumstances it was not immediately obvious that the money the administration was requesting for AIDS research was seriously inadequate. It was, however, as the record of congressional hearings and investigations makes plain, sufficiently obvious to make it worthwhile to examine what went wrong.

Lovett said that when he first started doing national political stories he was "stunned" to hear people say, "Thank God you're doing a story. Now maybe we'll have some action."[30] But this is typical of the way politicians and bureaucrats in the capital view the press—as an effective means to political goals. Yet in the case of AIDS, although coverage eventually built to a substantial volume, the Reagan administration moved at a glacial pace. An important contributing reason was that the efforts of members of Congress like Rep. Ted Weiss (D-N.Y.) and Rep. Henry Waxman (D-Calif.) to hold the administration accountable for its failures were not echoed in the media. Both Weiss and Waxman are usually good at getting press attention for issues they are interested in, but AIDS was an exception. A disease that affected drug addicts, most of whom were black and Hispanic, and gay men, did not capture the full attention of the mainstream press. In the case of EDB (see Chapter 2), or that of Alar, a chemical used to make apples ripen uniformly, the media were used to apply pressure on the administration, which led to hasty banning of the chemicals. Intense media scrutiny was the instrument used to change federal policy. With AIDS, however, there was no such scrutiny, even though Congress and the Congressional Office of Technology Assessment provided ample ammunition.

The first congressional hearing on AIDS was held in Los Angeles in April 1982 by a House Commerce Committee subcommittee chaired by Waxman. Harry Nelson covered the hearing for *The Los Angeles Times*. He wrote a lead that said: "An epidemic of rare diseases that first was noted among male homosexuals is now beginning to affect heterosexual males and females, a government scientist said Tuesday."[31] Nelson wrote that of the 300 sick persons identified, 10 were heterosexual females and 30 were heterosexual males. James Curran was quoted as saying at the hearing that the cases detected up to that point were "only the tip of the iceberg." It may be, as *New York Times* science reporter Lawrence Altman has said, that scientists were not pushing the panic button and predicting an epidemic, but forecasts of what was coming such as Curran's were beginning to appear. Nelson's article was thirteen paragraphs long, and it ran on page 22.

The next congressional hearing dealing with AIDS was held on May 9, 1983. At 10:00 A.M., Waxman convened his subcommittee on health and the environment in Washington to discuss emergency public health problems. In his opening remarks he cited comparisons, attributed to public officials, likening the AIDS "epidemic" to polio and smallpox. Waxman then went on to question Edward Brandt, the Reagan administration's assistant secretary for health. Waxman asked:

"Why is the administration's proposal for 1984 for AIDS work at the Centers for Disease Control to reduce it back to $2 million after we find that they have spent $4.5 million on AIDS research [in fiscal year 1983]?" Brandt's response in retrospect seems incredible but might not have seemed so to the same degree in May 1983. He said: "At the time that budget was being prepared, of course, we anticipated we would be a good way down the road to a solution of AIDS." Waxman also pointed out and Brandt acknowledged that it took almost two full years to get the NIH grant mechanism geared up to provide funds for AIDS research.

Of the newspapers and magazines surveyed for this chapter,[32] only *The San Francisco Chronicle* reported this hearing. It ran a nine-paragraph UPI story on page 8 that opened with Waxman citing the polio comparison and focusing on the California Democrat's criticism of the administration for failing to request adequate funds to combat the epidemic. By this time, of course, AIDS was being treated as a local story by the *Chronicle* because San Francisco's large gay community was already well on the way to being devastated by the disease. Nevertheless, the hearing contained hints of an important story, which with only a couple of exceptions would not be followed up. The story was the unwillingness of the administration to make the major commitment of money and manpower required to fight a burgeoning fatal epidemic. John Brownell, an assistant managing editor of *The Los Angeles Times*, had this to say of the post-1984 period:

> I think the big problem at that point in the AIDS story was people were reluctant, all through journalism, were reluctant to say, "Why isn't the federal government doing more?" because it gave you kind of an advocacy stand. The obvious answer is... that the federal government should be doing more, and that the argument you would hear against that quite often was that this is still a very isolated disease. It's unlikely to spread beyond the groups it has already infected, and at that time, we're talking homosexual patients and hemophiliacs. And so there wasn't a sense that we should be holding the government's feet to the fire on this issue.[33]

The pattern of coverage in major newspapers from 1983 to 1986 supports Brownell's analysis. Stories about congressional hearings and reports tended simply to balance critical comments with pro forma denials by federal officials, often leading with the denials. In fact, the handful of articles that were published support a stronger argument than Brownell's. In general, the stories do not treat the critics seriously.

Richard Flaste, who was science editor of *The New York Times* during this period, put it this way: "I don't give any credence to the notion of homophobia. What I do think is that there is this us-and-them kind of feeling that we weren't part of that group . . . that we were two separate cultures."[34] As a result of this culture gap, Flaste suggests, media coverage of what early in the epidemic was called the gay cancer and gay-related immune disease (GRID) was given relatively less attention than diseases like Legionnaires' disease and toxic shock syndrome that affected the white middle class. Flaste also argues persuasively that science journalists are highly sensitive to false alarms, whether burgeoning epidemics or miracle cures. As a result, even on stories with major public health implications, journalists would rather be slow than wrong. This contradicts the conventional wisdom that most journalists would rather be first than anything, but it is often true nonetheless.

The first full-scale hearings on AIDS were held on August 1 and 2, 1983, by the Intergovernmental Relations and Government Resources Subcommittee of the House Committee on Government Operations, chaired by Ted Weiss. Among the witnesses called were leaders of gay rights organizations who had been following the progress of the epidemic intensively from the outset. Virginia M. Apuzzo, executive director of the National Gay Task Force, said in her testimony that she would "point out some of the more shocking instances of the federal government conducting business as usual and thereby threatening the well-being of its citizens." She made three allegations, all of which were correct: it took more than two years for the government to begin funding research into the cause of AIDS; the CDC's AIDS effort had to rely on begging and borrowing from other programs and was still woefully underfunded; and public-information programs were late and inadequate.

The New York Times covered the opening day of the hearing with a four-paragraph Associated Press dispatch on page A10.[35] The article quoted Apuzzo but not her specific and well-aimed criticisms of the federal effort. *The Washington Post* story on the first day led with a physician testifying that federal health officials had acted on insufficient evidence when they identified Haitians as a high-risk group. It did not mention Apuzzo in any of its ten paragraphs.[36] The *Post*'s second-day article, which appeared on page A3, led with Assistant Secretary Brandt's testimony on the increase in federal spending for AIDS.[37] Except for a brief remark in the last paragraph about inadequate staffing for federal AIDS activities, the entire twelve-paragraph story was devoted to the administration's position. *The New York Times* also devoted its second-day story to the administration's position.[38]

Apuzzo's reference to "business as usual," which was accurate, spotlights the reason for the level of news coverage. News organizations are generally slow to recognize that a dramatic new development, or set of circumstances, like an epidemic, requires an unusual response. "Business as usual" also implies that government witnesses will put the best possible face on things, which often means dissimulating. Moreover, Apuzzo was a suspect source. She was an uncredentialed representative of a nonmainstream population and was perceived as having a clear bias in favor of increased funding for AIDS programs. Journalists were right to be sensitive to the possibility that her testimony was biased. But similar skepticism should have applied to Brandt's testimony. He, after all, had an administration position to defend. Brandt is a decent man who did what was in his power to increase funding for AIDS. But at this stage, in August 1983, he had little support within the Reagan administration. Apuzzo's presentation much more closely approximated reality than Brandt's. The news media did not reflect this fact, in part because little or no effort was made to find out who was right. There was simply an assumption that testimony by ranking government officials was more defensible under traditional standards reflecting both laziness and news judgment than testimony by gay activists.

The August 1 and 2 hearings on the federal response to AIDS and appropriations hearings held in April 1983 contained a rich lode of data for any reporter interested in examining whether or not the federal government was devoting sufficient resources to combating the epidemic. But no mainstream news organization provided the coverage. A few months later another news peg appeared. On November 30, 1983, the Weiss subcommittee issued its report titled "The Federal Response to AIDS." It made the following charges:

The committee has found that the Administration has not exercised sufficient leadership to ensure that adequate resources have been available for its number one health priority. Not only have funding levels been inadequate to undertake AIDS research and surveillance, but funding requests have also been delayed, hampering the ability of the Public Health Service scientists to effectively plan and carry out their work with the urgency demanded by this epidemic.

At the end of 1981, PHS officials were aware of the need for increased funding for AIDS research. The Administration, however, did not initiate requests for any additional funding for PHS activity to research and control the epidemic until May 1983. . . .

Both the House and the Senate, particularly their respective appropriations committees, have found it difficult to gather accurate and timely information about the resources needed by the PHS in pursuing AIDS activities. The history of AIDS funding includes the withholding of information about PHS resource needs from the Congress, and the belated communication of such information only after numerous attempts by Congressional committees and individual members to obtain it.[39]

These charges are documented in detail. For example, the subcommittee showed that only 10 percent of National Institutes of Health extramural research funds earmarked for AIDS research "were actually awarded to outside researchers specifically for AIDS work."[40] The subcommittee report also quoted a CDC AIDS Fact Sheet (December 1, 1982) setting out how the reprogramming of CDC funds to AIDS rather than appropriating new money was crippling "high priority disease investigation and prevention activities."[41] In retrospect the report seems well worth news coverage, even in a town that generates as much paper as Washington. It received none. And in May 1983, the Subcommittee on Health and the Environment of the House Energy and Commerce Committee held hearings on the Public Health Emergency Act (H.R. 2713), legislation intended to make funds instantly available to meet challenges such as AIDS. Brandt testified for the administration against the legislation, arguing that funds could be quickly reprogrammed or appropriated in response to emergencies. Committee chairman Waxman sharply disagreed. Despite the controversy, the hearing received virtually no news coverage.

On April 23, 1984, Secretary of Health and Human Services Margaret Heckler announced that the AIDS virus had been identified in an NIH laboratory by Dr. Robert C. Gallo. This assertion was immediately challenged on behalf of Dr. Luc Montagnier's Pasteur Institute laboratory in Paris. A long and acrimonious dispute followed over who first identified the AIDS virus, which will provide more than one chapter in the social history of science. What is important here, though, is that the identification of the virus changed the direction of AIDS research, increasing rather than reducing the need for funds. With this in mind, Brandt wrote a memo to Heckler on May 25, 1984, requesting just under $56 million in additional appropriations for AIDS activities. The request was turned down. On September 17, 1984, Waxman's subcommittee held a hearing in which this rejection of Brandt's request was examined.[42] Waxman found the administration's complex, confusing, and bureaucratic response to his questioning unpersuasive. It is likely that journalists would have found it unpersuasive, too, but there were no news stories.

Five months later, the Weiss and Waxman subcommittees held joint hearings to consider the "Office of Technology Assessment's Findings on the Public Health Service's Response to AIDS."[43] This was not a typical case of researchers competing for limited funds. The OTA had conducted a full-scale study and found that AIDS was being short-changed. Weiss characterized the OTA report this way:

> OTA has found . . . that the administration has continually refused to provide PHS scientists with the level of resources they indicated was urgently needed to address the AIDS epidemic. Although the Department continues to identify AIDS as its No. 1 health priority, its AIDS budget requests would suggest otherwise.
>
> Instead of requesting additional funds from Congress, the administration's policy has been to sacrifice the budget and staff of other important health programs in order to address the AIDS public health emergency. I believe the American public is ill-served by trading off one health need for another.[44]

Weiss went on to say that Congress had taken up the slack but had been forced to rely on "unofficial sources and leaks" to collect accurate budget information. *The New York Times* ran a six-paragraph story on the report four days after the hearing.[45] The story, which appeared on page A14, did not even mention the hearing. There was virtually no other coverage. Hearings held in July, September, and December of 1985 by Weiss's subcommittee of the Committee on Government Operations also received minimal coverage.

By this time AIDS was commanding large amounts of space in newspapers and magazines and significant amounts of time on the evening news programs. Some of this reporting was of relatively high quality, including a *Newsweek* cover story dated August 12, 1985. This major treatment, which took up nine full pages, devoted a single paragraph to federal funding. Predictably, *Time*'s cover that week was also on AIDS. The *Time* article was seven pages long. It had three paragraphs on the federal response, on the last page of the story. It had taken more, however, than just the mounting number of AIDS sufferers—by August 1985 there were 12,000—to stimulate cover stories in the major newsweeklies. It took an announcement by one very special sufferer: Rock Hudson. The actor had disclosed the previous month that he was dying of AIDS. That announcement dramatically altered the scope of AIDS coverage. According to J. Ronald Milavsky, "From July to December 1985, NBC broadcast over 200 stories on AIDS—three times as many as during the entire 1980 to 1984 period. The other news media reacted similarly."[46] So did the president of the United States.

According to Gen. John Hutton, President Reagan's personal physician, for five years the president "accepted [AIDS] like it was measles and it would go away." Then he read about Hudson going to Paris for treatment while he was recovering from colon cancer surgery. Reagan told Hutton: "I always thought the world might end in a flash, but this sounds like it's worse."[47]

The August 12, 1985, issue of *Newsweek* magazine was fairly typical of much of the coverage of Hudson's illness and death. The headline was a single word in large, eye-catching type: "AIDS." Underneath was a picture of a disease-ravaged Rock Hudson. Alongside the photograph was written: "It is the nation's worst public health problem. No one has ever recovered from the disease and the number of cases is doubling every year. Now fears are growing that the AIDS epidemic may spread beyond gays and other high-risk groups to threaten the population at large." Nowhere on the cover, and indeed nowhere inside the magazine, did it say that Hudson was gay. If there was an implication, it was that he was a member of "the population at large."

AIDS coverage had been increasing before Hudson disclosed that he had the disease, but it took a dying celebrity to fully capture the attention of the news media and the American people. According to *Newsweek*, "For many people the dramatic revelation that film star Rock Hudson had contracted the disease has put the problem in a new perspective." The newsweekly was right. People either cared about or were interested in Hudson. They "knew" him through the powerful media of movies and television. They were conditioned to empathize with his triumphs and travails, at that time mainly through his television romance with Krystle, the character played by Linda Evans on the ABC prime-time soap opera "Dynasty." If Hudson was vulnerable to AIDS, then at some level many people must have thought they were, too.

It is ironic that a gay man's death was the catalyst for widespread concern about the heterosexual spread of AIDS in the fourth year of an epidemic whose death toll was already more than 6,000, almost three-fourths of whom were gay men. There were other reasons for the attention the disease was getting from the media by the summer of 1985, not the least of which were the spreading of AIDS among women and children and the alarming slope of the disease's epidemiological curve, which was now too grave to be ignored. But it would be myopic not to see that Rock Hudson's infection, illness, and death concentrated the media's collective mind in a way that had been previously impossible.

Coverage, as Milavsky notes, did not remain at the peak it soared to after Hudson's announcement, but it did level off on a much higher plane than before the actor's illness brought AIDS home to America. Along with the personalization of the disease that came from Hudson's high-profile sickness, and ultimately his death in December 1985, a number of other factors combined to elevate AIDS to the status of a major running story. A perception was taking hold that AIDS was a disease that affected "us" as well as "them." The same month that Hudson announced that he had AIDS, an Indiana school superintendent, James O. Smith, told a local television reporter that he was about to order a 13-year-old boy to stay home from school because he was infected with the AIDS virus. As a result, Ryan White became a household name across the country. White's death in 1990 was featured on the evening news broadcasts. The slight 18-year-old had become a hero of the AIDS epidemic, admired for his courage and grace. In the fall of 1985 angry residents of two Queens, New York., school districts were featured regularly on the evening news protesting the fact that somewhere in the city of New York a seropositive second-grader was attending school. Stories on heterosexual spread of the disease also shot up in 1986, even though there was evidence from the outset that some heterosexual spread through means other than needle sharing was inevitable.[48] Some observers attributed this increase to Hudson's illness and death. Other matters, such as the safety of the blood supply, testing for infection as a civil rights concern, the availability of health insurance to members of high-risk groups, and the burden placed on hospitals and other municipal services by the mounting numbers of AIDS sufferers, combined to make AIDS big news.

AIDS had more dimensions than other epidemics such as influenza. As a result, it continued to generate news coverage. When the blood supply was found to be unsafe, stories were done about the risk to "innocent" victims of becoming infected through transfusions. The conflict over whether testing for AIDS should be mandatory received intensive coverage. These stories often pitted the right of the community to be protected from the spread of a fatal, incurable, but not easily transmitted disease against the right of individuals to decide not to know they are infected. The insurance stories frequently contrasted the plight of individuals facing a painful and futile struggle against the right of private industry to make prudent, unsentimental business decisions in a free-enterprise economy. The prospect of hospitals and their staffs physically overwhelmed by AIDS patients and economically overwhelmed by the cost of AIDS care was the source of regular stories. And the compelling human-interest accounts of mothers, lovers, and friends nursing their pain-wracked loved ones yielded hundreds of feature stories. Meanwhile, the science advanced, in fits and starts as science often does, providing another source of stories. Occasionally one of these added to the public's confusion. An example is the story that the AIDS virus had been found in tears.[49] Although it had been reasonably well established for about three years that AIDS could not be transmitted except through exchanges of blood or sexual inter-course, stories suggesting other routes of transmission were irresistible to many journalists.

By 1986, Marlene Cimons of *The Los Angeles Times* began covering AIDS policy as a full-time beat. She was not alone; reporters like Cristine Russell of *The Washington Post* and Robert Pear of *The New York Times* were also covering these stories, although less consistently than Cimons. Meanwhile, the administration's requests for AIDS money and the congressional response were following the same old pattern. In 1986 the Reagan administration asked for $213 million for AIDS activities in fiscal year 1987 and Congress appropriated $495 million. The respective figures for fiscal 1988 were $533.5 million and $950 million.

Conclusion

When federal officials and agencies are conducting "business as usual," Washington journalists often do not scrutinize their behavior very carefully. This is so even if it should be obvious that business as usual is not appropriate, as was the case for six years with the Reagan administration's response to AIDS, which in some ways was similar to the federal government's negligence in regulating the savings-and-loan industry. Part of business as usual in Washington is that the Office of Management and Budget reduces agency requests for money; interested congressmen learn about it and attempt to restore the funds. In general this process attracts little attention. In the case of AIDS, despite obstructionism and dissimulation by the administration, two congressional subcommittees and the Office of Technology Assessment discerned far greater need for AIDS funds than the administration was providing. From 1983 onward, Congress appropriated substantially more than the administration's funding request to meet those needs. For three years the news media paid virtually no attention to what was going on, despite efforts by congressional staff to sell the story. Randy Shilts reported in his book *And the Band Played On*:

> Tim Westmoreland [Henry Waxman's aide] felt vindicated to see the truth of the administration's duplicity on AIDS policy revealed as graphically as it was in the OTA report. The reporters would never be able to ignore this now.
>
> Although the real blood and guts of the hearing would come in the cross-examination, thirty minutes into the hearing, television crews started packing up. They had enough footage for their two-minute stories, and that was all they needed.
>
> As the crews trooped out, Waxman was chiding [CDC chief Dr. James] Mason for the budget reductions. Who decided spending, Waxman asked, doctors in the PHS or accountants at OMB?
>
> Of the AIDS funding figures, Mason said, "We did not write them— they were numbers that were written down."
>
> The reporters, however, weren't around to hear this. Once again, the media response to the OTA report and the hearing on the report was truly underwhelming. *The Washington Post* ignored the report altogether. In *The New York Times*, the report merited six paragraphs on page fourteen, which were not published until four days after the report was released.[50]

As a result, Westmoreland's feeling of vindication presumably turned to frustration. Earlier, Shilts reported, Westmoreland leaked a copy of the memo from Assistant Secretary Brandt to Secretary Heckler asking for an additional $55 million in AIDS funding. But he leaked it to a gay newspaper, the *Washington Blade*, rather than to a major general-circulation newspaper such as *The New York Times*, *The Washington Post*, or *The Los Angeles Times*, or, for that matter, to Shilts himself, who was covering AIDS full-time for *The San Francisco Chronicle*. If any of those papers had originated the story, it would have had a much better shot at influencing national policymakers. Shilts does not explain Westmoreland's strategy.[51]

Since intense coverage of important policy questions in most any area usually leads eventually to an administration response, it is a reasonable assumption that the case of AIDS would have been no different. It could be, of course, that Congress effectively took up the slack on its own and that a press-driven administration would have done no more.

NOTES

1. Michael Gottleib et al., "Pneumocystis Pneumonia—Los Angeles," *Mortality and Morbidity Weekly Report*, June 5, 1981, pp. 250–52.

2. Alvin Friedman-Kien et al., "Kaposi's Sarcoma and Pneumocystis Pneumonia among Homosexual Men—New York City and California," *Mortality and Morbidity Weekly Report*, July 4, 1981.

3. Task Force on Kaposi's Sarcoma and Opportunistic Infections, "Update on Kaposi's Sarcoma and Opportunistic Infections in Previously Healthy Persons—United States," *Mortality and Morbidity Weekly Report*, June 11, 1982, pp. 294–301.

4. Lawrence K. Altman, M.D., "Rare Cancer Seen in 41 Homosexuals," *New York Times*, July 3, 1981, p. A20.

5. Harry Nelson, "Outbreaks of Pneumonia among Gay Males Studied," *Los Angeles Times*, June 5, 1981, sec. I p. 3.

6. Lawrence Mass, M.D., "Disease Rumors Largely Unfounded," *New York Native*, May 18–31, 1981.

7. Lawrence K. Altman, M.D., science reporter, *New York Times*, interview, New York, April 21, 1989.

8. Associated Press, "2 Fatal Diseases Focus of Inquiry," *New York Times*, August 29, 1981, p. 9.

9. Altman interview.

10. Michael Gottleib, M.D., et al., "Pneumocystis Carinii Pneumonia and Mucosal Candidiasis in Previously Healthy Homosexual Men: Evidence of a New Acquired Cellular Immunodeficiency," *New England Journal of Medicine*, December 10, 1981, pp. 1425– 31.

11. Randy Shilts, "The Strange, Deadly Diseases That Strike Gay Men," *San Francisco Chronicle*, May 13, 1982, p. 6.

12. From a roundtable workshop on television coverage of health risks, Columbia University Graduate School of Journalism, New York, April 22, 1986.

13. J. Ronald Milavsky, "AIDS and the Media," paper presented to the Annual Meeting of the American Psychological Association, Atlanta, August 15, 1988.

14. Associated Press, "AIDS May Dwarf the Plague," *New York Times*, January 30, 1987, p. A24.

15. J. Ronald Milavsky, unpublished paper presented at a conference on "What Media Can Do to Alleviate the AIDS Problem," University of California at Santa Barbara, February 9, 1988.

16. Ibid.

17. Anthony Fauci, director, National Institute of Allergy and Infectious Diseases, interview, Washington, D.C., September 2, 1988.

18. Harry Nelson, 'Mysterious Fever Now an Epidemic," *Los Angeles Times*, May 31, 1982, p. 1.

19. Interview with CDC official who did not want to be identified.

20. David Shaw, "Coverage of AIDS Story: A Slow Start," *Los Angeles Times*, December 20, 1987, p. 38.

21. Dorothy Nelkin, "The Culture of Science Journalism," *Society*, September–October 1987, p. 23.

22. James Curran, M.D., team leader, AIDS Task Force, Centers for Disease Control, interview, September 28, 1988.

23. Altman interview.

24. For more on antigay attitudes in the media, see J. W. Dearing, E. M. Rogers, and X. Fei, "The Agenda-Setting Process for the Issue of AIDS," paper presented at the Annual Meeting of the International Communication Association, New Orleans, May 1988.

25. Joseph Lovett, producer, ABC's "20/20," interview, New York, August 10, 1988.

26. Malcolm Gladwell, "Failures Seen in Education on Safe Sex," *Washington Post*, June 24, 1990, p. A1.

27. Robert Bazell, "The History of an Epidemic," *New Republic*, August 1, 1983, p. 18.

28. Milavsky, unpublished paper, pp. 19–20.

29. Andrea J. Baker, "The Portrayal of AIDS in the Media: An Analysis of Articles in the *New York Times*," in Douglas Feldman and Thomas Johnson, eds., *The Social Dimensions of AIDS: Method and Theory* (New York: Praeger, 1986), p. 182.

30. Lovett interview.

31. Harry Nelson, "Epidemic Affecting Gays Now Found in Heterosexuals," *Los Angeles Times*, April 14, 1982, p. 22.

32. *New York Times, Los Angeles Times, Washington Post, San Francisco Chronicle, Time, Newsweek*, and the three television networks.

33. John Brownell, assistant managing editor, *Los Angeles Times*, interview, Los Angeles, February 6, 1989.

34. Richard Flaste, science editor, *New York Times*, interview, New York, April 21, 1989.

35. Associated Press, "Effort on AIDS Called Faulty," *New York Times*, August 2, 1983, p. A10.

36. John Wilke, "Physician Disputes Link of Haitians, AIDS Risk," *Washington Post*, August 2, 1983, p. A2.

37. John Wilke, "AIDS Mystery U.S. Priority, Officials Say," *Washington Post*, August 3, 1983, p. A3.

38. Associated Press, "Top Health Official Rebuts Bias Charge in Combatting AIDS," *New York Times*, August 3, 1983, p. B18.

39. Committee on Government Operations, "The Federal Response to AIDS," twenty-ninth report by the Committee on Government Operations together with dissenting and additional views, U.S. House of Representatives, November 30, 1983, p. 4.

40. Ibid. p. 6.

41. Ibid. p. 7.

42. Subcommittee on Health and the Environment of the House Committee on Energy and Commerce, hearings, U.S. House of Representatives, September 17, 1984.

43. Subcommittee on Intergovernmental Relations and Government Resources of the Committee on Government Operations, and the Committee on Energy and Commerce, hearings, U.S. House of Representatives, February 21, 1985.

44. Ibid. p. 2.

45. Associated Press, "Report Criticizes U.S. on AIDS," *New York Times*, February 25, 1985, p. A14.

46. Milavsky, "AIDS and the Media," p. 21.

47. "Reagan Was Slow to See Impact of AIDS, Doctor Says," *Washington Post*, September 3, 1989, p. A10. Reprinted from *Seattle Times*.

48. Of the 204 stories NBC ran about AIDS in 1986, only 38 referred to homosexuals, according to Milavsky. There were 21 stories devoted primarily to heterosexual spread, and many more touched on the subject.

49. Cristine Russell, "AIDS Virus Found in Patient's Tears," *Washington Post*, August 16, 1985, p. A7.

50. Randy Shilts, *And the Band Played On* (New York: St. Martin's Press, 1987), pp. 535–36.

51. More than a dozen phone calls were placed to Westmoreland requesting an interview for this book. None was returned. To this day I do not know why. The account of the leak to the *Washington Blade* appears on pages 466–67 of *And the Band Played On*.

7

Cholesterol:
What's in a Number?

THE partial text of a full-page advertisement in *The New York Times* of December 26, 1989, announced that "While you were checking your cholesterol... an entire decade went by." What an appropriate way to promote "Images of the 80s," a television retrospective of the period by Peter Jennings. After all, no population as healthy as the one to which the ad was addressed ever became so obsessed with its individual and collective health. And if the nation's obsession had a focal icon, it was the waxy alcohol called cholesterol.

Cholesterol, as almost everyone now knows, is associated with heart disease. The more you have in your blood, the greater the risk that you will have a heart attack. These two thoughts are part of medicine's conventional wisdom now. There is strong epidemiological, clinical, and biochemical evidence that the association expressed in the first statement is genuine. The second statement, however, requires qualification, as does much else concerning the relationship of cholesterol to coronary artery disease and mortality.

The current state of knowledge, for example, indicates that if the ratio of high-density to low-density lipoproteins in blood is favorable, the risk of heart attack may be less than if total cholesterol is relatively low but the ratio of high-density to low-density lipoproteins is unfavorable. (Lipoproteins are the particles in which cholesterol is transported through the arteries. Cholesterol from low-density lipoproteins appears to be deposited on the walls of arteries forming a plaque that slowly narrows the arterial passage. High-density lipoproteins appear to remove excess cholesterol from the arteries.) It is also true that your risk of coronary disease appears to be lower if you are a middle-aged female than if you are a middle-aged male. It is believed that this is because the female hormone estrogen (which cannot be manufactured by the body without cholesterol) inhibits heart attacks. No one is sure why this should be so. Your risk is also higher if you smoke, if you have high blood pressure, if you have diabetes, if you do not exercise, and if you are obese. And it is highest of all if you are genetically predisposed to high blood cholesterol levels.

The cholesterol story, then, is complicated. It is also very important. Coronary heart disease is the leading cause of death in this and many other countries. About a million and a half Americans have heart attacks annually, and a third or more of these heart attacks are fatal. Most specialists in coronary heart disease believe that by reducing blood cholesterol levels modestly through diet, or more dramatically where needed with drugs, a hundred thousand or more fatal heart attacks and tens of thousands of nonfatal heart attacks could be prevented annually. The basic price to be paid by individuals interested in lowering their risk of heart disease is eating a diet low in saturated fat and, in cases where the cholesterol level is very high, taking a drug daily for life. That's the price for nonsmokers who are not hypertensive or overweight. People with other risk factors such as high blood pressure or obesity must try to reduce or eliminate those risk factors, too.

Cholesterol represents a formidable public health challenge, much of which has to do with the difficulty of persuading millions of apparently healthy people to give up things they like to eat in return for benefits that, while significant for a substantial number of Americans, will be minimal or nonexistent for others. Moreover, for most people, the payoff is twenty or thirty years down the road.

In any public health campaign intended to reach virtually the entire population, studies have shown that personal physicians are viewed as the most credible sources of health-related information. According to one study completed in 1990, health professionals and mass media are roughly tied as the most frequent sources of health information.[1] In the case of cholesterol, many of these doctors were skeptical that cholesterol reduction would benefit most Americans, which translated into skepticism about the large-scale public health intervention eventually adopted by the government and the American Heart Association.

As a result, a major part of this campaign, known as the National Cholesterol Education Program, was targeted at practicing physicians.

The news media, probably the second most influential means of getting public health information to the general public, have rather accurately reflected the cholesterol debate as it has evolved in the expert community of researchers, at least quantitatively. Those who dissent from the near-consensus view that a quarter or more of the U.S. population would benefit from lowered serum cholesterol have been proportionately represented in news columns and perhaps even a bit overrepresented on op-ed pages. Qualitatively, the picture is a bit less bright, partly because the expert debate has become sharply polarized. Both sides often appear to overstate their cases. Journalists for the most part cannot resolve technical and scientific controversy, but some of them have the ability to present the debate with greater subtlety than is typically displayed. Many of these specialized health reporters often fall back on the traditional approach of giving a "fair hearing" to both sides, which usually means mechanical balancing even when the evidence strongly supports one "expert" position over another. And a few have become advocates for one side or another.

Though the public may have been confused by this debate, the behavior of millions of Americans has changed, apparently because they believe they will live longer if they lower their blood cholesterol. Press coverage certainly influenced the public's response to publicity about cholesterol, and especially to the National Cholesterol Education Program (NCEP), a large-scale public health initiative by the National Heart, Lung and Blood Institute to educate physicians and the public about the risks associated with high blood cholesterol. The NCEP's primary goal is to impress upon people the importance of lowering their blood cholesterol level if it is too high.

The History

In 1789, the year of the French Revolution and exactly 200 years before this writing, a scientist named De Fourcroy reported that twenty years earlier another scientist named Poulletier de la Salle had isolated from human gallstones a shiny substance that was similar to boric acid.[2] In 1816, another Frenchman, named Chevreul, dubbed the substance *cholesterine*, using the Greek for bile (*chole*) and solid (*steros*) to create the new word.[3] And in 1843, cholesterol was found in atherosclerotic plaque.[4] (Such plaque has been found in Egyptian mummies, and it was even described by Leonardo da Vinci in his *Dell'Anatomia*.) By the beginning of the twentieth century it was appearing in the literature as *cholesterol* in both French and English, and it had been identified in blood, brains, egg yolks, and tumors. By 1913 it had been demonstrated that atherosclerotic-like lesions could be induced in rabbits by feeding them dietary cholesterol, and by 1950 many physicians believed that there was an association between blood cholesterol and coronary disease. And the way to manage atherosclerosis, many thought, was through diet.

Over the next forty years a great many studies would attempt to prove the efficacy of a low-fat, low-cholesterol diet in controlling the development of atherosclerosis, or the buildup of fatty deposits on the interior walls of arteries that constrict blood flow. By 1990, there was widespread but not universal agreement that such a diet could lower blood cholesterol levels enough to have a significant impact on mortality from coronary heart disease. The judgment that the right diet has a salutary effect is based on a pooling of evidence from dozens of clinical trials and epidemiological studies. No study in itself has been big enough, comprehensive enough, or statistically significant enough to make a conclusive case on its own.[5]

The smaller number of researchers who dispute the evidence do so not on grounds that there is no relationship between diet, blood cholesterol, and heart disease, but on grounds that the relationships are weaker than claimed by the dominant group and that for preventive health purposes a therapeutic diet is likely to be helpful, if at all, only for those persons with seriously elevated serum cholesterol levels. They disagree about what are known as cut points: the number of milligrams of cholesterol in a deciliter of blood that should signal medical intervention either by diet or by drugs. Edward H. Ahrens Jr., M.D., of Rockefeller University says, "Those of us who are in the minority, and believe me, it's a very small minority, think you should focus on the people above 240. . . . If you move an individual from 240 to 180 you reduce risk very little."[6] The majority recommend dietary intervention when the reading is above 200. But these cut points are rough approximations that take no account of age, sex, or ratios of high-density to low-density lipoproteins, variables that for years now have figured prominently in the scientific literature on cholesterol.

This disagreement over cut points is the underlying basis for the argument by dissenting scientists that the National Cholesterol Education Program casts far too wide a net in trying to change the eating habits of about a quarter of the American population. As a result, these scientists contend, tens of millions of Americans are coerced into changing their diets unde an inadequately substantiated assumption that this will lessen their risk of suffering a potentially fatal heart attack.

Supporters of the NCEP make the following arguments: first, they contend that the statistical curve describing the association between blood cholesterol, heart disease, and coronary mortality is continuous and shows a sharp enough increase in disease and coronary mortality between 200 and 240 to merit reducing blood cholesterol; second, for a public health campaign to be maximally effective, the net must be cast widely; and third, the recommended diet works in reducing cholesterol, provides other health benefits, and has no known drawbacks.

Simply stated, the policy question these researchers disagree about is whether the evidence for a serum cholesterol–coronary disease connection is strong enough to warrant large-scale medical intervention in adults with total cholesterol levels below 240 or so. They disagree about what public action should be taken based on evidence that most researchers want to treat as very strong and others consider to be merely suggestive. For all practical purposes, the debate was won in 1985 when the majority group initiated the NCEP with the cooperation of the American Heart Association and thirty-six other governmental and nongovernmental agencies and institutions. Its direct costs are low at under $2 million a year, of which half or more are for media and publications, but indirect costs in the form of medical visits, laboratory testing, drugs, dislocations in the food industry, and so on, run into the billions of dollars.

When policy initiatives of this magnitude are undertaken—especially without public hearings or significant congressional review—the news media are the public's best hope of obtaining the information that makes it possible to participate—not directly, but by expressing their views to legislators—in the decision-making process. Not everyone, however, thinks that health policy decisions should be subject to the political process. For example, Daniel Steinberg, M.D., chairman of the consensus conference panel that launched the NCEP, wrote (but never sent) this response to an article in the ATLANTIC magazine by Thomas J. Moore that was sharply critical of the program: "Is Moore seriously suggesting that medical decisions about the health of the nation be allowed to become political decisions...? Surely you jest, Mr. Moore."[7] E. H. Ahrens, a clinical investigator, takes a different view: "I believe that as scientists we are expected by the public to render scientifically sound advice. Policy-makers must come to their own conclusions, and will do so for a complex of reasons—political, social and economic. That is their affair; ours is to be sound, as sound as current evidence permits, stating clearly where the gaps in knowledge exist."[8]

But when public health is involved, the matter is not so simple. It may be that only scientific experts have the intellectual authority to guide public health policy. And it may be that only scientists have the credibility to surmount the political obstacles to public health initiatives that conflict with powerful economic interests. Think of the cases of cigarette smoking and global warming (Chapters 5 and 8).

In the cigarette case the scientific evidence that smoking is unhealthy was solid long before a major public health campaign was launched. The tobacco industry was successful for decades in preventing the federal government from acting. Finally, in 1964, a physician, Surgeon General Luther Terry, using his authority as a scientist and the federal government's ability to command media attention, declared cigarettes devastatingly bad for our health. The press echoed the message across the land, and not long afterward cigarette smoking began to decline in the United States.

With global warming, James Hansen seems to have forced policy action by forcing the science just a bit. Hansen and senators Tim Wirth and Albert Gore also used the media to broadcast the message widely that global warming had arrived even though the evidence appears weaker than the evidence that heart disease can be prevented by lowering blood cholesterol. Nonetheless, Hansen's authority as a respected scientist led to substantial news coverage.

Cholesterol, like cigarette smoking and global warming, involves important economic and political interests. The drug industry, the medical profession, and the food industry are major stakeholders. In recent years a great deal has been written about cholesterol and health, but little of the news coverage has focused on how these interests have influenced cholesterol policy. For one thing, cattlemen and dairy and egg producers are less easily portrayed as villains than cigarette companies. Aside from the writings of Moore in the *Atlantic*,[9] Gina Kolata in *Science* magazine and *The Boston Globe*,[10] and a smattering of articles elsewhere, very little has been written or broadcast about how national policy on cholesterol was shaped. What follows is an account of what happened and an analysis of why such an important story went essentially uncovered.

The Cholesterol Policy Dilemma

Between 1934, when a researcher named S. R. Rosenthal analyzed twenty-eight epidemiologic papers on coronary disease, and 1970, when Jeremiah Stamler and others examined regional factors in the development of coronary disease, it became clear that there was a statistically significant correlation between diets high in saturated fat and the development of arterial plaque leading to disease. Animal studies supported this thesis. Perhaps the most influential data came from the now-famous Seven Countries Study directed by Ancel Keys. In 1976, a ten-year follow-up supported the earlier results of the Keys study: high-saturated fat intake is associated with high serum cholesterol, which in turn is associated with coronary heart disease.[11]

These epidemiologic and animal studies did not convince everyone, however. Edward R. Pinckney, M.D., and Cathey Pinckney wrote in 1973, for example:

> Since medical science has not, as yet, even come close to proving that cholesterol in the blood is the cause of heart disease, it becomes ridiculous to postulate that altering the amount of cholesterol in one's blood, especially through diet, will make any difference in the health of one's heart. Yet government agencies have allowed health associations and food industries to play havoc with the anxieties of millions and millions of people by permitting this unproved doctrine to be promoted.[12]

Other respected researchers were not satisfied with the epidemiological or experimental results. Not that they thought it was bad research, but for the most part they were clinicians, and they wanted clinical proof of what was already being called the lipid hypothesis, that saturated fat and dietary cholesterol raise blood cholesterol thereby causing heart disease.

These clinicians were even more skeptical of the growing belief that reducing blood cholesterol through a diet low in saturated fat and dietary cholesterol could cut the rate of heart disease. This jaundiced view was not out of the mainstream. It was supported by the report of a 1971 federal task force, which said that "the evidence is scientifically not entirely convincing" that a decrease in saturated fat in the diet will prevent heart attacks.[13] A year later, however, Congress passed the National Heart, Blood Vessel, Lung and Blood Act of 1972, which provided for the appointment of an assistant director of the National Heart and Lung Institute whose duties included placing "special emphasis" on "dissemination of information regarding diet" without specifying what that information should be. By 1977, a follow-up to the 1971 task-force report still displayed skepticism about the lipid hypothesis, but with a nuanced difference. "Although calories, dietary fat and cholesterol are important determinants of blood lipid and lipoprotein levels, much remains to be learned regarding their precise influence,"[14] the second study concluded. The federal government thus acknowledged that diet influenced blood cholesterol levels, but it was not yet ready to say that high blood cholesterol "causes" heart attacks.

In scientific controversies involving public health, however, as the 1972 legislation indicates, lawmakers are sometimes more willing than some administrations to get out in front of the scienctific evidence. In 1979, for example, Senator George McGovern held a hearing in which he said, "It is time to adopt as a personal health promotion objective the overall reduction of the adult blood cholesterol level to an average of 200 milligrams or less,"[15] hardly a consensus view at that time. But McGovern's star witness, Robert Levy, director of the National Heart, Lung and Blood Institute and an advocate for cholesterol lowering, said, "the problem here, Senator, is that we still have not proven conclusively that lowering cholesterol will prevent heart disease in man, and so we are left to presumption."[16] Levy, of course, was exercising caution not just as a scientist but as an administration official. The McGovern hearing got virtually no press coverage.[17]

Media interest was sharply stimulated at the end of May 1980, however, by the National Academy of Science's publication of a modest twenty-four-page pamphlet called "Toward Healthful Diets." The title seemed diffident enough to discourage much public debate. But the booklet's thesis—that since the "causes of atherosclerosis are unknown," fat consumption should not be linked to blood cholesterol but to "caloric requirements"—set off alarms. This was so because despite the lack of solid clinical evidence, and the opposition of such cardiac heavyweights as Michael DeBakey and Christiaan Barnard, the lipid hypothesis was rapidly taking hold within the research community. The epidemiologic and biological evidence by this time was becoming impressive, and coronary heart disease, while declining, continued to be the nation's biggest killer.

The prestige of the diet pamphlet's sponsoring body, the Food and Nutrition Board of the National Research Council of the National Academy of Sciences, gave the report credibility. But this authority was partly undermined and the controversy was heightened when the news media reported that the pamphlet had not disclosed that two board members received research funds from the food industry. *The Washington Post* ran a front-page story under the headline "2 on Food Panel Are Advisers, Dairy Industry among Clients."[18] The *Post* story said that "The two key members of a scientists' panel" were "paid consultants to the food producers affected by the study." None of the stories, however, offered evidence that scientists had tailored their research to fit their pocketbooks. Nor did they mention that some scientists who favored cholesterol reduction were consultants to drug companies that were developing cholesterol-lowering agents.

These hints of conflict of interest gave the running news story a little extra buoyancy and even led to a one-day congressional hearing, but it was the subject of the controversy itself, food and mortality, that guaranteed long-term media attention.

By 1980, most cholesterol news stories were about mounting evidence supporting the lipid hypothesis. While these stories generally indicated that there were still respectable dissenters among the experts, the thrust of coverage was that high cholesterol causes heart attacks. Much of the news coverage of the 1980 report emphasized the conflict between the nutrition board's findings and the slowly developing consensus view that a low-fat diet can reduce the risk of heart attacks.

The New York Times wrote editorials and news analyses with headlines like "A Confusing Diet of Fact"[19] and "Dispute on Americans' Diets: Although Panel Says Healthy Should Not Worry about Fat, Others Warn against Casual Attitude."[20]

Despite the confusion and dispute reflected in the headlines, however, the editorial and the news analysis were critical of the report and indicated that wise Americans should eat diets low in saturated fat. The editorial said that the report was "so one-sided that it makes a dubious guide to national nutrition policies."[21] Jane Brody, who wrote the news analysis, and the *Times*'s editorial writer had taken a clear stance behind the lipid hypothesis. So had *The Washington Post*, whose editorial of June 2 was even more critical of the report.[22] In response to the *Times* editorial, the chairman of the Food and Nutrition Board wrote:

A June 3 editorial condemned the board for not endorsing the view that a recommendation to reduce consumption of cholesterol and fat is an appropriate public policy action for lowering the instance of chronic degenerative diseases. Has the board been subjected to this coercive attack because it has had the effrontery to disagree with the established opinions of the editors? Are we to assume that the *Times* does not condone differences of scientific opinion?[23]

Both *Time* and *Newsweek*, on the other hand, gave the report a much less hostile reception. They illustrated their stories with a scoffing 1959 cartoon by Stan Hunt from the *New Yorker*. The drawing depicted a cocktail party setting with a woman asking a man sitting on a couch alongside her, "Are you a no cholesterol doctor or are you one of those no-cholesterol-is-all-bosh doctors?" *Newsweek*, under the headline "How Bad Is Cholesterol?" published a story that in general did not challenge the National Research Council report.[24] *Time*'s story was not challenging either, and it noted that "the council's food and nutrition board made a major plea for moderation" recommending that overweight persons cut down on dietary fat.[25] Only CBS of the three television networks carried anything on the report.[26]

There were mixed messages for the public and policymakers in the news reporting. This was partly because some researchers, adhering to strict standards of scientific evidence, were not prepared to make broadly based recommendations that would influence the lives of millions of people. Others, using more public-health-oriented standards, were. As Brody noted in another article, laboratory scientists, in contrast to epidemiologists, "tend not to think in public health or social policy terms."[27] She did not pursue the consequences of this assessment in her article, but years later she said in effect that scientists in government and certain kinds of journalists *should* think in both public health and social policy terms, as Lawrence K. Altman of *The New York Times* did in his reporting on AIDS. Brody implied that if they did not, the consequences might be very serious. "I'm a two-hatted person," Brody said: "a science writer and a public health columnist. As a columnist I applaud government agencies for acting. If we wait we could all be dead. It is important for government agencies to give advice and for us to report the advice."[28]

Echoing Brody's views, *The Washington Post*'s lead editorial June 2 on the controversy engendered by "Toward Healthful Diets" said:

> doctors and government agencies must constantly make recommendations on the basis of . . . incomplete but suggestive evidence. . . . Even when the precise cause of a disease is unknown, if a certain change in behavior will statistically lower the risk of it, and if the change does

not entail new risks or unacceptable economic costs, it should be recommended.[29]

The trouble is that 1980, the evidence supporting the lipid hypothesis was weaker than the conclusions being advanced by its proponents. This is not to suggest that the hypothesis was wrong, just that it was lacking evidence from clinical trials, and the existing epidemiological and animal data supported weak rather than strong claims for its validity. By promoting the majority view on cholesterol, on balance, the news media may have influenced public attitudes as measured by numerous polls.[30] By 1988, about 96 percent of Americans knew that high cholesterol levels were considered dangerous, and about 66 percent knew that a level of 300 was too high. On the other hand, 50 percent believed incorrectly that high blood cholesterol has been shown to cause cancer.

It didn't take long for the controversy generated by the Food and Nutrition Board's diet report to roil up again after a few quiet months at the end of 1980. In January 1981, the *New England Journal of Medicine* published a study[31] that got front-page coverage in *The New York Times*.[32] The *Times* headline said "Long-Term Study Links Cholesterol to Hazard of Early Coronary Death." And its fourth paragraph said:

> According to Dr. Oglesby Paul, a heart disease specialist at Harvard Medical School who was the study's first director, the findings are "at variance" with the advice issued last spring by the Food and Nutrition Board of the National Academy of Sciences, which concluded that otherwise healthy Americans need not reduce their intake of cholesterol and saturated fats.

The quote above is the only reference in Brody's story to disagreement within the scientific community about the link between diet and serum cholesterol. By contrast, Victor Cohn's story on page 14 of *The Washington Post* refers to this question as "one of the most controversial in medicine."[33] As for the study itself, the claims it makes are modest: "The correlations between dietary variables and serum cholesterol concentration in our study were small [but] it is reasonable to infer that the true associations were larger. . . . Clearly, however, other factors also affect the concentration of serum cholesterol." It also says:

> If viewed in isolation, the conclusions that can be drawn from a single epidemiologic study are limited. Within the context of the total literature,

however, the present observations support the conclusion that the lipid composition of the diet affects the level of serum cholesterol and the long-term risk of death from CHD [coronary heart disease] in middle-aged American men.[34]

Brody made no reference to the slightness of the evidence. Cohn, on the other hand, paraphrased the quote above. Because of these differences in treatment and play, the *Times*'s approach smacked somewhat more of advocacy than the *Post*'s. Which was closer to the ultimate truth about the correctness of the lipid hypothesis? Most researchers in 1990 would probably say the *Times*. Who covered the story better in 1981? The edge goes to Cohn for providing a better reflection of the state of the debate. Moreover, neither Brody nor Cohn was properly engaged in health-promotion activities. Both were supposed to be simply reporting a news event.

The idea of being right in this sense cannot properly be used to evaluate news stories. We can talk about news stories as being accurate, fair, balanced, substantially complete, understandable, and so on. But to test news stories for rightness—that is, that they draw the correct conclusion—when the evidence is inconclusive implies that they are essentially evaluative (as opposed to descriptive), which they are not meant to be. This is not to say that news stories should never include background paragraphs that rely on a reporter's judgment, only that these judgments should compromise as little as possible fair and accurate characterizations of the substance and details of the matter being reported on. The relatively few cholesterol stories that appeared in newspapers, in magazines, and on the air later in 1981 dealt with a range of subjects including U.S. government dietary recommendations, speculation about a link between low cholesterol levels and cancer, drug therapy, and genetic factors related to high cholesterol levels. One article worth noting was a discussion of a health-oriented cookbook by Jane Brody. Marian Burros, the author of the article, described how Brody disposed of "the problem of inconclusive evidence about the relation between diet and health, specifically fat and cholesterol," by saying that "if you're waiting to change your diet until there's an airtight case against fats and cholesterol, you may die waiting."[35]

In her own book, as in her *New York Times* columns, Brody was on journalistically firm ground when she took sides in the cholesterol debate. Some researchers argue that journalists like Brody lack the credentials to reach independent judgments about complex matters of health science. But when these matters are unsettled and laypersons have to make choices about how to behave, it seems entirely appropriate that a journalist with some training in science, who reads the scientific literature and interviews the researchers, should provide them with a considered judgment.

Throughout 1982 and 1983, there was very little cholesterol coverage in the nation's news media despite the fact that in 1982 results from research on the largest population ever studied for risk factors associated with heart disease were published. There were a few reports on a mini-scandal about the Agriculture Department suppressing diet advice under alleged pressure from meat and dairy producers and a couple more on a Norwegian study suggesting that massive coffee consumption raises blood cholesterol levels. But the major heart study, known as the Multiple Risk Factor Intervention Trial (MRFIT for short, which is pronounce "Murfit" or "Mister Fit"), received not a line in the national newsmagazines or *The Washington Post* and not a second of television air time. It did, however, get coverage in *The New York Times*[36] and *The Wall Street Journal*,[37] but deep inside these papers. And indeed the *Journal* article strained desperately to come up with a trivial and inappropriate lead about treating patients with heart abnormalities for its story on the study,[38] which was published in the *Journal of the American Medical Association.* To its credit, however, *The Wall Street Journal* published a story that explored some of the obstacles to mounting MRFIT.[39] But neither the *Journal* nor anyone else explored what role, if any, interested food producers played in pressing for a multifactorial study rather than a diet study so that the onus would not fall on their products alone.

The reason for the media's failure to provide extensive coverage of the MRFIT study is clear. The results were what scientists call negative but in general parlance would be designated inconclusive. The abstract at the beginning of the *JAMA* article put it dryly: "Mortality from CHD [coronary heart disease] was 17.9 deaths per 1,000 in the SI [special intervention] group and 19.3 per 1,000 in the UC [usual care] group, a statistically nonsignificant difference."[40] In other words, the trial did not demonstrate a beneficial effect on coronary heart disease or total mortality resulting from increased treatment for hypertension, counseling for cigarette smoking, and dietary advice for lowering blood cholesterol. Part of the reason for this lack of beneficial effect, the researchers speculated, was behavior change in the usual care group, some of which may have resulted from health education. The news media, of course, play a large role in the health-education process. (A long-term follow-up to the study shows significantly fewer heart attacks in the intervention group, but it is not certain that this can be attributed to the intervention.[41]

Inconclusive results do not make for a sharp news lead. Jane Brody's "Leaders of the largest study ever done on the value of trying to diminish the major risks associated with heart disease said today they had found no significant difference in deaths between a group that received special medical treatment and one that received more ordinary care" undoubtedly never had a shot at page 1. The phrase "no significant difference" doomed the story to burial on page 10.

By contrast, 1984 was a banner year for cholesterol. Before the middle of January, the results of a study were reported—by all three networks, all three newsmagazines, and most major newspapers—that effectively ended the cholesterol controversy as far as the media were concerned. It was called the Lipid Research Clinics Coronary Primary Prevention Trial (CPPT). It followed 3,806 middle-aged men, lasted ten years, and cost $150 million. Upon its completion, researchers from the National Heart, Lung and Blood Institute announced that for the first time they had demonstrated "conclusively" that lowering blood cholesterol reduces the risk of heart attacks in middle-aged men with blood cholesterol levels above 265 and low-density lipoprotein levels of 190 or greater. (Specificity in identifying the trial population is important because later questions would arise about the validity of generalizing the findings to other groups such as women and younger or older men.)

The CPPT study, using a drug called cholestyramine as the primary means of reducing serum cholesterol, showed that after seven years the men treated had 19 percent fewer heart attacks than the men who received placebo. George Lundberg, M.D., editor of *JAMA*, said, "These two articles [on the CPPT] will be looked at 25 years from now as the definitive articles that secured the cholesterol theory of coronary heart disease."[42]

The media did not need twenty-five years to reach that conclusion. References to the "cholesterol controversy," an obligatory element of most news stories about cholesterol, almost disappeared after the CPPT report appeared in *JAMA*. For example, Jerry Bishop of *The Wall Street Journal*, who has well-deserved reputation as a thoughtful and careful medical journalist, and who in the past had consistently noted that the lipid hypothesis was controversial, did not do so on March 15, 1984, in a story about cholesterol in children. Instead he included a paragraph saying that "a decade-long experiment . . . showed that for each 1% reduction in blood cholesterol levels, there was a 2% reduction in the risk of a heart attack,"[43] a conclusion drawn from the CPPT results that would be echoed widely in the media. *Time* magazine, in a cover story on cholesterol weighted toward the majority view, did, however, introduce an element of skepticism by quoting E. H. Ahrens twice.[44]

While the press was beginning to cover the diet–cholesterol–heart disease connection as a fact and devoting space on its food and health pages to "prudent" diets (promoted by the American Heart Association, one of the earliest advocates of cholesterol reduction, the U.S. government, and other organizations), the National Heart, Lung and Blood Institute (NHLBI) was beginning to discuss how to design and implement a large-scale program to educate the public about cholesterol. In preparation for this project, the NHLBI carried out a survey of both physicians and the general public to measure awareness and attitudes about the links among diet, cholesterol, and heart disease.

The poll takers discovered that a larger percentage of the public than of physicians was concerned about cholesterol. For example, 64 percent of the public said they believed that lowering high blood cholesterol would have a large effect on reducing the risk of coronary heart disease. But only 39 percent of doctors shared this view.[45] This disparity was attributed to a greater unwillingness on the part of physicians to make an endorsement in the absence of "conclusive" scientific evidence. One difference was that the physicians were getting much of their information from scientific journals, whereas the public was getting theirs from the lay press.

A Louis Harris poll conducted at about the same time, however, showed that cholesterol was way down on the list of what concerned ordinary Americans nutritionally. Only 5 percent of those surveyed named cholesterol as their number one concern, compared, for example, to 27 percent who said "chemical additives" and 24 percent who said "vitamin/mineral content." The percentage for "fat content" was 9.[46]

The NHLBI decided that both physicians and the public had to be reached. The mechanism selected to begin the process was a consensus development conference, which would bring together many of the leading scientists in lipid research along with a number of physicians in related fields and representatives of the public. The man chosen to organize the conference was Basil Rifkind, head of the NHLBI's lipid research branch. Rifkind would put together a planning committee, which would select a panel to draft the consensus document—if consensus was reached—and invite specialists to present papers and a distinguished audience to question and comment. With respect to the panel selection, he said, "We looked for people who had not taken strong partisan positions," adding, "you do go to people in the field, though."[47] The avowed purpose of the conference was to see if a scientific consensus could be reached, which in turn would permit a public health initiative to go forward. The assumption at NHLBI, where the lipid hypothesis was no longer seriously questioned, was that such a consensus would be achieved. Thinking about how to organize the public health campaign, therefore, moved ahead. Rifkind said, "Some of us have been conscious that . . . control of cholesterol . . . is a lifestyle problem. There was a population strategy embedded . . . no matter which way you went . . . so it was important to talk to the public as well as physicians."[48]

The conference, formally called the Consensus Development Conference on Lowering Blood Cholesterol to prevent Heart Disease, was held from December 10 to December 12, 1984, at the National Institutes of Health in Bethesda, Maryland. Some participants complained that it was structured to accommodate the preordained conclusion that the evidence supporting the lipid hypothesis was strong enough to treat the hypothesis as if it were a fact. The final report of the conference said: "It has been established beyond a reasonable doubt that lowering definitely elevated blood cholesterol levels (specifically, blood levels of low-density lipoprotein [LDL] cholesterol) will reduce the risk of heart attacks caused by coronary heart disease. There is no doubt that changes in our diet will reduce blood cholesterol levels."[49]

It requires no logical leap to see that a consensus had been reached that a change in the nation's eating habits would yield a reduction in heart attacks. There were, however, dissenters. Edward H. Ahrens Jr., an invited member of the audience and a lipid researcher since the early 1950s, said, "There was precious little discussion [at the conference]. I thought Dan [Dr. Daniel Steinberg, the panel's chairman] ran a very heavy-handed meeting. Paul Meier [a biostatistician], Michael Oliver [a British researcher], and I objected."[50] Ahrens asked for permission to write a minority report but was turned down, so he and Oliver published their views separately in the British journal the *Lancet*.[51] Oliver took the position that "well-orchestrated so-called consensus conferences . . . should be recognized as special pleading and evaluated as such."[52]

Ahrens, Oliver, and others took issue with a number of the conference report's findings and recommendations. They argued that the link between high serum cholesterol and coronary disease had been demonstrated in high-risk middle-aged men only and could not justifiably be extrapolated to women, children, and men in other age and risk groups; that benefits from change in diet would accrue unevenly with the largest number of people benefiting least; and that the link between diet and atherosclerosis, although theoretically sound, was unproved.

With these points in mind, Ahrens wrote:

> Since many unanswered questions remain about the role of nutrition in CHD [coronary heart disease] prevention, it is remarkable that the press in the USA has set out to sell the message that the diet-heart question has been solved by the LRC-CPPT. (In this process the press has had more than tacit support from many of the scientists concerned in the trial.) If this atmosphere prevails, there will be little encouragement for young medical investigators to probe more deeply into the mysteries of nutrition/CHD relations, and there will be increasing resistance by peer reviewers to approve funds for further study of these unsolved questions.[53]

The New York Times, The Washington Post, and *The Wall Street Journal* all covered the consensus conference, but the *Times* story was on page 1 compared to page 16 for the *Post* and 24 for the *Journal.* Moreover, Jane Brody's story for the *Times* was written in a tone exemplified by its first sentence: "In the most far-reaching public health recommendation yet made on cholesterol and heart disease, an expert panel yesterday advised dietary and other treatment for millions of Americans whose cholesterol levels [below 240] have until now been considered normal by many physicians."[54]

The *Post* and *Journal* stories are much more soberly written. But were they right, and was the *Times* wrong? This *was* very likely "the most far-reaching public health recommendation yet made on cholesterol and heart disease." Considering the number of people who would almost certainly be interested in and affected by the conference's recommendations, and the economic cost of implementing them, the *Times* would appear to have made the correct decision in running the story on page 1. But Brody's story leaves readers with the definite sense that the controversy is over. The *Post* and *Journal* stories do little to undermine that view, but they present it less starkly. Cristine Russell in the *Post*, for example, unlike Brody in the *Times*, quotes Steinberg as saying that the recommendations were "backed by the 'large majority' of research opinion."[55] In other words, there were still a few dissenters out there.

For an account reflecting the skepticism of this minority of researchers, one could have read *Science* magazine, in which Gina Kolata characterized the consensus development conference's conclusions quite differently from the way Brody and her lay press colleagues reported them. Kolata wrote:

> These conclusions sound so familiar that many commentators did not even mention that they are actually quite strong. But despite what the panel said there is no irrefutable evidence from clinical trials that cholesterol-lowering saves lives.
>
> The question is not whether people at high risk for heart disease should be concerned about their cholesterol levels. It is about whether the data are strong enough to recommend that the entire population, including children, go on low-fat diets.
>
> The critics are concerned that the panel exaggerated the evidence at hand and, in doing so, damaged their own credibility.[56]

Kolata's main point was not that the dietary recommendations, which included reducing dietary fat intake from 40 percent to 30 percent of total calories and saturated fat to 10 percent of total calories, were wrong, but that the evidence was weaker than the main conclusion that elevated blood cholesterol is a major cause of coronary heart disease. She ended the article with a quote from Paul Meier, who said, "My view—and I feel it very strongly—is that the dietary recommendations for adults are sound public policy. But none of this excuses misrepresenting the evidence. Our first obligation is to be honest and forthright."[57]

When such recommendations are issued, as Jane Brody has said, the news media have an obligation to report on them skeptically, recognizing that researchers like journalists sometimes become so committed to their theses that they overstate their conclusions. This may have been what happened at the Consensus Development Conference.

What usually happens in journalism was described by Sally Squires of *The Washington Post*, who has a master's degree in nutrition from Columbia University. Squires said, "As a reporter my job is to try to stay objective and listen to all the different types of evidence [but] when you get divergent information I have to go with what the majority of medical people say."[58]

The Consensus Development Conference set the stage for all kinds of diet considerations to become big news. Was oat bran, *The Wash-*

ington Post asked, "the next miracle food?"[59] No, the *Post*'s own editorial page responded tartly, "we don't think bran deserves the spotlight. When bran doesn't have bananas on it it is mere mulch and we can't think of a faster way to clear the theater than to confuse it with Madonna."[60] The *Post* notwithstanding, this was clearly the year in which the food industry concluded that cholesterol lowering was a major pathway to profit. Along with bran, fish oil was in, and so was olive oil. The public was being educated about omega–3 fatty acid, monounsaturated fats, polyunsaturated fats, triglycerides, good cholesterol, and bad cholesterol. The American Heart Association issued new dietary guidelines, an event that was covered by all three evening network news programs, and Jane Brody's columns about cholesterol during 1986 consisted almost entirely of advice on what to eat to avoid high blood cholesterol. Jeremiah Stamler, who directed the follow-up to the MRFIT study, was quoted in *The Washington Post* as saying, "I never talk about putting people on a diet. I like to talk about the pleasure of eating in a wiser, sounder and often tastier way."[61]

Not surprisingly, the public was getting confused about details such as the difference between dietary cholesterol and serum cholesterol, and between types of fats. Few people understood the importance of the ratio of high-density lipoprotein to total cholesterol. "Hydrogenated"—now let's see, does that mean it's good for me or bad for me? And was it 200 or 240 that was too high? Or maybe it was 180. Surveys by the National Cholesterol Education Program showed that "while the public is becoming better informed [about cholesterol and heart disease], this knowledge is superficial and myths and misconceptions abound."[62] Unless readers were getting their information from a single source with a consistent viewpoint like Jane Brody, they were bound to be somewhat hazy about these issues.

At the end of 1986, *The Wall Street Journal* reported that an "earthshaking" new cholesterol-lowering drug (lovastatin) was headed for the market.[63] But this article also quoted a cardiologist who said that "many doctors still aren't convinced lowering cholesterol is that helpful."

Nineteen eighty-seven was the year of fat substitutes, word that the stearic acid in beef might be good for us, a campaign against tropical oils, which are high in saturated fat, disclosure that many cholesterol tests were wildly inaccurate, an angiographic study showing regression of arterial plaque as a result of colestipol-niacin treatment,[64] FDA approval of lovastatin, issuance of the NCEP's first set of cholesterol guidelines, a study showing that raising the level of high-density lipoproteins in the blood reduces the risk of heart attacks,[65] the actress Cybill Shepherd moonlighting for the beef industry, and the continued feeling of some researchers that "an anti-cholesterol bandwagon is racing far ahead of what science can support."[66] This concern was manifested in a *New York Times* story by Philip M. Boffey, which made clear, however, that there was virtually no disagreement among cholesterol researchers that people with blood cholesterol levels above 240 should try to lower them. There was some dispute about just how much reduction a given individual might achieve through diet, but there was also widespread agreement that for adults a diet low in dietary cholesterol and saturated fat was healthy. The volume of news coverage expanded in 1987, at least partly in response to the National Cholesterol Education Program. Many stories were about NCEP initiatives, such as the program to standardize laboratory testing for blood cholesterol, and others can be attributed to the raised level of cholesterol consciousness among physicians and their patients, including journalists.

Neverthless, by the beginning of 1988, only 25 percent of Americans said they paid attention to the cholesterol content of their diet, and 39 percent said they paid attention to its fat content. Just 6 percent knew their cholesterol number. Among those surveyed, some "claimed to pay attention to cholesterol at every meal, but reported eating meals heavy in red meat and eggs."[67] Not all the reporting was informative. The Associated Press, for example, put a story out that noted: "Adding a bran muffin or a bowl of oat-bran cereal to a daily diet can cost about $250 a year, compared with some cholesterol-lowering drugs, which can cost as much as $1,450 a year."[68] What the story didn't say was that the drugs will lower your cholesterol; a muffin or a bowl of cereal will not. The story implied irresponsibly that normal portions of muffins or cereal could effectively substitute for cholesterol-lowering drugs.

Moreover, as Marian Burros pointed out in *The New York Times*, "The health profession keeps shifting signals" about what is healthy to eat.[69] For example, a paper on a small oat bran study published on January, 18, 1990, in the *New England Journal of Medicine* indicated that the fibrous cereal was no better than white wheat flour at reducing cholesterol. Two news reports on the study demonstrated how widely press accounts of scientific controversy can vary. Jane Brody's report appeared on page 24 of *The New York Times*, and its overall tone was skeptical. Malcolm Gladwell's story in *The Washington Post* appeared on page 1 and was far more receptive to the study's findings. Compare the two leads, looking at Brody's first:

The value of eating oat bran has been challenged by a small study that found eating oat fiber no more effective in lowering people's cholesterol levels than foods made from low-fiber refined wheat flour, which produced far fewer unpleasant side effects.[70]

Here is Gladwell's opening sentence:

Oat bran, one of the biggest health food fads of the last decade, does not play a significant role in reducing cholesterol, a group of Harvard University researchers has found.[71]

Brody says oat bran's value has been "challenged," not refuted, that the study was "small," and she does not mention Harvard in her lead. Gladwell calls oat bran a "fad," portrays the study's results as a finding by "Harvard" researchers, not as a "challenge," and he does not comment on the size of the study. These leads are reflective of the way the stories are written throughout.

A careful reader in 1988 might have been aware of certain subtleties, such as the fact that the strongest data on the risks associated with high blood cholesterol come from studies done on high-risk middle-aged men and that to keep the public health message simple, no effort was made to promote separate criteria by age and sex.

Meanwhile, the NCEP, the American Heart Association (AHA), and the food and drug industries were delivering messages about cholesterol by a wide range of promotional methods from posters in doctors' waiting rooms to highly sophisticated television commercials. The commercials ranged from a drug company ad that never mentioned drugs (Merck) to ads for oat bran cereal done in conjunction with the AMA (Kellogg). The AMA also linked up with Dr. Art Ulene of NBC to promote Ulene's book on cholesterol, the AHA started endorsing foods that met its dietary standards, and a book called *The 8-Week Cholesterol Cure* became a best-seller. News stories on the raising of low-cholesterol eggs and low-cholesterol beef were common, one could learn from the news media that bison were a source of low-cholesterol meat, and Warner-Lambert promoted a cholesterol-lowering candy bar whose taste an FDA staffer likened to a "pencil eraser."[72] The NCEP was directing its education toward the public and health-care professionals. "A good way to reach the professionals," said Dr. James Cleeman, the program's director, "is to educate the public... besides the professionals read [*Time* magazine] too." Leading NIH researchers like Basil Rifkind made themselves available to the press whenever necessary:

We believe in speaking to the world through the Jane Brodys and other responsible journalists. We take pains whenever there are major studies to make sure the media are aware of them. We participate in press conferences . . . to present material to the public so they will understand, given the complexities of science. Periodic conferences [at NHLBI] are structured to accommodate the press.[73]

Cholesterol, in other words, had become a full-fledged industry. It also became the subject of the weekly CBS news program, "48 Hours"[74] and a *Time* cover story.[75] By March 1989, Joan Gussow, a professor of nutrition education at Columbia University who was a member of the National Research Council, said, "The political climate has changed. The commodity producers are coming around. The meat industry has made a real effort to come to terms with this."[76]

During 1989, Americans were advised that one in three adults had a cholesterol level indicating a need for treatment and that a laxative called psyllium was better for us than bran; Malaysia's trade commissioner called the anticholesterol campaign a form of protectionism disguised as a health issue (Malaysia is a major palm oil exporter); egg sales were reported down a billion dollars or 25 percent from the 1984 level; there were hints that low cholesterol might be a factor in some kinds of cancer and stroke; boiled and decaffeinated coffee were linked to high cholesterol; and at the annual meeting of the American Heart Association, three new trials showed drug-induced regression of arterial plaque.

In this atmosphere, Thomas J. Moore, an experienced investigative journalist, set out to write a book about preventive medicine. The result was *Heart Failure*,[77] a volume about heart surgery and cholesterol. Much of what he had to say about cholesterol had been reported elsewhere in recent years, but he pulled it all together and made independent judgments about its significance. Most of the cholesterol segment of the book was excerpted by the *Atlantic* magazine, which published it as the cover story in its September 1989 issue. The headline that appeared on the cover was "The Cholesterol Myth," and additional copy on the cover said, "Lowering your cholesterol is next to impossible with diet, and often dangerous with drugs—and it won't make you live any longer." The cover illustration showed a man confronting a tabled loaded with fat- and cholesterol-laden foods, clutching a knife and fork in his hands, a napkin tucked into his collar like a bib, his mouth taped shut, and an apoplectic expression on his face.

This drawing overstated Moore's argument somewhat. He took issue with the National Cholesterol Education Program for its role in what he portrayed as coercing millions of Americans into inadequately differentiated regimens of treatment, by diet or drugs, based on either untested or insufficient evidence that such treatment was safe and would do any good. The twenty-five-page article presented a lot of material contradicting the conventional wisdom on the relationship between blood cholesterol levels and coronary heart disease, the relationship between diet and blood cholesterol levels, and the safety of cholesterol-lowering drugs. It never charged conspiracy between researchers and drug companies, but it insinuated that unduly tight relationships might exist. Talking about the researchers and the drug manufacturers, Moore said, "I believe these people formed too closed a loop and looked at the evidence in too closed a way."[78]

Moore is correct that the community of cholesterol researchers who fully subscribe to the lipid hypothesis (a near consensus among all cholesterol researchers) is close-knit. It is also true that many of these researchers do studies or consult for the companies interested in developing cholesterol-lowering drugs. And when policy action is considered necessary by a significant majority within the research community, this majority will tend to close ranks against the minority favoring delay. And when cholesterol-lowering drugs need to be tested in clinical trials, these leading cholesterol researchers are called on to do the studies. From a public-policy perspective, should it be otherwise?

Moore also charges what he might call the cholesterol-lowering cabal with ignoring evidence that conflicts with their thesis. He cites a 1970 report that was part of the Framingham Study, the longest ongoing study of heart disease in the United States: "There is, in short, no suggestion of any relation between diet and the subsequent development of CHD [coronary heart disease] in the study group."[79] The 1970 paper, however, goes on to say:

> It is important to be perfectly clear what these findings mean and what they do not mean. They mean that in the Framingham Study Group, diet (as measured here) is not associated with concurrent differentials in serum cholesterol level. It does not mean that the difference between Framingham and some other population (say the people of Japan) in serum cholesterol level is unrelated to differences between these populations in diet. Still less does it mean that serum cholesterol levels cannot be changed by changes in dietary intake.[80]

In effect, Moore does here what he accuses the researchers of doing by ignoring relevant information to bolster his position.

In pursuit of a point that could have some validity—that the consensus conference provided too little opportunity for those who opposed the conventional wisdom to express their points of view—Moore committed another distortion by omission. He quoted the comments of the director of the Heart, Lung and Blood Institute, Dr. Claude Lenfant, as follows: "Since the release of the CPPT we have been putting in place machinery to develop and implement a cholesterol education program."[81]

From this quotation Moore drew the inference that nothing that happened at the consensus conference would alter the course of events with respect to the education program. This might have been true, but here are the actual words delivered by an assistant on Lenfant's behalf: "Since the release of the findings of the CPPT last January, we have begun putting into place machinery to develop and implement a national cholesterol education program. However, the nature and scope of that program will be considerably influenced by what takes place here at this conference and the consensus development statement that emerges."

The newsmagazines, *The New York Times*, and *The Washington Post* responded to Moore, coming down in each case on the side of cholesterol monitoring. The news media's approach was more conventional than Moore's in that they sided with the near-consensus view in the scientific community. But Moore's article served a purpose by forcing the leading lipid researchers to respond to a critique that made telling points about the process by which scientific results are turned into public policy. However, the zeal with which he set about his task led to overstatements and misleading reporting, which undermined the effectiveness of his argument.

Conclusion

The only major policy initiative on cholesterol so far has been the National Cholesterol Education Program. Coverage of cholesterol since its launching, however, has expanded dramatically. Moreover, news reporting has reflected the viewpoint of the National Heart, Lung and Blood Institute, the American Heart Association, and the other thirty-six organizations participating in the program. Skepticism about what may not be an open-and-shut case on cholesterol has almost dried up.

Such reporting has served the government's public health goals, assuming that lowering blood cholesterol reduces coronary heart disease. Thomas Moore's contribution in reopening the debate, although useful, was seriously compromised because he overstated and somewhat sensationalized his case.

Future reporting would benefit from more careful attention to the research itself, questioning such things as the nature and size of the study group, the conclusions, the statistical tests applied, and the validity of the extrapolations made from the data. More attention might also be directed to bureaucratic factors that influence science, such as control of research funds. And finally, reporters should be wary of presenting as polarized the views of researchers that in fact differ only in degree. The cholesterol story will be with us for a long time because it deals with people's eating habits and it is complicated enough so that there are always new wrinkles to write about, which will breed new controversies among scientists and the press.

NOTES

1. National Knowledge, Attitude and Belief Survey, conducted for the National Institutes of Health by Prospect Associates, April 1989–February 1990.

2. De Fourcroy, Ann. chim. phys. [1]3, 242 (1789).

3. Henrik Dam, *Cholesterol, Chemistry, Biochemistry and Pathology*, Robert P. Cook, ed. (New York: Academic Press, 1958), p. 2.

4. Jeremiah Stamler, "Population Studies," in *Nutrition, Lipids and Coronary Heart Disease*, R. Levy, B. Rifkind, B. Dennis, and N. Ernst, eds. (New York: Raven Press, 1979), p. 29.

5. Herman A. Tyroler, M.D., of the University of North Carolina, states the case as follows: "Within-treatment group analyses (as observational epidemiologic studies) of the clinical trials and overview analyses of the aggregate outcome of the trials (as proper randomized experiments) are consistent with the results of population-based epidemiologic surveys: they disclose a continuous decrease in coronary heart disease risk with decreasing levels of total plasma cholesterol over a wide range of values." Tyroler, "Overview of Clinical Trials of Cholesterol Lowering in Relationship to Epidemiologic Studies," *American Journal of Medicine*, October 16, 1989, pp. 4A–14S–4A–19S.

6. Edward H. Ahrens Jr., M.D., interview, New York, December 15, 1989.

7. Part of a letter from Dr. Daniel Steinberg dated September 6, 1989,

that was not included in the version that was published in the January 1990 issue of the *Atlantic* on pp. 10, 11.

8. E. H. Ahrens Jr., "The Diet-Heart Question in 1985: Has It Really Been Settled?" *Lancet*, May 11, 1985, p. 1087.

9. Thomas J. Moore, "The Cholesterol Myth," *Atlantic*, September 1989, pp. 37–70. The *Atlantic* article was excerpted from Moore's book, *Heart Failure* (New York: Random House, 1989).

10. Gina Kolata, "Heart Panel's Conclusions Questioned," *Science*, January 4, 1985, pp. 40–41; and "Cholesterol Warning Called Too Broad," *Boston Globe*, January 14, 1985, p. 40.

11. For a history of the epidemiologic studies, see Stamler, "Population Studies."

12. Edward R. Pinckney, M.D., and Cathey Pinckney, *The Cholesterol Controversy* (Los Angeles: Sherbourne Press, 1973), p. 5.

13. *Arteriosclerosis*, a report by the National Heart and Lung Institute Task Force on Arteriosclerosis, DHEW, Vol. 1, June 1971, p. 14.

14. *Arteriosclerosis*, the report of the 1977 Working Group to Review the 1971 Report by the National Heart and Lung Institute Task Force on Arteriosclerosis, DHEW, p. 26.

15. "Heart Disease: Public Health Enemy No. 1," subcommittee on nutrition of the Committee on Agriculture, Nutrition and Forestry, U.S. Senate, May 22, 1979, p. 2.

16. Ibid., p. 6.

17. The networks, the national newsmagazines, the *New York Times*, and the *Washington Post* carried nothing.

18. Victor Cohn, "2 on Food Panel Are Advisers," *Washington Post*, May 31, 1980, p. A1.

19. "A Confusing Diet of Fact," *New York Times*, June 3, 1980, p. A18.

20. Jane E. Brody, "Dispute on Americans' Diets," *New York Times*, May 29, 1980, p. D18.

21. "A Confusing Diet of Fact."

22. "Cholesterol Does Count," *Washington Post*, June 2, 1980, p. A18.

23. Alfred E. Harper, "Fat Cholesterol and Free Scientific Inquiry," letter to *New York Times*, June 16, 1980, p. A22.

24. Matt Clark, with Mary Hager and Dan Shapiro, "How Bad Is Cholesterol?" *Newsweek*, June 9, 1989, p. 111.

25. "A Few Kind Words for Cholesterol," *Time*, June 9, 1980, p. 51.

26. "CBS Evening News" ran two pieces on the National Research Council report, one on June 2, 1980, and the other on June 9, 1980.

27. Jane E. Brody, "When Scientists Disagree, Cholesterol Is in Fat City," *New York Times*, June 1, 1980, p. E7.

28. Jane Brody, interview, New York, December 15, 1989.

29. "Cholesterol Does Count."

30. See polls by Roper and Louis Harris conducted between 1980 and

1989 as well as polls by *USA Today* (June 1988) and ABC News (April 1989); and Beth Schucker et al., "Change in Public Perspective on Cholesterol and Heart Disease, *Journal of the American Medical Association*, December 25, 1987, pp. 3527–31. Polling data supplied by the Roper Organization.

31. Richard B. Shekelle et al., "Diet, Serum Cholesterol, and Death from Coronary Heart Disease," *New England Journal of Medicine*, January 8, 1981, pp. 65–70.

32. Jane E. Brody, "Long-Term Study Links Cholesterol to Hazard of Early Coronary Death," *New York Times*, January 8, 1981, p. 1.

33. Victor Cohn, "Linking of Heart Disease to High-Cholesterol Diet Reinforced by New Data," *Washington Post*, January 8, 1981, p. A14.

34. Shekelle et al., "Diet, Serum Cholesterol, and Death."

35. Marian Burros, "Trimming the Fad Out of Diets," *Washington Post*, May 21, 1981, p. E1. Burros was writing about *Jane Brody's Nutrition Book ...A Lifetime Guide to Good Eating for Better Health and Weight Control* (New York: Norton, 1981).

36. Jane E. Brody, "Heart Disease Study Shows No Gain in Bid to Cut Risks," *New York Times*, September 17, 1982, p. A10. The *Times* also carried a follow-up story with a sidebar by Sandra Friedland, "Doctors Defend Heart Study That 'Failed,'" October 10, 1982, section 11, p. 1.

37. Burt Schorr, "Heart Abnormalities May Pose Some Risks in Hypertension Care," *Wall Street Journal*, September 17, 1982, p. 20.

38. The *Journal* lead said: "There may be an unsuspected risk to treating mild hypertension, or high blood pressure, in persons with heart abnormalities, a 10-year government study suggests."

39. Jerry E. Bishop, "Heart Attacks: A Test Collapses," *Wall Street Journal*, October 6, 1982, p. 32.

40. Multiple Risk Factor Intervention Trial Research Group, "Multiple Risk Factor Intervention Trial, Risk Factor Changes and Mortality Results," *Journal of the American Medical Association*, September 24, 1982, pp. 1465–77.

41. Jeremiah Stamler et al., "Is Relationship between Serum Cholesterol and Risk of Premature Death from Coronary Heart Disease Continuous and Graded?" *Journal of the American Medical Association,* November 28, 1986, pp. 2823–28.

42. Philip M. Boffey, "Study Backs Cutting Cholesterol to Curb Heart Disease Risk," *New York Times*, January 13, 1984, p. 1.

43. Jerry E. Bishop, "Cholesterol Levels in American Children Should be Lowered, Heart Specialists Say," *Wall Street Journal*, March 15, 1984, p. 8.

44. Claudia Wallis, "Hold the Eggs and Butter," *Time*, March 26, 1984, pp. 56–63.

45. Beth Schucker et al., "Change in Public Perspective on Cholesterol and Heart Disease," *Journal of the American Medical Association*, December 25, 1987, p. 3529 (Table 2).

46. Louis Harris Associates, survey for Food Marketing Institute, conducted between January 14 and January 24, 1983.

47. Basil Rifkind, chief, Lipid Metabolism-Atherogenesis Branch, Division of Heart and Vascular Diseases, National Heart, Lung and Blood Institute, interview, Bethesda, Md., December 11, 1989.

48. Ibid.

49. Consensus Development Panel, Daniel Steinberg, M.D., chairman, "Lowering Blood Cholesterol to Prevent Heart Disease," *Journal of the American Medical Association*, April 12, 1985, p. 2080.

50. Ahrens interview.

51. Ahrens, "The Diet-Heart Question," pp. 1085–87; and M. F. Oliver, "Consensus or Nonsensus Conferences on Coronary Heart Disease," *Lancet*, May 11, pp. 1087–89.

52. Oliver, "Consensus or Nonsensus," p. 1089.

53. Ahrens, "The Diet-Heart Question," p. 1087.

54. Jane E. Brody, "Panel Says Cholesterol Level in Many Is Dangerously High," *New York Times*, December 13, 1984, p. 1.

55. Cristine Russell, "NIH Panel Recommends Lowering Cholesterol," *Washington Post*, December 13, 1984, p. A16.

56. Gina Kolata, "Heart Panel's Conclusions Questioned," *Science*, January 4, 1985, p. 40.

57. Ibid., p. 41.

58. Sally Squires, interview, Washington, D.C., December 18, 1989.

59. Sandy Rovner, "Oat Bran May Be the Next Miracle Food," *Washington Post*, January 15, 1986, p. E1.

60. "Fiber," *Washington Post*, March 3, 1986, p. A10.

61. Sally Squires, "The Cholesterol Connection," *Washington Post*, December 16, 1986, p. 12 (Health).

62. Sally Squires, "Cholesterol: Increasing Awareness," *Washington Post*, October 14, 1986, p. 7 (Health).

63. Michael Waldholz, "New Cholesterol Drug Enhances Merck's Role As a Leader in Research," *Wall Street Journal*, December 23, 1986, p. 1.

64. D. H. Blankenhorn et al., "Beneficial Effects of Combined Colestipol-Niacin Therapy on Coronary Atherosclerosis and Coronary Venous Bypass Grafts," *Journal of the American Medical Association*, June 19, 1987, pp. 3233–40.

65. M. Heikki Frick et al., "Helsinki Heart Study: Primary-Prevention Trial with Gemfibrozil in Middle-Aged Men with Dyslipidemia," *New England Journal of Medicine*, November 12, 1987, pp. 1237–45.

66. Philip M. Boffey, "Cholesterol Debate Flares over Wisdom in Widespread Reductions," *New York Times*, July 14, 1987, p. C1.

67. Marian Burros, "What Americans Really Eat: Nutrition Can Wait," *New York Times*, January 6, 1988, p. C1.

68. Associated Press, "Oat Bran Found to Lower Cholesterol More Cheaply Than Drugs," *Washington Post*, April 19, 1988, p. 22.

69. Marian Burros, "Eating Well," *New York Times*, January 13, 1988, p. C4.

70. Jane E. Brody, "Small Study Challenges Role of Oat Bran in Reducing Cholesterol," *New York Times*, January 18, 1990, p. A24.

71. Malcolm Gladwell, "Oat Bran's Claims Weakened," *Washington Post*, January 18, 1990, p. A1.

72. Michael Waldholz, "Candy Bar Medicine Has 2 Companies Ready to Square Off," *Wall Street Journal*, December 21, 1988, p. B3.

73. Rifkind interview.

74. "Beating Heart Disease," "*48 Hours*," CBS News, with correspondents Dan Rather, Robert Arnot, M.D., Faith Daniels, Richard Schlesinger, and Susan Spencer, May 12, 1988.

75. David Brand, "Searching for Life's Elixir," *Time*, December 12, 1988, pp. 62–69.

76. Marian Burros, "Diet and Health: Old Lesson in New Detail," *New York Times*, March 2, 1989, p. A1.

77. Thomas J. Moore, *Heart Failure* (New York: Random House, 1989).

78. Thomas J. Moore, interview, November 28, 1989.

79. Moore, *Heart Failure*, p. 42.

80. "The Framingham Diet Study: Diet and the Regulation of Serum Cholesterol," April 1970, p. 24–14.

81. Moore, *Heart Failure*, p. 63.

8

Blowing Smoke

JUST before Christmas of 1953, executives in the New York office of Hill and Knowlton finished drafting a strategy memorandum for the tobacco industry. The document got right to the point. It began:

> Because of the grave nature of a number of recently highly publicized research reports on the effects of cigarette smoking, widespread public interest has developed, causing great concern within and without the industry.
>
> These developments have confronted the industry with a serious problem of public relations. Obviously, that problem would be quickly solved if the adverse publicity would cease and people would stop talking about the whole matter.
>
> But there is no evidence that the publicity has abated, or is about to abate, or that research workers who are critical of cigarettes are going to cease these criticisms. . . . There is nothing the manufacturers can say or refrain from saying that can stop people from being interested in their health, nor allay their fear of cancer.[1]

The nine-page memo contained a detailed proposal for combating news reports on a growing number of increasingly persuasive studies linking cigarette smoking to lung cancer, heart disease, and premature death. Speculation and even statistical evidence strongly suggesting a smoking-health connection were not new. The speculation dates at least from the beginning of the seventeenth century, and during the 1920s and 1930s numerous studies were published indicating a link among tobacco, illness, and early death.[2] But the first statistically significant, systematic study demonstrating that smoking shortens life appears to have been carried out in 1938 by Dr. Raymond Pearl, a biologist at Johns Hopkins University.[3] Pearl studied a group of 6,813 white males selected at random except for their smoking habits. He concluded that "the smoking of tobacco was statistically associated with an impairment of life duration, and the degree of this impairment increased as the habitual amount of smoking increased." Pearl showed, for example, that of his subjects between the ages of 30 and 60, 61 percent more heavy smokers died than nonsmokers.

So the fact that cigarette smoking could have unhealthy consequences was not news to the cigarette manufacturers in December 1953. Indeed, in November 1938, just seven months after Pearl's study appeared in *Science*, Philip Morris ran an ad in the *Pennsylvania Medical Journal* that said: "You may have questions on the physiological effects of smoking. . . . If you have not already read the studies on the relative effects of cigarette smoke, may we suggest that you use the request blank below? And also that you try Philip Morris Cigarettes yourself."

Awareness was at least fifteen years old. The real news, as far as the industry was concerned, appeared in the first sentence of the Hill and Knowlton document. It was that the most recent research had been "highly publicized." A study using the *New York Times* Annual Index to gauge press coverage of smoking and health noted that "By the late 1940s there were articles suggesting a link between cigarette smoking and both lung cancer and heart disease; and in 1953, 9 of 15 smoking items linked cigarettes to lung cancer."[4] But it was on December 21, 1953, just three days before the date on the Hill and Knowlton memo, that the *Times* ran its first front-page story on smoking and health. It was about Governor Thomas E. Dewey requesting funds for research.[5] It was this press coverage to which the cigarette industry and Hill and Knowlton were responding.

Until the late 1940s, there had been almost no coverage of the health consequences of smoking. Press critic George Seldes noted in 1943 that "the American press and radio—at least 99 percent of each— have suppressed the facts, scientifically established, that the more tobacco a person uses the earlier he dies."[6] Seldes was referring principally to the failure of the press to adequately report on the 1938 Pearl study. His 99 percent figure does not appear to reflect exhaustive research and should probably be treated as less than precise. But it seems reasonably indicative of the lack of attention by most daily newspapers and weekly newsmagazines to stories about smoking and health until just before 1950. Exceptions included a story on page 17 of *The New York Times* of October 26, 1940, which began by saying that "An assertion that the increase in smoking of cigarettes was a cause of the rise in recent years of cancer of the lung... was made today at the closing sessions of the Annual Clinical Congress of the American College of Surgeons."[7]

By 1953, however, news about research linking smoking to health was being widely reported. About three weeks before Hill and Knowlton delivered its strategy memo to the tobacco industry's top leadership, *Business Week* magazine published the following:

> The slow fuse that has been burning under the cigarette industry for several years reached the powder last week.
>
> The sputtering began in earnest a couple of weeks ago when it began to be apparent that this year's sales of cigarettes are going to run about 1% behind last year's.... What made this stand out is the fact that for 20 years the cigarette industry has had a charmed life of steadily increasing sales and markets.
>
> The unexpected setback brought to the surface an ugly phrase that has been lurking underneath people's consciousness for several years— lung cancer. To many observers it has looked very much as though the chief reason for the setback was the spreading fear that cigarettes cause lung cancer, a fear that has made a lot of people cut down their smoking.
>
> Then the top blew off:
>
> *Reader's Digest*, a long-standing foe of the industry, published an article called "Can the Poisons in Cigarettes Be Avoided?"[8] which bluntly stated that "used to excess tobacco may... even shorten life."
>
> *Time* magazine came through with an article on cancer research that points a finger straight at cigarettes as a major cause of lung cancer, the incidence of which has quadrupled during the 20 years that cigarette consumption has shot up from 100-billion to about 400-billion a year.[9]

The *Business Week* article was published partly in response to the increasing number of epidemiological studies in scientific journals linking cigarette smoking to cancer and other diseases. More importantly, though, like the Hill and Knowlton memo, it was responding to newspaper and magazine articles about those studies. *Business Week*, after all, is not a journal whose main concern is public health. Its main interest is the health of industry, including the multi-billion-dollar cigarette industry. The real animus for the article, therefore, was that cigarette sales were slipping for the first time in twenty years, apparently because the press was alerting the public to the dangers of tobacco. And the public was getting the message, not only from *Time* and *The New York Times*, but through stories like "Cancer by the Carton" in the *Reader's Digest*[10] (which were a lot more accessible than "Etiology of Lung Cancer: Present Status" in the *New York State Journal of Medicine*)[11] and in occasional articles in such magazines as the *Nation*, the *New Republic*, and *U.S. News and World Report*. A Gallup poll in June 1954 asked: "What is your opinion—do you think cigarette smoking is one of the causes of lung cancer, or not?" Forty-one percent of the respondents answered "yes," and only 29 percent answered "no." Thirty percent were undecided.

Despite a lag of more than a decade after Raymond Pearl's pioneering study, other researchers found that cigarette smoking was unhealthy, and the press reported it. The people were getting the word, but for reasons that will be explored later, not everyone drew the correct conclusions from the published reports. And among those who did, relatively few took the indicated action, which was to stop smoking.

As the years went by and the evidence mounted that cigarette smoking caused lung cancer, heart disease, emphysema, and a range of other illnesses, the media continued to report the story, as long as there was something new to say. When the Gallup organization surveyed again in July 1957, it found that 77 percent of the respondents were aware of an important American Cancer Society report on "the effects of smoking," and this time 50 percent of them answered "yes" to the question "What is your opinion—do you think cigarette smoking is one of the causes of cancer of the lung?"

This rising level of awareness, for which the media were largely responsible and which by 1990 was almost complete, has had a major impact on public health in the United States. More than 35 million people who would probably still be smoking without the widespread news coverage have given up cigarettes. Moreover, 90 percent of all those Americans who do smoke cigarettes say they would like to quit. By almost any standard, it would seem, the American media should be congratulated for a job well done. However, critics such as Alan Blum, M.D., of the Baylor College of Medicine, and Kenneth E. Warner, Ph.D., of the University of Michigan's School of Public Health, contend that for a number of reasons, not the least of which is a desire to retain cigarette advertising revenue, the media, with notable exceptions, have covered the health risks of smoking poorly. Their arguments imply that with proper coverage there would not be 55 million cigarette smokers in this country in 1990, even though for at least thirty-five years it has been painfully evident that smoking causes cancer and a host of other diseases.[12] These critics point to anecdotal evidence like that which was presented in the *Cipollone* trial, a 1988 civil suit against three tobacco companies. Stories about smoking and health represented only .05 percent of the total number of stories that appeared in Rose Cipollone's regular newspaper, the Bergen County (N.J.) *Record*, and *Life* magazine, to which she subscribed.[13]

Observers such as Michael Pertschuk, chairman of the Federal Trade Commission in the Carter administration, have made the direct link not just between press coverage and public behavior but between coverage and government policy on smoking. Pertschuk said, "The ultimate political weapon of the public health forces is broad, sustained public outrage provoked and stimulated by a responsible press."[14] In other words, press coverage influences public opinion, which in turn influences government policy.

The criticisms of Blum and Warner and the observation of Pertschuk raise important questions about the duties of the news media, the definition of news, and the ability of the media to influence both thought and action. Pertschuk's comment, for example, strongly implies that public health officials must use the news media to provoke "sustained public outrage" if they hope to change policy and seems to suggest that a "responsible press" will not only acquiesce in being used in this way but will willingly become part of the process. And Blum and Warner argue in journal articles and on public platforms that even in the absence of new developments, the smoking-and-health story is news because there are 55 million smokers in the United States, about 2,500 to 5,000 teenagers start smoking daily,[15] and about 400,000 Americans die annually from smoking-related diseases. Both men are antismoking activists who want the smoking-and-health story to be news because they believe that sustained media coverage can influence behavior and policy in ways that could save hundreds of thousands or even millions of lives. The Blum-Warner and Pertschuk views dovetail. The two academics say the story was, is, and will continue to be there for the foreseeable future. The former congressional aide and FTC chairman agrees but adds that it is up to advocates and activists like Blum and Warner to shape the news and get it reported if they expect it to have an influence on policy.

Assuming Pertschuk is right, what role do the news media play in the politicized process of informing the public and influencing policy? In the interest of fairness and balance, should they convey the tobacco industry's message that no cause-and-effect relationship has been established between smoking and lung cancer, although dozens of carcinogens have been identified in cigarette smoke? When should the media have accepted the overwhelming evidence that smoking causes lung cancer and stopped "balancing" that evidence with specious cigarette industry counterclaims? What was the moment for heart disease? Emphysema?

The history of what was once widely known as the smoking-and-health "controversy," and is still occasionally referred to that way ("Morning Edition," National Public Radio, January 9, 1989), provides an opportunity to answer these questions. Moreover, it is an example of the difficulties inherent in using the media to shape public attitudes, behavior, and policy. A careful analysis shows why it took members of the smoking public thirty years to begin to act on their knowledge that cigarettes had been proved deadly and to create an environment in which effective antismoking policy could be made. And it demonstrates why, despite the difficulties, the media are so often the field on which decisive health policy battles are fought.[16]

The *Cipollone* Case

Hill and Knowlton's 1953 Christmas Eve memo to the leaders of the cigarette industry surfaced during the discovery process at a trial known as *Antonio Cipollone individually and as executor of the estate of Rose D. Cipollone, Plaintiff,* v. *Liggett Group, Inc., Philip Morris Incorporated, and Lorillard, Inc., Defendants.* The *Cipollone* trial, which took place in federal district court in Newark, New Jersey, in the spring of 1988, was important for two reasons. It was the first time a cigarette company had been ordered to pay damages in a tobacco liability suit (overturned by the Third Circuit, a new trial has been ordered). Perhaps more important, through the discovery process, much of the hidden history of the cigarette industry's campaign to protect its profits irrespective of the cost in lives was made public. During the trial, in response to a motion by the defendants for a directed verdict, Judge H. Lee Sarokin commented on this history:

> The evidence indicates... that the [cigarette] industry of which these defendants were and are a part entered into a sophisticated conspiracy. The conspiracy was organized to refute, undermine, and neutralize information coming from the scientific and medical community and, at the same time, to confuse and mislead the consuming public in an effort to encourage existing smokers to continue and new persons to commence smoking.

In this regard plaintiff has presented evidence, again, mainly from the files of the defendants themselves, which demonstrates a deliberate intent and purpose to challenge all adverse medical and scientific evidence regarding smoking, irrespective of its truth or validity.

The most subtle evidence of misrepresentation comes from the creation of the Tobacco Institute Research Committee (Council for Tobacco Research). The foregoing was created and highly publicized as the industry's good faith effort to search for the truth, learn the risks of cigarette smoking, and then supposedly report those findings to the general public. Plaintiff has presented evidence from which the jury could reasonably conclude that the creation of this entity and the work performed was nothing but a hoax created for public relations purposes with no intention of seeking the truth or publishing it.[17]

What Sarokin described was a deliberate attempt to mislead, confuse, and dupe the public about the hazards of smoking. He called this purposeful and extended campaign by the cigarette industry a "sophisticated conspiracy." The principal vehicle for implementing the "conspiracy" was the news media. William Kloepfer Jr., for twenty-one years a leading spokesman for the cigarette industry, offered a different perspective. He denied there was any conspiracy. Kloepfer said the industry was simply responding to "What I regarded, I think, as a lack of full understanding on the part of the media of the issues that had arisen as a result of some scientific studies."[18] Still another perspective was expressed by the majority of the jurors in the *Cipollone* trial:

a majority of the jury though that Rose Cipollone didn't deserve one penny from the cigarette makers. They viewed her as an independent woman who made her own informed decision about smoking and who was responsible for her own death. They agreed to award damages only after two of the six jurors refused to give in unless a compromise— granting her husband some small amount—was reached.[19]

Based on a plethora of news articles introduced as evidence by the defense, the jury concluded that the public, including Rose Cipollone, should have known for decades that smoking was hazardous: "for most of the three men and three women who deliberated, [plaintiff's lawyer Marc Z. Edell's] portrayal of an 'evil-minded conspiracy' just didn't wash."[20]

The Early Days

Before enough scientific studies accumulated, the known health effects of smoking were indeed uncertain. The Pearl study, which was reported in *The New York Times* on page 14 (February 28, 1938), was impressive but hardly conclusive. It had been preceded by Dr. Alton Ochsner's research from 1936 onward linking smoking to lung cancer, and it was followed by studies and pronouncements in 1939 and throughout the 1940s, when Mrs. Cipollone started smoking. The work of Ochsner, an unusually prescient researcher, was reported on the inside pages of the *Times* and hardly noticed elsewhere. Lung cancer was rare in the first third of the twentieth century, so rare that Ochsner first saw it as a medical student when his whole class was summoned to witness the autopsy of a man who had died of it. He made the connection between smoking and cancer seventeen years later when he saw nine cases of lung cancer in one six-month period and noticed that all nine men had been smokers.[21] In at least one instance during that period the *Times* published an article linking smoking to cancer, but there was no follow-up.[22]

In the early 1950s, however, the circumstances began to change rapidly. On May 27, 1950, Dr. Evarts A. Graham and Ernst L. Wynder, a medical student at Washington University in St. Louis, where Ochsner had also been a medical student, published a study in the *Journal of the American Medical Association* titled "Tobacco Smoking as a Possible Etiologic Factor in Bronchiogenic Carcinoma" (lung cancer). Graham and Wynder studied 605 hospitalized men with lung cancer to see if there was an association between smoking and the disease. Graham did not expect to find such an association. He noted wryly that "one could draw a similar correlation between increased lung cancer and the sale of silk stockings."[23] To Graham's surprise, however, he and Wynder did find a significant statistical association, as a result of which they concluded: "Excessive and prolonged use of tobacco, especially cigarettes, seems to be an important factor in the induction of bronchiogenic carcinoma."[24] An article about the Graham-Wynder research appeared on page 34 of the *Times*. It was eight paragraphs long, the last two of which dealt with another study yielding similar results.[25]

In September 1950, Richard Doll, M.D., and A. Bradford Hill, a professor of medical statistics, analyzing data from twenty London hospitals, published an article in the *British Medical Journal* whose findings were quite close to those of Graham and Wynder.[26] Doll and Hill published a more detailed study with similar findings in 1952 in the *British Medical Journal*.[27] That same year, Ochsner and three colleagues, one of whom was Michael DeBakey, later to become a world-famous heart surgeon, published a study in *JAMA* concluding that "There is a distinct parallelism between the sale of cigarettes and the incidence of bronchiogenic carcinoma."[28] In 1953, Wynder and Graham reported that they had produced cancer in a strain of mice by painting their backs with cigarette tar.[29] The cigarette companies and their consultants were paying close attention to this research. In a report dated December 31, 1956, Arthur D. Little Inc. told its client Liggett and Myers that an in-house effort to repeat the mouse-painting experiment yielded an "incidence of carcinoma" that was "statistically significant," indicating further investigation. Reacting to the Wynder and Graham study, Ochsner "predicted that 'In 1970 cancer of the lungs will represent 18 percent of all cancer . . . one out of every 10 or 12 men.' Ochsner's prediction was amazingly accurate. In 1970, lung cancer accounted for 19.7 percent of cancers."[30] Despite his prescience, Ochsner's views remained so controversial that "prior to an appearance on 'Meet the Press' in the mid-1950s, he was told he would not be permitted to mention on the air the possible relationship between cigarette smoking and lung cancer."[31] This was the case despite the fact that Graham, Wynder, Hill, Doll, and others had all demonstrated at the very least a strong statistical relationship between cigarettes, cancer, and other diseases.

Why were these data so controversial? The scientists producing the research were respected; the mounting evidence of an association between cigarette smoking and disease was fast becoming undeniable, or at least should have been; and some newspapers were reporting the facts adequately, delivering a powerful, explicit antismoking message while printing in every article a boilerplate industry disclaimer that the smoking-cancer link had not been proved. Yet with the exception of a brief blip linked to reports on the major studies of the early 1950s, cigarette sales continued to surge, although less rapidly than between 1922 and 1952, when sales rose by 639 percent while the population was growing by only 54 percent. (Between 1954 and 1963, cigarette sales increased only two and a half times as fast as the population grew.)[32] Meanwhile, Congress and the Eisenhower administration were paying little attention to a national habit that, it was rapidly becoming clear, was killing tens of thousands if not hundreds of thousands of men annually. And since the 1920s, cigarettes had become progressively more popular among women, who also were beginning to die of their effects. ("Between 1930 and 1967, the proportion of women in the adult population who were smokers rose from 10 percent to an estimated 35 percent. And in that same period the rate of lung cancer among women increased approximately fourfold.")[33] Although the important scientific research on smoking and health was being widely reported in the mass media, neither the press nor the public seemed able to draw the proper conclusions, at least not nearly to the extent warranted.

Nevertheless, by the end of 1953, the cigarette industry already had cause for concern, and, of course, worse was still to come. On June 25, 1954, *The New York Times* reported that the lung cancer death rate among doctors who smoked was increasing at a "significant and steadily rising" rate.[34] This was the finding of a new study by Doll and Hill. But Doll and Hill's data paled when compared to those disclosed three days earlier and reported on the front page of the *Times*[35] and of papers around the world.[36] Dr. E. Cuyler Hammond, chief statistician for the American Cancer Society, told the American Medical Association's convention in San Francisco that a two-pack-a-day smoker was twenty-five times more likely to get lung cancer than a nonsmoker. Hammond's announcement would have been dramatic in almost any circumstances, but it was especially so because it was based on a prospective study of 187,000 men. No one had ever assembled and examined so much information on the health effects of smoking as Hammond and his coresearcher, Dr. Daniel Horn. Moreover, as Richard Doll wrote in the June 1, 1984, issue of the *Journal of the American Medical Association*:

> Hammond and Horn's study broke new ground in [that] it showed that smoking was associated with a much wider variety of ills than had been previously suspected, that the association was, in nearly all cases, much closer for smoking cigarettes than for smoking tobacco in other forms, and that among regular cigarette smokers, smoking might be responsible for anything up to 40% of their total mortality.
>
> The 15 causes of death that were associated with cigarette smoking included several of the most common causes and the suggestion that smoking might contribute to causes of death that together accounted for two thirds of all deaths came as a considerable shock.[37]

It stands to reason that the shock hit hardest in tobacco country, from the flue-curing barns of North Carolina to the burley fields of Kentucky, from corporate headquarters in Winston-Salem and Louisville to those in New York and London. Public statements on the spate of tobacco-and-health studies by cigarette industry spokespersons were few and far between. According to several accounts, the first came on November 26, 1953, from Paul Hahn, president of the American Tobacco Company. *Business Week* magazine characterized Hahn's remark at the time as follows: "The burden of [Hahn's statement] was that the case against cigarettes has not been proven, either statistically or in the laboratories. He scored [sic] 'much loose talk on the subject as reported in the press during the recent months.' "[38]

R. J. Reynolds and Philip Morris weighed in shortly afterward with similar comments, but the other three members of the Big Six that dominated the industry—Liggett and Myers, P. Lorillard, and Brown and Williamson—remained silent. The industry might have been relatively quiet, but it had not been stunned into inaction, which was clear from Hill and Knowlton's Christmas Eve memo. And it was not without some potent strategic advantages in the battle for which it was preparing. One observer, writing about the American Cancer Society, made the following acute and generalizable comment about the risks of taking on the tobacco industry:

> When it finally discovered that smoking was statistically associated with ill health, especially lung cancer, the society found itself in a painful position. The statistics invited it to tangle with one of the country's most affluent industries, and inform millions of Americans that one of their favorite pastimes had suicidal aspects. No voluntary health agency had ever engaged in such controversy.[39]

This applies equally well to government. Michael Pertschuk, the former FTC chairman, is fond of saying that "malaria didn't have a lobby" when discoursing on the difficulties of getting people to stop smoking and getting governments to make antismoking policy and pass antismoking legislation. His point, of course, is that tobacco, unlike malaria, has powerful legions and exceptional resources, both financial and political, to promote its distribution. To get a sense of the economic power of the tobacco companies, consider that the sale of one cigarette a day to each of the country's 63 million smokers in 1953 earned the cigarette industry more than a quarter of a billion dollars. Multiplied by the pack a day the average smoker consumed, the total revenues of the Big Six manufacturers were more than $5 billion annually.[40] Moreover (although they didn't know it), 63 million Americans were addicted to nicotine, for which the slim white tubes of tobacco on which they sucked were the delivery system. By 1970, tobacco was "a ten-billion-dollar-a-year consumer product, from which federal and state governments derive[d] four billion dollars a year in tax revenues, and tobacco advertising... accounted for about eight percent of the entire advertising revenues of the television networks."[41] Because smokers were addicted to nicotine, because they liked cigarettes for reasons ranging from taste to self-image, and because the case against smoking was not airtight in the 1950s, it was easy for a determined industry to take advantage of these human and evidentiary weaknesses to maintain and, as it turned out, even to steadily increase sales. The Hill and Knowlton memo laid out the strategic problem and recommended several tactical approaches to pursuing a media-oriented campaign to protect the cigarette industry's market and to keep it from stagnating.

The memo itself was intended for limited internal consumption. Each page is stamped "Confidential." Nevertheless, it is written circumspectly, apparently to conceal any intent to counteract legitimate studies adding to the body of existing research already demonstrating the strong statistical association between smoking and lung cancer and other diseases. The memo says on page 2: "The underlying purpose of any activity at this stage should be reassurance of the public through wider communication of facts to the public. It is important that the public recognize the existence of weighty scientific views which hold there is no proof that smoking is a cause of lung cancer."[42]

Similarly, the memo says that the first public statement of a new industry committee formed to deal with the public relations challenge "should be designed to clarify the problem and reassure the public that (a) the industry's first and foremost interest is the public health; (b) there is no proof of the claims which link smoking and lung cancer..." The incompatibility of (a) and (b) is self-evident. To reassure the public that "there is no proof" that smoking causes lung cancer, despite strong evidence that smoking probably does cause lung cancer, is antithetical to the claim that the industry's "first and foremost interest" is the public health.

The main piece of advice contained in the memo was that the industry set up a committee to sponsor tobacco research and respond to the press and the public. The main purpose of the committee, the memo makes abundantly clear, was to "offset anticigarette propaganda and to give justified reassurance to the public."[43]

A number of long-term scientific studies were in progress during the mid-1950s. Several of them hit the newspapers and the airwaves in the same year, 1957. The first to appear ran on page 1 of *The New York Times* under the headline "7 Experts Find Cigarettes a Factor in Lung Cancer." The article said:

> There is a direct cause and effect relationship between cigarette smoking and lung cancer, according to a report by seven experts who have made a thorough review of the scientific evidence.... "The sum total of scientific evidence establishes beyond reasonable doubt that cigarette smoking is a causative factor in the rapidly increasing incidence of human epidermoid carcinoma of the lung.... The evidence of a cause-effect relationship is adequate for considering the initiation of public health measures.[44]

The report was the work of a Study Group on Smoking and Health organized by the American Cancer Society, the American Heart Association, and the Cancer and Heart Institutes of the National Institutes of Health. It said among other things that "one of ten men who smoked more than two packs a day would die of lung cancer" and that the comparable figure for nonsmokers was one in 275. A spokesman for the tobacco industry was quoted on an inside page as saying that the "statistical" evidence provided was neither new nor conclusive. The *Times* also published the text of the report.

On June 5, 1957, the *Times* published a story at the top of page 1 with the headline "Cigarette Smoking Linked to Cancer in High Degree." The article began:

> A report to the American Medical Association yesterday showed a high degree of association between cigarette smoking and total death rates. It added that there was an "extremely high" association between cigarette smoking and death from lung cancer.... In addition to noting a high degree of association between cigarette smoking and total death rates, the report said "extremely high" associations were found between cigarette smoking and deaths from cancer of the lung, larynx and esophagus.[45]

This was the final report of Hammond and Horn, which was subsequently published in two parts in the *Journal of the American Medical Association* on March 8 and 15, 1958. The fifth paragraph of the *Times* article was devoted to a quotation from a tobacco industry representative that "the causes of cancer and heart disease are not yet known to medical science." The *Times* published a text of the report and the tobacco industry's full statement.

On June 28, 1957, the *Times* published a story on page 4 with the headline "Britain to Warn of Smoking Peril."[46] It said the British government would support the circulation of a report "that concludes that cigarette smoking is a direct cause of lung cancer." The British equivalent of the Tobacco Industry Research Council, as the American industry group that promoted research favorable to tobacco interests was then known, was quoted in the eleventh paragraph as follows: "The manufacturers do not know of the presence of any carcinogenic substance in tobacco smoke in quantities which conceivably could cause cancer in human beings from smoking."

The cigarette industry received another blow on July 12, when the surgeon general of the United States Public Health Service, L. E. Burney, held a televised press conference in which he said that there was "increasing and consistent evidence" that "excessive cigarette smoking is one of the causative factors of lung cancer."[47] This statement was challenged in the fourth paragraph of *The New York Times* account of the press conference by Dr. Clarence Cook Little, chairman of the Scientific Advisory Board to the Tobacco Industry Research Committee, who said that "three years of research by his group 'has produced no evidence that cigarette smoking or other tobacco use contributes to the origin of lung cancer.'" The importance of the surgeon general's statement was twofold: the federal government had stopped equivocating over the mounting evidence that smoking and disease were inextricably linked, and the surgeon general had used the mass media to deliver the message to the public forcefully and pervasively. Six and a half years later another surgeon general, Luther Terry, was to play an even more important role because he recognized even more fully than Burney that he could only reach the public effectively through the news media.

Two things are evident from the events between 1950 and 1957: the link between cigarette smoking and lung cancer and other diseases had become progressively stronger, and the cigarette industry recognized that it had a major public relations problem on its hands, to which it responded in 1958 by setting up the Tobacco Institute to counter the scientific evidence and to promote cigarettes in the press. *The New York Times* covered the major events fully. Other papers covered these events, too, but less consistently, less thoroughly, and less prominently; radio and television devoted still less time to smoking, and, with a few exceptions like *Reader's Digest,* general-circulation magazine coverage was almost negligible. The cigarette industry was given its say in each story, but the prevailing message was that cigarettes are bad for people. Americans continued to smoke in sharply increasing numbers during this period, and no policy decisions of any consequence were made, except for an FTC ban on health claims for tobacco products. Aside from that ban, the closest the federal government came to action was the recommendation in the study cosponsored by the Cancer and Heart Institutes of NIH that public health measures be considered. More than four years after the tobacco companies began mounting their defensive campaign, the first congressional hearings related to smoking and health were held. Rep. John A. Blatnik (D-Minn.) was directing an effort to redefine the responsibility of the FTC "for enforcing standards of truthfulness in advertising claims relating to the effectiveness of cigarette filters."[48] *The New York Times* covered the Blatnik hearings on page 1, *The Washington Post* ran a much shorter story on page 16, and *Newsweek* carried six paragraphs on page 71.

Between 1958 and 1962, news coverage declined sharply and cigarette sales increased, but with a notable exception. An August 1959 survey shows that physicians, who were not dependent on the mass media for information about smoking and health, had already cut back significantly on their cigarette smoking or had changed to filter cigarettes, which were just beginning to become a factor in the market. And about two-thirds of them were also advising patients with respiratory and circulatory ailments to stop smoking.[49] Meanwhile, the cigarette manufacturers were fighting the battle on three fronts—in the news columns, through increased advertising and promotion (which by 1963 totaled a quarter of a billion dollars annually), and in the laboratory, where among other things they were trying to develop better filters and tobacco-less cigarettes.[50]

Between 1957 and 1962, the companies had a rather quiet stretch with no important new studies to try to discredit and declining press coverage. But on Ash Wednesday of 1962, the venerable Royal College of Physicians in Britain issued a major report whose release ran at the top of column 1 of *The New York Times* under the headline "War on Smoking Asked in Britain."[51] The report said that the "facts are discussed and none of them is found to contradict the conclusion that cigarette smoking is an important cause of lung cancer."[52] The report notes "a great increase in deaths from this disease" and that "men are much more often affected than women," adding that "heavy smokers may have 30 times the death rate of non-smokers." Commenting on the cigarette industry's latest confrontation with medical science, *Business Week* wrote:

Once again a dark cloud, no bigger than a puff of cigarette smoke hangs over the tobacco industry.

It hung over the industry's shares on the New York Stock Exchange this week and prices tumbled although later rallying. It hung over the industry in Great Britain, and sales of cigarettes declined and the industry was moved to restrict its advertising. . . .

The tobacco industry in this country is somewhat nonplussed by it all. It knows what started the sudden resurgence of mentioning cigarettes and cancer in the same breath—but it doesn't understand why the move has gathered such momentum.

All of the new discussions associating cancer and cigarettes apparently began a little more than a month ago with the publication in England of a report by a special committee of the Royal College of Physicians.[53]

The First Big Media Event

While the Royal College report was being prepared in Britain, ten members of an advisory committee to the surgeon general in the United States were working on a document that would have greater impact on public attitudes about smoking, and eventually on public behavior, than any of its predecessors. This document broke no new scientific ground. It did not add to the weight of the evidence. Indeed, it was not really a scientific document at all. It was partly political, but mostly it was a "media event." It was calculated to capture the attention of journalists and, through them, the public.

A number of voluntary organizations and a member of Congress, working separately, had been trying to promote the establishment of an advisory committee on smoking and health. On June 1, 1961, the American Cancer Society, the American Heart Association, the American Public Health Association, and the National Tuberculosis Association (now the American Lung Association) wrote to President John F. Kennedy asking that he appoint a commission to examine "widespread implications of the tobacco problem."[54] Shortly afterward, Senator Maurine Neuberger (D-Ore.) introduced Senate Joint Resolution 174 requesting the president to set up a similar commission. Kennedy, who did not care to embroil himself in the politics of tobacco, ignored both the letter and the resolution. But the president was not able to sidestep the issue when it was raised by a reporter at a press conference. The reporter asked Kennedy the following:

Mr. President, there is another health problem that seems to be causing growing concern here and abroad and I think this has largely been provoked by a series of independent investigations, which have concluded that cigarette smoking and certain types of cancer and heart disease have a causal connection. I have two questions: do you and your health advisors agree or disagree with these findings, and secondly, what if anything should or can the Federal Government do in the circumstances?

Kennedy, apparently unprepared for the question, replied:

That matter is sensitive enough and the stock market is in sufficient difficulty without my giving you an answer which is not based on complete information. . . . I would be glad to respond to that question in more detail next week.[55]

Kennedy asked Surgeon General Luther Terry to respond, which he did two weeks later by announcing that he would appoint an advisory committee to examine the evidence and issue a report. From the outset Terry seemed to understand that if this committee was to have any impact, it would have to be credible and it would have to have a high public profile. According to Robert H. Miles, "Terry began to create a 'stage presence' for his commission by the method he chose to select its members. . . . Terry heightened the suspense . . . by taking extraordinary precautions against 'leaks' . . . and by the time the report was ready to be released, all the major news agencies of the nation focused their attention on the Advisory Committee."[56]

All members of the committee had to be selected unanimously by the interested parties, including voluntary organizations such as the American Cancer Society, various government agencies, and, of course, the industry. Of 150 names submitted, 10 men were selected. They were mainly physicians, but among them were a statistician, a chemist, and a pharmacologist. Terry served as nominal chairman but did not participate in the deliberations of the group. Despite its professional composition, it is clear from the way the committee came into being, and from the already overwhelming evidence that cigarette smoking caused cancer and other diseases, that the body had not been created simply to add to the existing mass of scientific evidence. According to medical historian Stanley Joel Reiser:

It is apparent that the committee's purpose was extrascientific. The advisory committee may be regarded as a *deus ex machina* [whose purpose was] to pacify, to postpone, to gain support, and to camouflage. In the committee, the Surgeon General presumably saw a political shield which would protect him from the congressional backlash sure to follow proposals for remedial legislation on cigarettes. The wrath of opposing legislators, he could hope, might be deflected from himself if he could claim "lack of responsibility" for its findings. Having said this in one breath, however, he might indicate in the next that he was compelled to seek restrictive legislation in light of *public awareness* [my italics] of the committee's findings.[57]

In other words, the strategy for getting legislation through a Congress in which tobacco state legislators wielded substantial power was to promote "public awareness." The only practical instrument for making the public aware was the press. That Luther Terry understood this is clear from the way he released the report. He described the event, its goals, and its immediate results as follows:

The report was released on Saturday, January 11, 1964 at a press conference held in the conference room of the State Department, which was chosen because of its communications facilities. Congress was not in session and we were assured of the full attention of the press.

All those attending the press conference were required to remain for the entire presentation. Each person was given a copy of the final report. After allowing an hour for the press to study the report, the members of the committee, a few members of my staff, and I held an open press conference. The report hit the country like a bombshell. It was front page news and a lead story on every radio and television station in the United States and many abroad. The report not only carried a strong condemnation of tobacco usage, especially cigarette smoking, but conveyed its message in such clear and concise language that it could not be misunderstood.[58]

The New York Times account of Terry's press conference ran under a three-column, three-line headline and then jumped inside, covering almost two full pages, which included the full text of the report's executive summary and brief biographies and photographs of the committee's members. It said in part:

The long-awaited Federal report on the effects of smoking found today that the use of cigarettes contributed so substantially to the American death rate that "appropriate remedial action" was called for....

The report dealt a severe blow to the rear-guard action fought in recent years by the tobacco industry. It dismissed one by one the arguments raised to question the validity of other studies....

A spokesman for the committee told the press conference there was no valid evidence that filters helped reduce the harmful effects.[59]

The Surgeon General's Report, as it came to be known universally, was planned and executed successfully. It got the media coverage it was intended to get, and regulatory and legislative action followed. Throughout the 1960s and the early 1970s, acts were passed mandating health warnings on cigarette packages, and a broadcast advertising ban was put into effect. But public behavior was another matter. There was a short, sharp decline in cigarette sales in the months immediately after the report was issued, and then they began to rise again.[60]

Why did the report not have a more devastating effect on the cigarette industry and a correspondingly more salutary one on the smoking public? In large part, it was because the industry was alert to its "public relations problem," and it was taking a wide range of measures to influence news coverage and thereby public opinion about cigarettes and health. Consider this April 9, 1962, memo on the subject of what was blandly called the "TIRC [Tobacco Industry Research Committee] Program":

> Historically, it would seem that the 1954 emergency was handled effectively. From this experience there arose a realization by the tobacco industry of a public relations problem that must be solved for the self-preservation of the industry. . . .
> To date the TIRC program has carried its fair share of the public relations load in providing the materials to stamp out the brush fires as they arose. While effective in the past, this whole approach requires both revision and expansion. The public relations problem created by Hammond, et al. was like the early symptoms of diabetes—certain dietary controls kept public opinion reasonably healthy. When some new symptom appeared, a shot of insulin in the way of a news release, a . . . television rebuttal, etc., kept the patient going. Again characteristic of the same disease with age; the problem becomes more complex, response to treatment is slower and treatment far more complex. Troublesome symptoms are appearing in the almost constant reference to cigarette smoking or the use of tobacco in some form in practically every article written about chest disease (all forms of lung disease as well as cardiovascular disease), tumor formation of the upper respiratory tract, gastrointestinal disorders, e.g., ulcer, etc.[61]

There is no discernible trace of irony in the extended medical metaphor chosen to describe the tobacco industry's "public relations problem." The memo goes on to recommend a "five-year plan" of image building, calling among other things for more research funds because "The public's knowledge of advertising costs while selling tobacco products does leave John Q. Public with the feeling he is being 'suckered' a little. A more substantial allocation of hard money would improve the industry 'image.'"

The media have been criticized for failing to report adequately on efforts by the TIRC and the Tobacco Institute to manipulate public opinion through advertising and by framing the cigarette-and-health issue as a controversy years after it was no longer scientifically controversial. But there were a few notable exceptions. For example, a 1963 account in *The New York Times* said: "Surprisingly the furor over smoking and health failed to send the industry into a slump. Instead, it sent it into an upheaval that has resulted in unforeseen growth and profits. Behind this growth has been the anxiety of the average smoker and the agility of the major tobacco companies."[62] The *Times* story went on to describe the roles of the Tobacco Institute and the Tobacco Industry Research Committee. With respect to the committee, it said:

> No one denies that the Tobacco Industry Research Committee has sponsored valid research, some of which could even be cited by the anti-smoking forces. But tobacco's critics do not fail to note that the industry's total scientific investment through the committee, $6.25 million to date, would hardly be enough to promote a single new brand on the national market....
>
> "If you spend $6 million on a problem that you say doesn't exist," one critic asserted, "and if $5.5 million goes to proving that it doesn't exist, you can hardly expect to solve it."
>
> "When the tobacco companies say they're eager to find out the truth, they want you to think the truth isn't known," an official of the American Cancer Society declared. "They want to be able to call it a controversy."[63]

The Role of the Media

For anyone who wanted information, then, it was available in detail before the landmark 1964 Surgeon General's Report. A *New York Times* reader, for example, was exposed to clear accounts of the relevant scientific studies. At the same time, major news media like the *Times* gave the industry its say in almost every story of more than a few paragraphs. The concept of "balance" is deeply ingrained in American journalistic practice, making it unlikely that stories critical of an industry would be run without providing space for an industry response. By the early 1960s, however, there was a journalistic problem and a public health problem with this balancing approach in stories about smoking and health: (1) the cigarette industry's claim that a cause-and-effect relationship between smoking and disease had not been proved was either false or irrelevant, depending on how the word *proved* was being used, and (2) most smokers would grasp at any straw to justify their continued use of cigarettes (government studies between 1964 and 1966 showed that between 70 and 75 percent of Americans agreed that "Cigarette smoking is enough of a health hazard for something to be done about it.[64] But they weren't doing anything about it themselves, i.e. stopping smoking.) The balancing had either become mindless, or it served as a mechanism to prevent the news organization from losing its cigarette advertising. There is a clear correlation between the amount of cigarette advertising and the amount and type of smoking-and-health coverage within a given news organization or medium. Newspapers, which have never depended on cigarettes for more than a percentage point or so of their total advertising revenue, have covered smoking and health more thoroughly than magazines, which often derive 15 percent or more of their advertising revenues from tobacco companies. Magazines like *Reader's Digest* and *Good Housekeeping*, which take no cigarette ads, have covered smoking and health better than *Time* and *Newsweek*, which are heavily dependent on cigarette advertising. Kenneth Warner has analyzed this subject extensively.[65]

Traditionally, American journalists, in contrast to many of their European colleagues, have posed as neutral conveyors of information with no social or policy agenda. They claimed no expertise and contended that they should not attempt to resolve controversies, especially scientific controversies. This posture, while noble, made the media vulnerable to manipulation by interested parties, especially those with well-conceived public relations strategies and substantial economic leverage who sold products that tens of millions of Americans enjoyed, indeed to which they were at the least habituated and perhaps addicted, and which contributed to a positive self-image for the users. In the case of cigarettes, the industry benefited from (1) the fact that the evidence used to demonstrate that cigarettes were unhealthy was epidemiological (it could not be demonstrated experimentally and reproduced; therefore, it was more deniable, at least psychologically); (2)

the fact that people took great pleasure in smoking and indeed may have been addicted to cigarettes; (3) the notion of the individual's right to smoke; (4) the identification of cigarettes with sex and sophistication, as promoted in movies and advertising; (5) the identification of the tobacco industry with traditional American values like attachment to the land; and (6) its advertising clout. All of this could be used to manipulate the media to cast doubt on the ever-increasing evidence that cigarettes were killers. Manipulation is at the heart of the evolving contemporary debate about press responsibility, but resistance to manipulation is rarely recognized as a core issue. Although critics talk about the power or the influence of the press, they often miss the point—more influence is wielded through the media by the parties to a controversy on which the press is reporting than by the journalists doing the reporting. For these parties the press is an instrument with which to pursue their goals by creating events (a Surgeon General's Report), framing issues ("statistics are not proof"), disparaging adversaries and their positions, and so on. In the case of tobacco, it was the most effective instrument either side had.

During the next fifteen years, the main theater of action moved from medical science to Congress and the regulatory agencies, but the press remained a (if not *the*) key battlefield. The most active agency was the Federal Trade Commission under the chairmanship of Paul Rand Dixon. Within a week of the release of the Surgeon General's Report, the FTC announced that it planned to issue a rule mandating a health warning on all cigarette packs and advertisements. On March 16, 1964, the agency began three days of public hearings during which H. Thomas Austern, the industry's senior counsel, apparently inadvertently acknowledged that cigarettes were harmful.[66] Both Robert Wald, a lawyer for the industry, and Philip Elman, an FTC commissioner at the time, recall that Austern argued that no warning label was necessary because everyone already knew that cigarettes were unhealthy. Wald said that the industry's representatives "looked like they were in shock." Austern himself contends that he qualified his comment by the use of a word like "alleged," and he acknowledges that he filed a motion to amend the official record. According to Elman, his fellow commissioners took pity on Austern and agreed to alter the record.

The industry argued during the FTC hearings that the proposed rule making would exceed the agency's authority. The strategy was to move the activity to Congress, where tobacco had many powerful friends. The cigarette makers were prepared to accept a mild warning label on packs but not on advertising, a goal they believed they could accomplish in the House and the Senate. Aside from the tobacco state members of the two houses, who were among the best log rollers on the Hill, the industry was also well connected with the White House. One of President Lyndon B. Johnson's closest friends, Earle C. Clements, was a lobbyist for the Tobacco Institute. Clements, a former senator and governor of Kentucky, was an enormous political asset. Another one of Johnson's closest friends and political allies, Abe Fortas, was a top legal adviser to the industry, then and later.

An important player on the other side was Michael Pertschuk, a 29-year-old Senate Commerce Committee staff member, who by his own account was so charmed and befogged in his first run-in with the slick, affable, and politically experienced Clements that he let damaging compromises weaken the legislation. It took a little more than a year, but the industry got almost everything it wanted from the Cigarette Labeling and Advertising Act: a mild warning label that said only "Smoking *may be* [italics added] hazardous to your health," a four-year (as opposed to permanent) preemption against any warning in advertisements in print or on the air, and a preemption of the right of states to add or substitute warnings of their own, either on packs or in advertising. *The New York Times*, however, was not taken in. It said in an editorial:

> Congress has now virtually completed action on a shocking piece of special interest legislation. . . . The bill forbids not only the F.T.C. but also state and local governments from regulating cigarette advertising in any way for the next four years. As a maneuver to distract attention from this surrender to the tobacco interests, the bill also directs that cigarette packages carry an innocuous warning that smoking *"may* be hazardous" [italics added].
>
> Contrary to an unctuous and misleading statement by Senator [Warren G.] Magnuson [D-Ore.], the bill is not "a forthright and historic step toward the responsible protection of the health of this nation's citizens." Rather, it is a bill to protect the economic health of the tobacco industry by freeing it of proper regulation.[67]

An even franker account of the impact of the bill, which was especially interesting because of its sources, appeared in the *Times*'s advertising column. Two ad agency executives were quoted as follows:

> The bill doesn't mean a damn thing. Congress took the cigarette industry off the hook by making the bill meaningless.

The first thing you learn about labels in this business is that people don't read them. This issue has been so thoroughly thrashed out in public that I can't believe that anyone's mind will be changed with a few words on a label.[68]

In Michael Pertschuk's words, "The industry had given an inch to gain ten years,"[69] something it was to do again and again as the public slowly began to accept the truth about smoking.

The *Times* reported the story with political sophistication and editorialized with justified outrage. Since the Surgeon General's Report, almost everyone had gotten the message. Even in Congress, where tobacco was strongest, and with a president with strong political ties to tobacco interests in the White House, it was still possible to get the first smoking-and-health legislation passed. It wasn't much, but an effective antismoking coalition was slowly building. The public was continuing to smoke cigarettes, but there were hints of change. Overall cigarette consumption fell 2.9 percent in 1964 as the result of a roughly 20 percent decline in the two months immediately after the release of the Surgeon General's Report. Between 1965 and 1966, consumption increased by 2.9 percent, and from 1966 to 1967 it was up by an additional 2 percent. But these relatively small increases came during a period (1964 to 1967) in which the adult population increased by about 10 percent.

Despite the fact that the industry had gotten precisely the legislation it had sought, concern about the future was mounting among cigarette manufacturers. A Council for Tobacco Research (formerly the Tobacco Industry Research Committee) memo in August 1965 laid out a continuing strategy for using the media to reinforce the desire of smokers and potential smokers to believe that a controversy still existed over whether cigarettes were unhealthy.[70] The memo recommended continued research to demonstrate "that questions regarding tobacco use and health are far from being resolved"; the use of personal contacts to get stories favorable to tobacco written in "friendly publications" such as the Richmond, Charlotte, and Louisville newspapers and in a few medical publications such as Dr. Fishbein's *Medical World News* (ironically, the Charlotte and Louisville papers were to publish two of the most thorough and forthright series of articles on tobacco ever written by the American press);[71] paying for journalists to visit the council and write about it; and the use of a number of other more or less conventional public relations techniques geared to getting favorable news coverage.

On January 1, 1966, the cigarette-labeling legislation took effect. No available research data suggest that it did any good. In June 1967, however, the Federal Communications Commission issued a ruling that seemed much more promising to the growing antismoking lobby. As a result of the efforts of a lawyer named John F. Banzhaf III and an FCC official named Henry Geller, the FCC ruled that its fairness doctrine applied to cigarette advertising. The fairness doctrine provided free air time for response to controversial views of public importance. The cigarette industry and the broadcasters fought hard, as Banzhaf knew they would, to prevent the application of the fairness doctrine to cigarette advertising. They used First Amendment arguments, which they hoped would be popular with print media, and slippery slope arguments such as "Will people who claim that cars are unsafe get a chance to respond to automobile ads on the air?" But the cigarette manufacturers and broadcasters bought only time in the courts. As of September 15, 1967, radio and television stations were required to air antismoking commercials, not on an equal-time basis but roughly one to every four cigarette commercials. Of course, the cigarette commercials were running in prime time, and the antismoking commercials "were being broadcast at times like 2:30 A.M. or 6:38 A.M. WNBC-TV's explanation for running anti-smoking spots at 6:38 A.M. was that it wanted to reach children with them before they left for school."[72] Some of these commercials were very powerful, and it is likely that they were responsible for part of the decline in smoking that began in the late 1960s. However, the Tobacco Institute's new vice president for public relations, William Kloepfer Jr., contested this view, and he is supported by a 1981 FTC study.[73] In a later interview, Kloepfer said that state taxes on cigarettes were increasing, antismoking reports in the media were becoming more frequent, and the downturn in smoking actually ended before the heaviest concentration of antismoking messages was aired.

Kloepfer, who was director of public relations for the Pharmaceutical Manufacturers Association before joining the Tobacco Institute in 1967, said he thought the media's attitude toward the tobacco industry was "hostile" and that "as far as the media were concerned, the communication job was going to be very difficult." To deal with the situation, he organized a small road show to promote the message that cigarettes had not been proved to be unhealthy. Two-man teams from the Tobacco Institute visited twenty-four cities around the country and held press conferences, complete with a slide show, in what Kloepfer described as "a minor hospitality setting." He said this technique was effective and that "Reporters and correspondents would say to us, 'Golly, where have you fellows been?'" As a result of their success, Kloepfer said, these traveling press conferences became a regular activity of the Tobacco Institute, to which four employees devoted full-time.

Under Kloepfer's direction, the institute papered newsrooms with press releases promoting research that served the industry's interests. It was also early in his tenure that a public relations man for the Brown and Williamson Tobacco Company named Joseph Field paid $500 to a writer named Stanley Frank to produce an article casting doubt on the evidence that smoking was hazardous to health. Frank wrote the article, *True* magazine published it on January 15, 1968, and a public relations firm representing the tobacco industry named the Tiderock Corporation paid for the distribution of 608,000 reprints. A shortened version of the Frank article appeared in the *National Enquirer* under the byline Charles Golden. By the time the *True* article appeared, Frank was working for Hill and Knowlton, the tobacco industry's main public relations firm. Elizabeth Whelan of the American Council on Science and Health commented that "The most important part of the *True* story is not the fact that the tobacco industry did it—but that they were apparently under so much pressure that they had to use such a desperate measure."[74] Articles such as Frank's, and others placed by more legitimate means, permitted pro-cigarette forces to cite published sources in their efforts to counter the results of epidemiological and animal studies.

Another Decade

On July 1, 1969, when the Cigarette Labeling and Advertising Act of 1965 expired, *The New York Times* urged passage of legislation to ban cigarette advertising on radio and television, to toughen the package warning label, and to include the warning in print advertising.[75] The *Times*'s wish list was granted by Congress in the Public Health Cigarette Smoking Act of 1970. But this would be another example of giving an inch to gain ten years. For one thing, the industry, despite Kloepfer's comments on the lack of efficacy of antismoking commercials, was glad to see them off the air, even if the price was to take cigarette commercials off the air as well. According to Michael Pertschuk, Earle Clements had advised the industry that it would be in its interest to take the whole smoking-and-health issue "out of the living room."[76] Kloepfer said that as far back as 1967 the industry was discussing the wisdom of reducing the volume of television advertising.[77] The first time cigarette smoking declined on a per capita basis for four consecutive years was between 1967 and 1970, the period of the antismoking commercials. According to Kenneth Warner, between 1970 and 1973, when there were neither cigarette nor antismoking commercials on radio and television, per capita consumption turned upward again. It then began to decline slowly with the onset of the nonsmokers' rights movement. Warner contended that every time per capita smoking declined, it was linked to a major news event and that the media's "failure to cover smoking and health more thoroughly" and by implication more consistently has resulted in fewer smokers quitting than would otherwise have been the case.[78] Another consideration is that when the ads went off the air, legislative activity stopped for more than a decade.

A less intrepid industry might have caved in by the beginning of the 1970s had it had less at stake, more social conscience, less skillful political support, and less faith in its ability to continue to manipulate the majority of the nicotine-habituated or addicted smoking public through paid (advertising) and free (news) media channels. Another source of comfort for the cigarette industry was the likelihood that it could promote the legitimacy and desirability of cigarettes well enough to attract new smokers from the ranks of teenagers and minority groups.

On May 1, 1972, a Tobacco Institute vice president named Fred Panzer wrote a memorandum directed mainly to the media-related concerns of the industry. It was addressed to Horace R. Kornegay, a former North Carolina representative who had become president of the Tobacco Institute. The memo, which caused a stir at the *Cipollone* trial, said in part:

> It is my strong belief that we now have an opportunity to take the initiative in the cigarette controversy, and start to turn it around.
>
> For nearly 20 years, this industry has employed a single strategy to defend itself on three major fronts—litigation, politics and public opinion.
>
> While the strategy was brilliantly conceived and executed over the years helping us to win important battles, it is only fair to say that it is not—nor was it intended to be—a vehicle for victory. On the contrary, it has always been a holding strategy consisting of

—creating doubt about the health charge without actually denying it

—advocating the public's right to smoke without actually urging
them to take up the practice

—encouraging objective scientific research as the only way to resolve
the question of health hazard.[79]

Each of the three tactics cited by Panzer was intended at least in
part to manipulate public opinion through the media. The first used
techniques ranging from taking advantage of the news media's reflex
notion of balance to cast doubt on solid epidemiological evidence, to
promoting deceptive articles as in the *True* magazine example. The
second tactic took advantage of a libertarian strain in American society,
to which journalists were no less receptive than other Americans, by
framing the smoking issue as having to do with individual rights rather
than health. And the research mentioned in Panzer's last point was
intended to keep alive a false perception of scientific controversy. Another industry memo noted that "smoking and health research programs have not been selected against specific scientific goals, but
rather for various purposes such as public relations. . . . Thus, it seems
obvious that reviews of such programs for scientific relevance and
merit in the smoking and health field are not likely to produce high
ratings."[80]

On the next page of Panzer's memo, he made a number of critical
observations:

On the public opinion front . . . our situation has deteriorated and will
continue to worsen. This erosion will have an adverse effect on the other
fronts, because it is where the beliefs, attitudes and actions of judges,
juries, elected officials and government employees are formed. . . . The
public . . . must perceive, understand, and believe in evidence to sustain
their opinions that smoking may not be the causal factor [in causing
lung cancer and other diseases]. . . . There are millions of people who
would be receptive to a new message, stating:

Cigarette smoking may not be the health hazard that the antismoking people say it is *because other alternatives are at least as
probable.*

Panzer went on to recommend "research" that would support the
"alternatives" thesis and that could be released "as a book in both hard
cover and paper back version, hopefully published by a legitimate
house. In effect, such a volume would be a counter–Surgeon General's

Report.... And best of all, it would only have to be seen—not read— to be believed... just like the Surgeon General's Report." This book was never published, but Panzer was right about the Surgeon General's Report. People did not have to read it to believe it. They believed it because it had the imprimatur of authority.

Panzer was also right about the tide having turned. After 1973, per capita cigarette smoking went into steady decline, dropping to 3,400 in 1984 from 4,100 in 1973, and at various times in the 1980s between 70 and 90 percent of all smokers said they wanted to quit. The word was out. Like the industry's original strategy, which Panzer said was never intended to be "a vehicle for victory," the latest strategy, too, was an effort to gain as many years of profitability as possible. Even though it was fighting a rear-guard action on the media front, by cutting costs and raising prices the industry made the cigarette an increasingly profitable product.

In 1974, the industry used its clout to cancel a press conference by one of its own researchers, who was planning to use the media to charge that "the tobacco industry was attempting to suppress important scientific information about the harmful effects of smoking."[81] And a little later in the year, a P. Lorrillard internal memorandum noted that "the public and political attitude toward smoking has seriously decayed with respect to the tobacco industry, and scientific and political attack has become intense.... Thus, we see the litigation threat of much lesser importance than that of legislative and public acceptance of cigarette smoking."[82] Legislative and public acceptance were, as the industry recognized, inseparable. On the regulatory front in the mid–1970s, the FTC was beginning to look into deceptive advertising practices in an industry that was spending about a billion dollars a year on advertising and promotion. By 1984, tobacco manufacturers were spending $2 billion a year to promote their products, more than any other industry. Overall sales (not per capita) continued to rise, as did profits, throughout the 1970s.[83]

The 1979 Surgeon General's Report

The decade was to close on a sour note for the cigarette manufacturers. Secretary of Health, Education and Welfare Joseph A. Califano, a Washington insider who fully understood the importance of the press in accomplishing legislative and other political goals, presided over the mòst successful antismoking media event since the 1964 Surgeon General's Report: the issuance of the 1979 Surgeon General's Report. But the industry was not yet toothless. Califano paid with his job for his antismoking zeal. Although he had quit smoking as a gift to his 11-year-old son on October 21, 1975, Califano contends that when he was appointed secretary by newly elected President Jimmy Carter, he had "never thought about smoking as a serious health issue."[84] He was, however, interested in preventive health care. Shortly after his appointment, he scheduled a series of interviews with experts inside and outside his department to help determine where he should focus his efforts. One of those interviews was with Daniel Horn, who with Cuyler Hammond had done the first major prospective study showing that cigarette smoking and lung cancer were strongly associated. Horn was director of the tiny Atlanta-based National Clearinghouse on Smoking and Health, the government's token antismoking office (budget: $750,000). Horn told Califano that cigarette smoking was responsible for more than 300,000 premature deaths a year and that it was the nation's major health problem.[85] Califano got the same message elsewhere and concluded that an antismoking campaign would be an important element of his tenure at HEW. Califano said that "By the time Dr. Julius Richmond became the Surgeon General and the Assistant Secretary for Health in July 1977, he and I had decided to issue a new Surgeon General's Report on smoking in January, 1979, to celebrate the 15th anniversary of the original report on smoking issued by Dr. Luther Terry in 1964."[86]

During his first year in office, Califano shopped for approaches. He floated the idea of phasing out tobacco price supports while answering a press conference question from CBS News correspondent Barry Serafin in June 1977, but quickly discovered that he might as well have tried to change the colors of the American flag. Finally, he decided to "stick to a highly visible anti-smoking campaign to alert the public to the dangers."[87] "Highly visible" meant media. As Califano developed his antismoking program, with a release date set for January 11, 1979, he imposed tight security to develop suspense and heighten the interest of the press. Journalistic speculation about the program made the Tobacco Institute edgy, and it had the same effect on the White House. Califano said that "the President's White House health aide, Dr. Peter Bourne, moved to distance Carter from the effort." Advance copies of Califano's speech announcing the new program were very closely held. Even though the Tobacco Institute's executives failed to get a copy, they decided to hold a preemptive press conference on January 11, in which they denounced Califano for not giving them an advance copy of the text.

The text of that speech did more than present the outlines of a program. It framed the smoking-and-health issue for the press and for the future. It did so by careful crafting and by a single headline-grabbing phrase written by Califano's speechwriter, Ervin Duggan: "slow-motion suicide." This phrase was reused in the secretary's preface to the 1979 report and appeared in a page 1 *Washington Post* headline a year after Califano first used it.[88] Califano characterized the program's approach in his book, *Governing America*:

> The theory of the campaign announced in the speech was that a choice is free only if it is informed, a decision genuinely voluntary only if it is based on all the relevant information. Its key was to offset the billions of dollars for seductive advertising spent each year by the tobacco companies. There was no hope that we could approach in federal funds the investment of the tobacco industry. But we could mount an effective public education campaign through the media if we marshaled our limited federal resources [and] made it newsworthy and interesting.[89]

The media were to be the battleground on which the campaign would be fought to educate the public and pressure Congress to legislate against the will of the powerful tobacco state committee chairmen. Califano picked John Pinney, the young, good-looking, articulate head of the National Council on Alcoholism, to head the reconstituted Office of Smoking and Health in Washington. "One of the first things that was done with me," Pinney said, "as part of my training, was to be prepared by Eileen Shanahan to meet the press."[90] Shanahan, a former correspondent in the Washington bureau of *The New York Times*, was Califano's assistant secretary for public affairs. Pinney said he found this training not only relevant but essential, adding that "one of the few things public health officials have in countering the cigarette companies is the press."

Indeed, the press was also to be Califano's instrument for dealing with the White House and Congress. In *Governing America*, Califano quoted a "high-ranking White House aide" as saying, "With all the problems Carter has in North Carolina [a reference to the court order to desegregate its higher education system that HEW was enforcing], he doesn't need an anti-smoking campaign."[91] Bourne was saying what he could publicly to soothe the tobacco state legislators, anonymous

White House press leaks labeled Califano a dissident within the administration, and Carter himself made two speeches in North Carolina, one at Wake Forest University in the R. J. Reynolds headquarters city of Winston-Salem and the other in a tobacco center named Wilson. The president cracked jokes at Califano's expense and said everything he could to ingratiate himself with the cigarette manufacturers, tobacco growers, other North Carolina voters, and their representatives in the Senate and the House of Representatives.[92]

In May 1978, between the two Carter speeches, a sequence of events took place that illustrates graphically the use of the news media by government officials as an internecine weapon. At the annual World Health Assembly in Geneva, the Saudi Arabian delegation offered an antismoking resolution that Califano and the U.S. delegation supported but that Bourne and other White House advisers including Anne Wexler sought to soften on political grounds. Califano told it this way:

> I told [HEW deputy undersecretary for international affairs Peter] Bell . . . to get Bourne to call the State Department and ease the White House pressure. "Bourne's a doctor. He can't stand public exposure of such blatant support of the tobacco interests."
>
> Bell convinced Bourne that a vote against the Saudi resolution would do Carter more political harm than good. Bourne called the State Department. He also agreed to argue our side of the case with Hamilton Jordan's political section in the White House. But Bell and I feared he was not strong enough to counter other pressure State had received from the White House.
>
> We had one last resort to trim the White House staff sails. We leaked to a reporter that White House staffers Wexler and Bourne were trying to put Tobacco Institute language into a Saudi resolution against smoking at the World Health Assembly, or to force the U.S. delegation to vote against it. The reporter called me later that afternoon. "There's nothing there," he said. "They strenuously deny any attempt to weaken the Saudi resolution on smoking or to get HEW to vote against it. Unless you go on the record, there's no story."[93]

"No story," of course, was exactly what Califano wanted. Peter Taylor, author of *The Smoke Ring*, writes that Bell persuaded Bourne to drop his opposition to HEW's position by telling him that a unanimous vote on the Saudi resolution "wouldn't have gotten an inch of space in an American newspaper," whereas a "vote against the Saudi resolution . . . would have been a story because of the political motivation in the vote."[94] A master of press politics like Califano, as this story demonstrates, can use the media to accomplish his goals without a word appearing in print or broadcast over the airwaves.

The 1979 Surgeon General's Report was to be another matter, however. It was designed to garner as much type and air time as possible. It was conceived of and explicitly labeled as a "media event" in the original proposal recommending a fifteenth-anniversary report. In describing the objectives of the document, Robert Hutchings, the man whose idea it originally was, said: "We did, indeed, want this information to get out to the public.... That was the purpose of the report.... The press was a vehicle, maybe the only available vehicle [to] reach those people who would really rather not know."[95] John Pinney, the director of the Office of Smoking and Health who oversaw its production, said, "Joe [Califano] looked at the 1979 Surgeon General's Report as the foundation of the credibility of his initiative [on smoking].... He called me on a number of occasions, at odd hours of the day or night, to find out how it was going.... He said, 'It's got to be good. It's got to be credible.'" Pinney went on to say that the report had to be "so conclusive" that it would lay to rest the notion that there was such a thing as a "smoking controversy." Califano said that even the cosmetics were important. When asked if the 1,200-page document should be bound in two volumes, he said, "No way. I don't care if it falls apart after it's been published. I want one volume. I want to have one monster book that ... someone can ... give to the press and say, 'You may think there's some controversy; this is only a fifth of the studies that we've actually reported on. These are just the best. This is only scratching the surface. There is no controversy.'"[96]

Califano had been told that he was on his own as far as the smoking campaign was concerned. The president wanted no part of it. He had told Califano in a private meeting in the Oval Office to "keep" the smoking program "off my desk."[97] Although Califano understood the political implications of his antismoking campaign and the upcoming Surgeon General's Report, he did not try to tone down the publicity surrounding the report's release. On the contrary, he did everything he could to enhance it. "In an attempt to saturate the mass media from Thursday until Sunday," Califano wrote in *Governing America*, "we identified anti-smoking programs in every media market for local television and radio stations and newspapers to broadcast and write about."[98] Meanwhile, the manufacturers prepared a response. The Tobacco Institute launched an attack in the press on January 10 even though they did not know what was in the report. This hardly mattered, though, because the object was not so much to criticize the document as to manage the news. According to William Kloepfer, "That was the one time that the ... tobacco industry's story [that the scientific evidence linking cigarette smoking to cancer, heart disease, and other diseases was inconclusive] was number one on each of the network newscasts."[99] The same day, White House press secretary Jody Powell called Califano from National Airport before boarding a plane for a Democratic Party fund-raising meeting in North Carolina. When Califano told Powell about the report that was going to be released in less than twenty-four hours, and added that he didn't know what Powell could do to defend the administration against the inevitable flak in North Carolina, the press secretary replied, "Smoke. I'll just smoke like hell while I'm down there."[100] Powell's ignorance of the upcoming report illustrates just how isolated the White House was keeping itself from Califano's crusade, not to mention its attitude toward it. Califano described the release of the report itself exclusively in media terms:

> When Richmond and I walked into the press conference on the morning of January 11, the HEW auditorium was filled with more reporters and cameras than on any occasion until I was to meet the press after President Carter asked me to resign. The evening television coverage was extensive, and the next day the NBC *Today* show gave an hour to the subject and *Good Morning, America* did a forceful piece of extended coverage. Local television coverage was enormous, and so was the play in the newspapers. Only magazine coverage was moderate or light, perhaps because of the enormous amounts of cigarette advertising they carried.
>
> The impact was stunning. A special HEW survey revealed that, in the two weeks following the release of the Surgeon General's Report, more Americans tried to quit smoking than in any other two-week period since the release of the first report in 1964.
>
> For the President, there was one unfortunate aspect of the television coverage. After reporting the case against cigarette smoking, the three networks showed footage of Carter amidst the tobacco leaves in the Wilson, North Carolina, warehouse, talking about making smoking "even more safe." After viewing the broadcasts, Vice President Mondale, who never lost his wry sense of humor, called me. "Jeez," he said, "those guys in the White House really have it positioned—the President's for cancer and you're for health."[101]

The report got the kind of media attention it was meant to get—a banner headline across the top of *The Los Angeles Times,* a two-column headline in the upper left corner of page 1 in *The New York Times*, a two-column front-page headline in *The Washington Post*. And that was no accident. John Pinney said, "We spent hours with the report in its draft form saying, 'What's the story?' And the second question we asked was, 'What are the policy implications?' We made a conscious effort to define well in advance what the story was and what the policy implications were. . . . We were thinking like reporters at several stages along the way."[102] Pinney went on to say:

> We did not go so far as to formulate specific policy recommendations [because] we decided that it would never get through the White House, [but we looked for] the things that we can tell people that will really make a difference in formulating policy. . . . More attention on kids, more prevention activity . . . that women had been totally overlooked and were a major source of concern and were subject to the same consequences as men. . . . We were criticized by the industry . . . for conducting a media blitz. There was a media blitz. It worked.

Califano concluded the section on smoking in *Governing America* with these words:

> The anti-smoking campaign generated more mail to me than any issue I faced as Secretary, more than ten thousand letters. Fifty-four percent supported the anti-smoking campaign, 35 percent (mostly from tobacco states) opposed the campaign. . . .
> And the campaign had an impact. Its success was measured by a decline in per capita cigarette consumption in the United States in 1979 to its lowest level in twenty-two years and a decline in the consumption of tobacco that same year to the lowest in 46 years. From 1977 to 1979, there was a 25 percent drop in the percentage of teenage boys who smoked regularly, while the decline among teenage girls was only 9 percent. There are demonstrable cultural changes in American society about smoking as well. The smoker who used to say, "Have a cigarette," now asks, "Do you mind if I smoke?" An increasing number of teen-agers—two-thirds by 1979—disapprove of smoking. No-Smoking areas abound in aircraft, trains, restaurants and other public enclosed spaces. Children are urging their parents not to smoke, as my own son Joe successfully encouraged me when he asked me to quit as a present for his eleventh birthday.[103]

Just over six months later, on July 19, 1979, Joe Califano was fired as secretary of Health, Education and Welfare largely because, as a front-page story in *The New York Times* put it, Califano had "offended powerful political interests in the South with his campaign against cigarette smoking."[104]

The very legitimacy of the cigarette as a product was increasingly challenged by adverse news coverage. By 1988 this challenge had advanced so far that a headline in *The New York Times* could ask without a trace of irony, "Is Smoking Becoming Taboo?"[105] A Philip Morris interoffice memorandum from March 1981 said that the tobacco industry's "Communications Committee is committed to instituting national advertising to reinforce the smoker, his choice to smoke and the custom of smoking."[106] In other words, the whole culture of cigarette smoking badly needed shoring up.

The 1980s have seen the rise of a nonsmokers' rights movement, which has capitalized on increasing evidence that side-stream smoke from the cigarettes of others is hazardous. The industry has fought back for "smokers' rights" with multi-million-dollar campaigns in states and local communities to defeat antismoking ordinances. Industry spokespersons say they win these battles about 90 percent of the time at the state level and 75 percent of the time at the local level. In 1988, however, a $20-million campaign failed to defeat a twenty-five-cent-a-pack increase in the cigarette excise tax in California.[107] And in response to the American Cancer Society's Great American Smokeout, which according to society vice president Irving Rimer "has made tremendous impact in the news,"[108] the industry has come up with the "Great American Welcome," an effort to mobilize the economic clout of smokers through the media and grass-roots canvassing.[109] And in the 1980s, C. Everett Koop, a surgeon general like no other before him, a man with an Old Testament face and military bearing to go with his commanding voice and military uniform, emerged on the American scene. Koop used the news media as virtually his sole weapon to attack cigarettes with the zeal of a crusader. He issued provocative, news-making Surgeon General's Reports on the health consequences of smoking for women, nicotine addiction, and passive smoking; he gave frequent congressional testimony; and he coined memorable phrases about cigarettes such as "the chief, single, avoidable cause of death in our society and the most important public health issue of our time." Koop even made the papers once by not testifying in favor of legislation to ban tobacco advertising. White House chief of staff Donald T. Regan banned his testimony.[110]

Policy goals have been accomplished, most notably the Comprehensive Smoking Prevention Education Act of 1984, which provided for four health warnings to be rotated randomly on cigarette packs. The legislative hearings for the act were designed, as such hearings often are, as a media event. Matt Myers, staff director of the Coalition on Smoking or Health, described it this way:

> It was recognized that the hearings [were] an effective mechanism for educating the American public and . . . we got very good coverage of the issue. . . . At the first hearing, American Heart Association, American Lung Association, Cancer Society brought in people like Amanda Blake, who was Miss Kitty on Gunsmoke . . . Bob Keeshan, who plays Captain Kangaroo, and . . . John Forsythe, the star of "Dynasty" . . . and their presence, more than the presence of the eminent scientists who followed them, was the key to getting the hearing on the nightly network news, on the front page of newspapers all over the country.[111]

In his book *Giant Killers*,[112] Michael Pertschuk recounts the battles of the 1980s, especially in Congress. What Pertschuk's fascinating tale of lobbying and legislative maneuvering demonstrates above all is that in Congress, too, the cigarette had been progressively delegitimized through the media. The "tobacco family," made up of six economically powerful cigarette manufacturing conglomerates, a politically powerful coalition of tobacco-state senators and representatives, tobacco farmers, people in dependent industries, an army of lobbyists and public relations and advertising specialists, and 55 million smokers, could no longer keep its collective finger in the dike. The American public, albeit slowly, was giving up smoking. And the American government was legislating and regulating on behalf of a large majority of increasingly militant nonsmokers.

Media as Battleground: An Analysis

There can be little doubt that from the mid-1950s to the mid-1980s, major battles in the cigarette war were fought in the media. And there is strong evidence that the media battles have influenced millions of people to quit smoking, and bureaucrats and lawmakers to regulate and legislate against smoking. How should we rate the performance of the press itself during a thirty years' war fought on its turf that is not over yet? The news media, of course, have no direct responsibility to modify behavior or promote legislation. Nor are they in the dispute-resolution business. It is their business, however, to provide timely, fair, accurate, understandable, and substantially complete accounts of matters of legitimate public concern, which obviously includes public health.[113] Because news media are the beneficiaries of special constitutional and statutory rights and privileges based on the premise that only they can serve the public's need for information citizens must have to provide for their welfare and participate in the political process, they have a corresponding moral duty to try to provide this information, unmanipulated by interested parties, in a way that promotes free and informed choice, even when doing so might entail a loss of advertising revenue.

It is clear that some national news organizations met the five criteria—timeliness, fairness, accuracy, understandability, and substantial completeness—cited above, and others did not. Kenneth Warner demonstrates that newsmagazines such as *Time* and *Newsweek*, which are far more dependent on cigarette advertising than newspapers, performed poorly. He calls attention, for example, to special health sections that appeared in the November 7, 1983, *Newsweek* and the October 8, 1984, *Time*. The "AMA-*Newsweek* supplement," he wrote, "mentioned cigarettes in only four sentences, none of which explicitly identified smoking as a health hazard. The same issue of *Newsweek* contained 12 pages of cigarette advertisements, worth close to $1 million in revenues." Warner went on to say that "*Time* published a similar special health supplement, produced in cooperation with the American Academy of Family Physicians. The text contained no references to cigarette smoking. The Academy claims that *Time* removed discussion of the health hazards of smoking without the knowledge of the Academy. . . . The October 8 issue of *Time* contained eight pages of cigarette advertisements."[114] (*Reader's Digest*, the one large-circulation magazine that consistently reported on smoking and health, had been dropped by its advertising agency in July 1957 at the insistence of the American Tobacco Company.)[115]

It may be because large daily newspapers derive only about 1 percent of their revenue from cigarette advertising that they did better than the magazines. Since the 1950s, *The New York Times* has covered smoking and health in a way that should have alerted thoughtful readers to the dangers of smoking. At various times from the 1964 Surgeon General's Report onward, papers such as *The Los Angeles Times*, *The Washington Post*, and *The Boston Globe* have provided strong coverage. Most of the stories in the late 1980s and into the 1990s have focused on antismoking ordinances, airline smoking bans, and the efforts of cigarette companies to sell their products abroad, especially in Asia.

Television has a mixed record. Edward R. Murrow, who perpetually had a cigarette dangling from his lip, did a "See It Now" documentary on smoking and health as early as 1955, but for the most part, up to the broadcast ban on cigarette advertising, very little critical of smoking was aired.[116] There have been a number of documentaries since, some of which, including "The Smoking Wars" ("48 Hours"), have been quite good. But as recently as the late 1970s, network news programs insisted on "balancing" an appearance by John Pinney, for example, with a representative of the Tobacco Institute. Today's tobacco companies are, of course, units of vast consumer conglomerates that own food companies like Nabisco, General Foods, and Kraft. These conglomerates control billions of dollars' worth of advertising. According to Tony Schwartz, a media consultant who makes antismoking commercials, New York radio station WMCA "was threatened by [advertising] agencies who represented companies that were owned by the cigarette companies, and they were told, 'If you run any antismoking ads, we will not put our advertising on your station.'"[117]

Allan Brandt, a historian of science who is writing a social history of smoking, said that "as the general social attitudes [toward] and meaning of the cigarette shifted . . . I think the press began to report it in a more serious way, and this is in large measure a result of the Surgeon General's Report" of 1964.[118] Editors such as A. M. Rosenthal of *The New York Times* have correctly noted that the news media regularly fail to recognize major social or scientific trends until they are well under way; it is a truism that the way to know a trend or fad has peaked is to see a cover story about it in *Time* magazine. In the case of cigarettes, the product was popular, the early evidence that it was unhealthy was relatively weak, and the industry was wealthy and willing to kick and bite to defend itself. Moreover, there was a strong congressional delegation from the tobacco states that wielded influence that was disproportionate to its size, cigarette advertising was an economic factor, and many journalists were smokers.

With a few exceptions, such as Morton Mintz of *The Washington Post*, journalists are not comfortable with the role of attacking popular products and demanding corporate responsibility. As a result of this and other factors mentioned above, no major American newspaper, magazine, or network ever mounted a sustained, full-fledged, crusading investigation of the tobacco industry, even though all the elements of a terrific investigative story were present, including an audience of tens of millions of smokers who said they were eager to quit. It could also be, as Thomas Schelling of Harvard's Kennedy School of Government said, that "smoking is a very boring subject. About all you can say about smoking is that it is bad for people."[119]

By 1991, of course, tens of millions of smokers had quit. One reason for that might have been a flaw in the cigarette industry's strategy to manipulate the public through mass media channels, both news and advertising. Inevitably, the industry's efforts to frame the smoking-and-health issue as a controversy led to more news coverage because controversy about issues of public interest is, by definition, news. The industry contributed to keeping the smoking-and-health issue controversial and before the public in a wide range of ways, including sponsoring research, developing and promoting low-tar and low-nicotine cigarettes, and challenging scientific findings that cigarettes are unhealthy. Each of these techniques was meant to use the media to manipulate the public into believing that the health risks of smoking were nonexistent, negligible, or controllable. But when a story appeared in the media, the public was usually reminded, more effectively than by easily ignored warning labels, that smoking was hazardous. Tobacco companies had tried to burnish their images in ways that did not directly call attention to cigarettes by sponsoring athletic and cultural events. And Philip Morris even incorporated the Bill of Rights into a promotional campaign. In one case, though, an antismoking activist turned the tables on the huge cigarette-manufacturing conglomerate. Ann Seibert, a Vermont legislator, collected sixty-five Philip Morris calendars featuring attractive women smokers and the Bill of Rights that had been sent to the state house in Montpelier. She then "distributed them to teachers in the state who would use them to teach students about addiction and substance abuse and about media manipulation and gender bias."[120]

What conclusions should be drawn about the overall performance of the news media in reporting on smoking and health between 1950 and 1990? First, predictably, it was mixed. Second, the press was much more an instrument of the parties at interest than an independent actor. Third, because of a wide range of factors, it took many years before the information put before the public by the media began to influence attitudes, behavior, or policy, but it eventually did. And fourth, for a long time the elite media reported inadequately on the efforts of the industry to perpetuate a deadly habit that was killing hundreds of thousands of Americans annually. This last indictment reflects a general tendency on the part of most America news media to underreport derelictions of corporate responsibility.

NOTES

1. "Preliminary Recommendations for Cigarette Manufacturers," memorandum prepared by the public relations firm Hill and Knowlton for the cigarette industry and disclosed as plaintiff's exhibit 2700 during the 1988 trial in Federal District Court in Newark, N.J., known as *Cipollone* v. *Liggett Group, Inc., et al.*

2. King James I proclaimed that tobacco was a noxious weed in 1604 (A Counterblaste against Tobacco). An example of an early epidemiological study was the one carried out by Drs. Herbert L. Lombard and Carl R. Doering, who wrote in the *New England Journal of Medicine* (April 26, 1928, p. 485): "The use of tobacco has long been considered a factor in the incidence of cancer of the buccal cavity." Lombard and Doering went on to say that their research "suggests that heavy smoking has some relation to cancer in general" (p. 486.).

3. Raymond Pearl, "Tobacco Smoking and Longevity," *Science*, March 4, 1938, pp. 216–17.

4. Ronald A. Troyer and Gerald E. Markle, *Cigarettes: The Battle Over Smoking* (New Brunswick, N.J.: Rutgers University Press, 1983), p. 54.

5. Warren Weaver Jr., "Lung Cancer Tests Planned by State," *New York Times*, December 21, 1953, p. 1.

6. George Seldes, *Facts and Facism* (New York: In Fact, 1943), p. 268.

7. William L. Laurence, "Lung Cancer Rise Laid to Cigarettes," *New York Times*, October 26, 1940, p. 17. The article reports on a study by Dr. Alton Ochsner, one of the pioneers in the field of smoking and health.

8. Clarence William Lieb, M.D., "Can the Poisons in Cigarettes Be Avoided?" *Reader's Digest*, December 1953; condensed from *Safer Smoking* (New York: Exposition Press, 1953).

9. "Cigarette Scare: What'll the Trade Do?" *Business Week*, December 5, 1953, pp. 58–68.

10. Roy Norr, "Cancer by the Carton," *Reader's Digest*, December 1952, pp. 7–8; condensed from *Christian Herald*, December 1952.

11. Morton L. Levin, M.D., "Etiology of Lung Cancer: Present Status," *New York State Journal of Medicine*, March 15, 1954, pp. 769–77.

12. E. Cuyler Hammond, Sc.D, and Daniel Horn, Ph.D., followed a cohort of 187,783 white males between 50 and 69 years of age, some of whom smoked and some of whom didn't, for forty-four months. By mid–1954, their most important results were released. Total mortality among cigarette smokers was found to have been increased by 68 percent. Final results were published in the *Journal of the American Medical Association* on March 8 and March 15, 1958.

13. Morton Mintz, "Witness Questioned on Study of Tobacco Ads," *Washington Post*, April 13, 1988, p. F3.

14. Michael Pertschuk, "The Politics of Tobacco: Curse and Cure," *New York State Journal of Medicine*, December 1983, p. 1277.

15. Extrapolation based on statistics developed by Kenneth Warner. See *Selling Smoke: Cigarette Advertising and Public Health* (Washington, D.C.: American Public Health Association, 1986), p. 64.

16. The implication of the media-battlefield analogy is that the media play an instrumental rather than a participatory role in the policy process. The participants try to use the media to their advantage as military strategists try to use terrain. The relevant difference is that, unlike terrain, which is morally neutral, the media are responsible to the public. This implies a duty to avoid being used in ways that result in the public being misinformed or manipulated. The account that follows is intended to assess the role the media played in the smoking-and-health controversy according to these criteria.

17. Opinion of Judge H. Lee Sarokin rejecting defendants' motion for a directed verdict in *Antonio Cipollone* v. *Liggett Group et al.*

18. William Kloepfer Jr., senior vice president and director of public relations, Tobacco Institute, from 1967–1988, interview, Chevy Chase, Md. November 8, 1988.

19. Amy Singer, "They Didn't *Really* Blame the Cigarette Makers," *American Lawyer*, September 1988, p. 31.

20. Ibid., p. 32.

21. Alan Blum, "Alton Ochsner, MD, 1896–1981," *New York State Journal of Medicine*, December 1983, p. 1251.

22. Laurence, "Lung Cancer Rise." See Ronald J. Troyer and Gerald E. Markle, *Cigarettes: The Battle over Smoking* (New Brunswick, N. J.: Rutgers University Press, 1983), p. 54.

23. Elizabeth Whelan, *A Smoking Gun* (Philadelphia: George F. Stickle, 1984), p. 80. The quotation is from Whelan, who paraphrased Graham.

24. Evarts A. Graham and Ernst Wynder, "Tobacco Smoking as a Possible Etiological Factor in Bronchiogenic Carcinoma," *Journal of the American Medical Association*, May 27, 1950, p. 336.

25. "Smoking Found Tied to Cancer of Lungs," *New York Times*, May 27, 1950, p. 34.

26. Richard Doll and A. Bradford Hill, "Smoking and Carcinoma of the Lung," *British Medical Journal*, September 30, 1950, p. 739.

27. Richard Doll and A. Bradford Hill, "A Study of the Aetiology of Carcinoma of the Lung," *British Medical Journal*, December 13, 1952, pp. 1271–86.

28. Blum, "Alton Ochsner, MD."

29. E. L. Wynder, E. A. Graham, and A. B. Croninger, "Experimental Production of Carcinoma with Cigarette Tar," *Cancer Research*, December 1953, pp. 855–64.

30. Whelan, *A Smoking Gun*, p. 85.

31. Blum, "Alton Ochsner, MD."

32. Thomas Whiteside, "Smoking Still," *New Yorker*, November 18, 1974, p. 134.

33. Thomas Whiteside, "Cutting Down," *New Yorker*, December 19, 1970, p. 45.

34. "Tobacco Tied to Rising Death Toll in British Doctors' Lung Cancer," *New York Times*, June 25, 1954, p. 3.

35. Lawrence E. Davies, "Cigarettes Found to Raise Death Rate in Men 50 to 70," *New York Times*, June 22, 1954, p. 1.

36. The account of the Hammond and Horn study that follows is based largely on chapter eight of *Crusade* (New York: Arbor House, 1987), the official history of the American Cancer Society by Walter Ross; and "Smoking and Death Rates," a landmark perspective by Sir Richard Doll in the June 1, 1984, issue of the *Journal of the American Medical Association*.

37. Sir Richard Doll, "Smoking and Death Rates," *Journal of the American Medical Association*, June 1, 1984, pp. 2854–57.

38. "Cigarette Scare: What'll the Trade Do?" *Business Week*, December 5, 1953, p. 58.

39. Walter Ross, *Crusade* (New York: Arbor House, 1987), pp. 56–57. The man quoted, Richard Carter, is identified as "a critical observer of U.S. philanthropies."

40. "Cigarette Scare," p. 64.

41. Thomas Whiteside, "Annals of Advertising," *New Yorker*, December 19, 1970, p. 43.

42. "Preliminary Recommendations for Cigarette Manufacturers," Hill and Knowlton, December 24, 1953, p. 2.

43. Ibid., p. 5.

44. Harold M. Schmeck Jr., "7 Experts Find Cigarettes a Factor in Lung Cancer," *New York Times*, March 23, 1957, p. 1.

45. Harold M. Schmeck Jr., "Cigarette Smoking Linked to Cancer in High Degree," *New York Times*, June 5, 1957, p. 1.

46. "Britain to Warn of Smoking Peril," *New York Times*, June 28, 1957, p. 4.

47. Bess Furman, "U.S. Links Cancer with Cigarettes," *New York Times*, July 13, 1957, p. 1.

48. A. Lee Fritschler, *Smoking and Politics* (Englewood Cliffs, N.J.: Prentice-Hall, 1975), p. 27.

49. "Doctors and Smoking (IV)," a study of the National Physicians' Advisory Panel, Medimetric Institute. The study, dated August 1959, was commissioned by Hill and Knowlton for the Tobacco Industry Research Council.

50. Industry memo, Dr. R. N. DuPuis and Dr. C. V. Mace, July 24, 1958, which acknowledges that "the evidence is building up that heavy cigarette smoking contributes to lung cancer." DuPuis and Mace were researchers for Philip Morris. The memo discusses both filters and smokeless cigarettes.

51. James Feron, "War on Smoking Asked in Britain," *New York Times*, March 8, 1962, p. 1.

52. "Smoking and Health," Report of the Royal College of Physicians, 1962, p. 85.

53. "British Report Sparks Cancer-Smoking scare," *Business Week*, April 14, 1962, p. 42.

54. Letter to Kennedy, quoted in Ross, *Crusade*, p. 64.

55. Ibid.

56. Robert H. Miles, *Coffin Nails and Corporate Strategies* (Englewood Cliffs, N.J.: Prentice Hall, 1982), p. 41.

57. Stanley Joel Reiser, "Smoking and Health: The Congress and Causality," in *Knowledge and Power*, Sanford A. Lakoff, ed. (New York: Free Press, 1966), p. 295.

58. Luther Terry, "The Surgeon General's First Report on Smoking and Health," *New York State Journal of Medicine*, December 1983, p. 1255.

59. Walter Sullivan, "Cigarettes Peril Health, U.S. Report Concludes; 'Remedial Action' Urged," *New York Times*, January 12, 1964, p. 1.

60. According to Thomas Whiteside, writing in the *New Yorker* of November 18, 1974, "between the end of 1963 and the end of 1970 . . . the adult population increased at the rate of one and nine-tenths percent a year, but total sales of cigarettes increased at the rate of only eight-tenths of one percent a year."

61. Memorandum to C. C. Little, from J. M. Brady, April 9, 1962, from discovery material in *Cipollone* trial.

62. Joseph Lelyveld, "Cigarette Makers Prosper Despite Debate on Hazards," *New York Times*, November 29, 1963, p. 59.

63. Ibid.

64. Fritschler, *Smoking and Politics*, pp. 38–39.

65. See, for example, Kenneth E. Warner, "Cigarette Advertising and Media Coverage of Smoking and Health," *New England Journal of Medicine*, February 7, 1985, pp. 384–88; Kenneth E. Warner and Linda M. Goldenhar, "The Cigarette Broadcast Ban and Magazine Coverage of Smoking and Health," *Journal of Public Health*, Spring 1989, pp. 32–42; and *Selling Smoke: Cigarette Advertising and Public Health* (Washington, D.C.: AHPA, 1986), pp. 71–84.

66. The account that follows is taken from Peter Taylor, *The Smoke Ring* (New York: Pantheon, 1984), pp. 169–70.

67. "Cigarettes vs. F.T.C.," *New York Times*, July 9, 1965, p. 28.

68. Walter Carlson, "Advertising: Scorn for Cigarette Labeling Bill," *New York Times*, July 14, 1965, p. 47.

69. Michael Pertschuk, interview, Washington, D.C., October 28, 1988.

70. Memorandum from Simon O'Shea to W. T. Hoyt, subject Planning, August 18, 1965.

71. The *Louisville Courier-Journal* ran an extensive series of articles

November 11–15, 1984. The series, compiled by Richard Whitt and Phil Norman, included additional sections and prominent highlights. The *Charlotte Observer* ran a twenty-page section titled "Our Tobacco Dilemma" on March 25, 1979. The *Observer* even offered additional copies of the report to interested readers.

72. John W. Banzhaf III, quoted by Whiteside, "Cutting Down," p. 55.

73. Federal Trade Commission, Staff Report on the Cigarette Advertising Investigation, May 1981.

74. Whelan, *A Smoking Gun*, p. 113.

75. "Cigarette Deadline," *New York Times*, July 1, 1969, p. 40.

76. Pertschuk interview.

77. Kloepfer interview.

78. Warner, "Cigarette Advertising and Media Coverage," p. 387.

79. Memo from Fred Panzer to Horace Kornegay, May 1, 1972.

80. Lorillard memorandum, from A. W. Spears to C. H. Judge, June 24, 1974.

81. Memo released during *Cipollone* trial, dated April 22, 1974, addressed to Henry-Tom (Henry H. Ramm and W. Tom Hoyt) and signed L.S.Z. (Leonard S. Zahn, a consultant for the Council for Tobacco Research).

82. Spears-Judge memo.

83. Kenneth E. Warner, "Promotion of Tobacco Products: An Overview of the Issues," paper delivered February 12, 1986, at a meeting of the Interagency Committee on Smoking and Health, p. 1.

84. Joseph A. Califano, *Governing America* (New York: Simon and Schuster, 1981), p. 183.

85. Donald Shopland, public health advisor, National Cancer Institute, who was executive editor or managing editor of more than a dozen surgeon general's reports, interview, Silver Spring, Md. October 11, 1988.

86. Califano, *Governing America*, p. 183.

87. Ibid. The main outlines of the story of Califano's tenure come from *Governing America*. Most additional notes will be reserved for information from other sources.

88. "Action Vowed against 'Slow-Motion Suicide,'" *Washington Post*, January 12, 1979.

89. Califano, *Governing America*, p. 186.

90. John Pinney, interview, Washington, D.C., October 17, 1988.

91. Califano, *Governing America*, p. 187.

92. Speeches by President Jimmy Carter, Wake Forest University, March 17, 1978, and Wilson, N.C., August 5, 1978, presidential documents, Administration of Jimmy Carter.

93. Califano, *Governing America*, pp. 191–92.

94. Taylor, *The Smoke Ring*, p. 220.

95. Robert Hutchings, associate director of the Office on Smoking and Health, interview, Silver Spring, Md. October 31, 1988.

96. Pinney, interview.

97. Califano, *Governing America*, p. 190.

98. Ibid., p. 194.

99. Kloepfer interview. All three networks led with the story. ABC devoted 4:50 to the piece, including coverage of Tobacco Institute press conference held the morning before the report was released. They also addressed the difficulties Califano was having fighting the industry. The ABC piece was reported by Margaret Osmore and Charles Gibson. CBS's Susan Spencer reported a 2:20 piece, listing statistics from the report and noting TI's criticisms. William Dwyer, TI vice president at the time, was interviewed. Andrea Mitchell did a three-minute piece for NBC, outlining the report and TI's response. TI president Horace Kornegay and Dwyer both commented.

100. Califano, *Governing America*, p. 194.

101. Ibid.

102. Pinney interview.

103. Califano, *Governing America*, pp. 196–97.

104. Robert Reinhold,"Califano Cites Feuds and Politics; Blumenthal Denies Being Coerced," *New York Times*, July 20, 1979, p. 1.

105. David S. Wilson, "2 Ballot Issues Raise Question: Is Smoking Becoming Taboo?" *New York Times*, October 25, 1988, p. A17.

106. Philip Morris interoffice correspondence, from J. J. Morgan to H. H. Cullman and J. C. Bowling, March 24, 1981.

107. Douglas C. McGill, "Cigarette Industry Financing Wide War on Smoking Bans," *New York Times*, December 24, 1988, p. A1.

108. Irving Rimer, vice president for public relations, American Cancer Society, interview, New York, October 25, 1988.

109. Douglas C. McGill, "Tobacco Industry Counterattacks," *New York Times*, November 26, 1988, p. 31.

110. David Hoffman, "Regan Bars Koop's Testimony for Bill to Ban Tobacco Ads," *Washington Post*, July 16, 1986, p. A1.

111. Matt Myers, staff director, Coalition on Smoking or Health, interview, Washington, D.C., November 8, 1988.

112. Michael Pertschuk, *Giant Killers* (New York: W. W. Norton, 1987).

113. See Stephen Klaidman and Tom L. Beauchamp, *The Virtuous Journalist* (New York: Oxford University Press, 1987), pp. 32–56, for an account of what it means for news stories to be fair, accurate, understandable, and substantially complete.

114. Warner, "Cigarette Advertising and Media Coverage," p. 385.

115. Ben H. Bagdikian, *The Media Monopoly* (Boston: Beacon Press, 1983), p. 173. The agency was Batten, Barton, Durstine and Osborn.

116. The following documentaries were found in Daniel Einstein, *Special Edition: A Guide to Network Television Documentary Series and Special News Reports, 1955–1979* (Metuchen, N.J.: Scarecrow Press, 1987):

5/31/55: "See It Now," CBC, "Report on Cigarettes and Lung Cancer," Part 1. This is the famous Murrow piece.

6/7/55: "See It Now," Part 2.

9/15/62: "The Teenage Smoker," CBS Reports. A look at development of smoking among American teens.

1/11/64: "Report on Smoking and Health," CBS; "Report on Smoking," ABC; "Smoking and Health," NBC. These were in response to the release of the Surgeon General's Report. Einstein did not identify lengths of the programs.

4/14/64: "Cigarettes: A Collision of Interests," CBS Reports. This was an examination of the industry's reaction to the report, including interviews with farmers, manufacturers, advertisers, experts from the FTC labeling hearings, the governors of North Carolina (Sanford) and Virginia (Harrison), and a representative of the National Association of Broadcasters.

3/7/65: "Sunday," NBC. One segment examined trends in smoking habits since the issuance of the report.

1/18/66: "The National Health Test, Part 1," CBS. Viewer-participation quiz. Smoking and health was one topic.

Complete lists from all of the networks were not available. However, CBS's "48 Hours" aired a program on September 8, 1988, titled "The Smoking Wars." Also, series like ABC's "Nightline" and "20/20" have occasionally devoted programs to various aspects of the smoking issue, with a frequency of about one program a year.

117. Tony Schwartz, interview, New York, October 25, 1988.

118. Allan Brandt, interview, Cambridge, Mass., October 26, 1988.

119. Thomas Schelling, interview, Cambridge, Mass., October 26, 1988.

120. Don Oldenburg, "A Smoky Ethical Issue," *Washington Post*, June 29, 1990, p. B5.

9

Interpreting the News

A S the cases in this volume illustrate, even when journalists are able to resist manipulation and translate science into lay language with reasonable success, many health-risk stories remain maddeningly hard to evaluate. Reporters and editors must grapple with uncertain scientific results that resist interpretation, fundamental assumptions that are hidden and untested, undisclosed values that underlie important regulatory decisions, and the clandestine substitution of illegitimate economic or political goals for the public interest. As a result, even the most thoughtfully reported and composed stories can be a challenge to untangle. And they rarely, if ever, are able to provide the definitive answers the public is seeking. They may report instead findings like these: "If you eat five biscuits a day containing X parts per billion of EDB over seventy years, you will increase your chance of getting cancer by Y in a million." What should news consumers make of that? Probably not much, because the news media, even when they do their very best, are often likely to convey a value-laden, politically and economically influenced rough estimate of health risks that may or may not be based on valid assumptions.

This should not be understood as criticism of the news media. It is an assessment of the enterprise of health-risk reporting. It is intended to provide a sense of what readers and viewers are entitled to expect of "elite" news organizations with specialized health reporters such as *The New York Times*, *Newsweek*, and the "CBS Evening News." In general, even less can be expected of smaller, less affluent news organizations that cannot afford specialized reporters or costly investigations. When readers and viewers know what to expect, they can begin to identify and extract the nuggets of useful information embedded in health-risk stories.

News stories about health risks are not unique in their complexity. They are similar in many ways to stories about arms control, international economics, or the competition to build a better microprocessor. In each of these other cases, a limited group of sufficiently motivated readers and viewers acquires the expertise and sophistication necessary to follow fairly detailed newspaper or television accounts on the subject in which they are interested. They learn to read between the lines; to evaluate sources, named and unnamed; to recognize political motivation; and to understand, at least on a basic level, technical aspects of the specified field. The same is true of health-risk stories. There is a limited number of persons who know how to read them. The problem is that, unlike arms control or microprocessors, practically everyone is more than casually interested in health risks; but many, if not most, of these interested Americans are functionally illiterate in science.

All is not lost, however. There are some generalizable patterns in health-risk stories that if identified can help readers and viewers interpret their meanings. The cases in Chapters 2 through 8 of this book lay bare some of the elements that make health-risk stories so complex. Once this background is exposed, these patterns become apparent. What follows is a chapter-by-chapter guide to recognizing the patterns and thereby gaining a better understanding of health-risk stories.

Early in Chapter 2 William Ruckelshaus, who had just been appointed director of the Environmental Protection Agency, traveled to New York to visit CBS anchorman Dan Rather. Ruckelshaus elected to call on Rather personally even before he took office so that his agenda for the agency would be clear. This kind of attention to the media is typical of individuals and institutions that consistently get favorable coverage, as Ruckelshaus did throughout the EDB controversy. Ruckelshaus, as it happened, performed well. But it is worth remembering that public figures who are attentive to media considerations are usually given the benefit of the doubt by jounalists. The tipoff to unduly favorable treatment can be as subtle as the use of a respectful adjective or a flattering camera angle. The lesson is to concentrate on the substance of what newsmakers say and what they do, irrespective of how favorably or unfavorably reporters portray them.

Chapter 2 also calls attention to the fact that the actual risk to the public from ingesting EDB at the levels at which it was present in citrus fruit and grain products was unknown. The suspicion that there was any risk at all was based on high-dose animal studies. It may well have been good public policy to remove the chemical from the food chain, although there does not appear to have been any immediate danger. But many news stories about EDB conveyed a sense of urgency with phrases such as "massive doses of a cancer-causing pesticide," "one of the most potentially hazardous pesticides known to man," and "there is poison in paradise." The bias to write a "good story," high in drama and human interest, may lead to this kind of linguistic excess. Look for evidence that the chemical has done or can do harm to humans. If studies are cited as evidence, pay attention to the size of the study; whether it was done on animals or humans; if it was done on animals, whether it was limited to a single species; and so on. In other words, do not uncritically accept assertions, even if they are attributed to an apparently reputable scientist, that a chemical or other agent is safe or unsafe.

The EDB chapter also describes how high-impact videotape, even if it is irrelevant to the health hazard at issue, can be used to dramatize news stories and promote fear. The description of a grain worker shaking uncontrollably while trying to give an interview was used by the NBC program "First Camera" to make the point that EDB is highly toxic. But the worker was exposed to more EDB in an hour than most people would be exposed to in a lifetime. He also came into regular contact with substantial amounts of other toxic chemicals. His illness may or may not have been related to high-dose EDB exposure, but it surely was not related to the health risk of an average person who is exposed to minuscule amounts of EDB in a biscuit or a slice of chocolate cake. It requires alertness to notice that compelling television pictures often are not relevant to the health risk they purportedly illustrate. But it is worth the effort, because the EDB example is hardly unique.

Pictures with even greater impact were shown on the nightly news programs when companies began recalling their well-known brands of cake, biscuit, and pancake mixes. The strong implicit message was that if these products were coming off the shelves, they must be unsafe. The pictures were newsworthy, but the real reason for the recall was the bad publicity about EDB, not the magnitude of the hazard. The media had become an important part of the story, which was now feeding on itself. It is difficult to specify precisely how this phenomenon can be identified, but alert readers and viewers may sense it.

This will add still another dimension to their understanding of health-risk stories.

Although the examples from Chapter 2 deal with the apparent exaggeration of a health risk, they should not be understood as an endorsement of EDB or as an indication that the news media never underestimate hazards. Exaggeration of risk, however, is probably substantially more common than underestimation, because it is consistent with the media's bias for dramatic stories and their role as guardians of the individual citizen's interest.

In Chapter 3, a high-level radon risk in Clinton, New Jersey, got much less attention in the state press than a very low-level radon risk in Vernon, New Jersey, largely because an outraged and media-wise group of Vernonites dramatized the story and emphasized their role as citizens abused by the state. In Clinton, the mayor and the town's citizens quietly organized remediation efforts. With the exception of some misleading television reports suggesting that unusual numbers of houses were for sale in Clinton, news coverage was unsensational.

A major difference between the Vernon and Clinton situations was that in Vernon the radon problem was manmade and the Vernonites were resisting the exportation of a suburban New York problem to their semirural community. There was conflict, insensitive treatment of the community by the state, and an industrial villain, albeit one long gone from the scene. In Clinton, the radon was naturally occurring; therefore, there was no conflict and no villain. Human and political conflict and the perception of injustice, especially when the state is seen to be treating citizens unfairly, are guaranteed to focus the media's attention. In the Vernon case, this concentration on political conflict and injustice resulted in a failure on the part of most news organiztions to report thoroughly on the radiation risk itself, which was almost certainly negligible under the state's disposal plan. The lesson is to keep your eye on the ball. Do not confuse politically motivated characterizations of health risks with science. Be sensitive to the possible motives of sources cited in news stories, especially if the sources are unnamed.

Radon may represent a case in which on balance the news media have underplayed the health risk. There is disagreement in the scientific community about how much radon exposure under what conditions poses an unacceptable risk of lung cancer. But there does seem to be enough evidence that radon is a major preventable cause of death to warrant more sustained coverage. Nuclear power (the subject of Chapter 4), on the other hand, has been covered as a health hazard for twenty years or more. It is one of the classic examples of a health risk mired in political and economic conflict.

Because nuclear plants pose a risk of large-scale disaster, albeit a minuscule one, any reference to accidents associated with these facilities generates fear of a catastrophe. It is in the nature of journalism to alert readers and viewers to the worst possible outcomes. But it is not clear how useful these worst-case scenarios are in making choices about the acceptability of health risks, even when they are accompanied by equally detailed accounts of the remoteness of the risk. Suppose, for example, a newspaper reports that during the operating life of a nuclear plant the risk is 1 in 10,000 that there will be an accident in which several thousand persons will die, mostly horrible, lingering deaths from radiation sickness; or, to put it the other way around, the odds are 10,000 to 1 that such an accident will *not* occur. How should a rational reader factor this information into a decision about whether to support or oppose construction of the plant?

One way is to compare the risk with other risks, but unless the newspaper story provides some comparisons, most persons will be unprepared to do this. Books such as *Of Acceptable Risk* by William Lowrance provide comparisons for anyone sufficiently interested to buy a copy. But for the average person who has no means of comparison at hand, a gut reaction to the media characterization is the likely alternative. The acceptability of 1 chance in 10,000 of a catastrophe occuring may be hard to evaluate intellectually, but a vision of irradiated corpses littering the landscape is guaranteed to elicit a visceral response. The lesson is not that this emotional response should be ignored, but rather that it should be recognized for what it is and evaluated in light of the remoteness of the risk. A final decision will also properly take into account non-health-related information such as the cost of plant construction, the price of oil, the risks of American dependency on uncertain Middle Eastern supplies, and the availability and cost of other energy sources.

There are two additional health-related factors: the risks of energy alternatives such as burning fossil fuels and improvements in training and technology that may make nuclear plants safer to operate. From time to time news reports include assessments of the risks to workers, especially those who mine coal, and the morbidity and mortality associated with burning coal. Since there is no evidence that anyone has ever died as the result of a civilian nuclear accident in the United States, it stands to reason that many more people have died as a result of mining and burning coal. Most stories about nuclear power do not include a reminder of this fact. It is worth remembering in all such stories that no technologies are risk-free.

It is also worth remembering that almost all potentially catastrophic nuclear accidents will be the result of human error or plumbing failures or some combination of the two (as was the case at Three Mile Island) leading to the melting of fuel in the reactor core. Careful attention should be paid, therefore, to stories about better training and higher standards for reactor operators; improved techniques for welding pipe, manufacturing valves, backing up electrical systems, and designing control panels; and innovations intended to prevent fuel from melting. The lesson is to pay attention to the technical details, even those that seem mundane—they are the ultimate keys to safety.

Finally, assume that there are no disinterested parties. In an environment as politically charged as the one surrounding nuclear power, every source should be viewed as an advocate. The nuclear industry and its supporters in government have a long history of papering over safety problems, and the antinuclear lobby has an almost equally long history of playing on the public's fears of a catastrophic accident. Journalists try to take this into account when they write their stories or prepare their television pieces, but clever advocates are often able to insinuate subtle messages into news stories by manipulating the sympathies or ambitions of even the most perspicacious journalists.

Health-risk issues are especially manipulable because of the high level of uncertainty that is typical of them. Chapter 5 has less direct connection with health hazards than the other chapters in this volume, but the threat of global warming presents a good example of how the media can be used to transmute scientific uncertainty into political reality. It would be too cynical to suggest that senators Albert Gore and Tim Wirth did not believe in the seriousness of the threat of global warming, which they promoted as a political issue in the 1980s. But it would be naive to think that they didn't recognize that the data on which they based their belief were somewhat soft and subjective. At the same time, the political process moves slowly, and if actions such as reducing the release of carbon dioxide into the atmosphere were going to have a chance of succeeding, they believed they would have to get started right away. Since cutting back on carbon dioxide meant doing battle with two of the country's most powerful industries—oil and automobiles—the two senators recognized that they would have to build a broad-based public constituency for their cause. There was only one way to do that: use the news media.

The technique was to get a respected scientist or scientists to deliver a message about global warming that was sufficiently scary to get large numbers of ordinary people worried—worried enough to accept the economic consequences of a major cutback in the use of fossil fuels, which is the only way to significantly reduce carbon dioxide emissions. In this they succeeded when James Hansen of NASA announced at a congressional hearing that the impact of the greenhouse effect was already being felt. Hansen was virtually alone among climatologists in this view when he made his statement. But that did not keep the news media from treating the story as a major breakthrough. Hansen, after all, was the first respected scientist to make such a claim. The lesson is to beware of scientific breakthroughs, especially when they are announced in political forums. The primary motivation for such announcements is unlikely to be the advancement of science. Hansen did not choose to disclose this startling information in a peer-reviewed journal in the time-honored fashion because it would have been dismissed and would have had no impact. He chose to make it public at a hearing he knew would be covered by *The New York Times* because he knew it would be treated as a breakthrough and have substantial political impact. Two years later, Hansen was still isolated in his view, and the greenhouse effect's impact on planet Earth was a uncertain as ever, but global warming was firmly on the public agenda.

The impact of AIDS, the subject of Chapter 6, on those infected with the virus became clear early on—they grew ill and died. Nevertheless, for a couple of years this devastating yet medically fascinating disease got very little attention from the news media. Why was it that the epidemiologists who were predicting a full-scale epidemic did not attract as much interest as Hansen did with his assertion that global warming had arrived? Was it because the early victims of AIDS were social outcasts—homosexuals, drug addicts, and poor Haitian immigrants—and the media thought their "mainstream" audience wouldn't care? (If Hansen was right about global warming, it would affect everyone, rich and poor, white and black, straight and gay.) Or perhaps it was that the epidemiologists were predicting the future, whereas Hansen had announced the present. Or could it have been that the disease's primary mode of transmission in the early days—gay sex—was not something the "mainstream" media wanted to deal with? For years journalists avoided explicit descriptions of how AIDS was transmitted even though education was the only weapon available against the spread of the disease.

All of these factors probably influenced the way AIDS was reported, although none of them was readily discernible from the stories that were published and broadcast. The lesson is to think beyond what appears on the page or on the screen to what does not appear. Journalistic reports frequently are not transparent. Stories are shaped by elements as diverse as a newspaper's conception of the willingness of its audience to accept sexually explicit material and the values, goals, and ambitions of individual reporters and sources. Some of the best reporting on AIDS, for example, was done by reporters with a strong personal stake, like Randy Shilts of *The San Francisco Chronicle*, who is gay, and Vincent Coppola of *Newsweek*, whose brother was dying of AIDS. This does not mean that other reporters such as Marlene Cimons of *The Los Angeles Times* and Lawrence K. Altman of *The New York Times* did not soon recognize the magnitude of the story and perform exceptionally well. They did. What it does mean is that coverage can be spurred and shaped by motives unknown to readers and viewers.

In the case of AIDS, it is also notable that the science was covered well from the beginning. But the social and political aspects of the story did not begin to get the coverage they deserved until the epidemic was several years old. The reason may be that the science could be treated in a relatively detached and academic fashion without graphically describing a sexual culture that many Americans view at best as bizarre. These research-oriented stories did not require readers and viewers to think about the religious, moral, and economic questions that would eventually strain the fabric of American society. Newspapers, newsmagazines, and the electronic media are essentially conservative. They do not want to challenge the mores of their audience. And they do not want to be wrong. It is useful to keep in mind this institutional conservatism—which may be at odds with the liberal leanings of individual journalists—when evaluating the way in which the social and political aspects of controversial stories are covered.

Unlike AIDS, cholesterol poses a health risk to a large segment of the population as a result of behavior that up until recently has been considered absolutely normal by just about everyone: eating fatty food. The problem is that researchers are unsure how much cholesterol in the blood is unhealthy as Chapter 7 indicated. Hundreds of studies have been done. They show a clear association between very high blood cholesterol and coronary artery disease. But at the levels chosen for intervention by the National Heart, Lung and Blood Institute, the association is less clear. And the possibility of prolonging life through dietary change is still less clear. Setting aside the question of children, which is unsettled, there do not appear to be detrimental side effects associated with low-cholesterol diets, so a strong public health argument can be made for an aggressive campaign to try to reduce borderline cholesterol levels through diet. But it is difficult to make a persuasive argument that for any given individual with borderline blood cholesterol a reduction in saturated fat consumption will lengthen or improve the quality of his or her life.

What this means for journalists who write about cholesterol is that they find themselves under pressure to take sides. Jane Brody of *The New York Times* believes borderline blood cholesterol is bad for you and that diet can make a difference. Thomas J. Moore, author of *Heart Failure*, does not. These views come through clearly in what the two journalists have written on the subject. Other reporters such as Sally Squires of *The Washington Post* and Philip Boffey of *The New York Times* have remained more circumspect. All four of these reporters have read the important studies in the field and interviewed the prominent researchers on both sides of the question. The lesson for readers is twofold: (1) With a subject as complicated and important as cholesterol, do not trust a single journalist or news organization. Read widely. And (2) do not expect a clear-cut answer. Readers will have to evaluate the conflicting evidence for themselves and weigh it against the importance of well-marbled steak in their personal lives.

Rarely, if ever, has anything as unhealthy as the cigarette been so important in the personal lives of so many people. And rarely, if ever, has a health risk been so bound up with the economics and politics of the nation (and the news media) as cigarette smoking. Add to this the addictive nature of the product, and it becomes easy to see why it took so long for the media to do their job, as shown in Chapter 8. The lessons are manifold. (1) When there is a lot at stake, expect a lot of manipulation. (2) When a health risk comes packaged as a popular product, it will have a powerful lobby that will use free media (news columns and programs) to promote it as well as paid media (advertising). (3) When industry spokespersons make much of the fact that a cause-and-effect relationship between a product and a disease has not been demonstrated, look for epidemiological evidence of a strong statistical association between the product and the disease. (4) Pay attention to the sources of studies. If a study is sponsored by the Tobacco Institute Research Committee, the words *Tobacco Institute* may render the words Research Committee untrustworthy. This body does not become more trustworthy by changing its name to the Council for Tobacco Research. (5) Question the relevance of research to health effects, especially research that yields negative results. A study that fails to find a cause-and-effect relationship between cigarette smoke and lung cancer, for example, does not prove that cigarette smoke does not cause lung cancer. (6) If the industry is rich enough and politically powerful enough, it may wear out the media, at least in the short run. Journalists will not keep running a story unless there is something new to report. (7) Be sensitive to language. If a news story refers to "the smoking-and-health controversy," make sure there really is a "controversy" among qualified researchers about the health effects of smoking. (8) Remember that when an industry is a source of billions of dollars in tax revenue, government will think long and hard before taking it on. And (9) when an industry is the source of billions of dollars a year in advertising revenue, the media will think long and hard before taking it on. (10) The media's reverence for balance leads to the mindless inclusion of misleading statements in news stories such as those contending that there is no causal link between smoking and disease.

As Chapters 2 through 8 demonstrate, there is room for improvement in coverage of health risks, even by America's best news organizations. But there may be even more room for improvement in the way Americans interpret and understand news. Just as attentiveness and skepticism are essential attributes in journalism, they are necessary for anyone who wants to read newspapers or view television news more than superficially. A critical intelligence is required for substantially complete understanding. But it must be accompanied by an awareness that underlying stories like the ones in this volume exist, and an ability to piece them together from the evidence, even that which is omitted. (Remember Sherlock Holmes' dog that didn't bark.)

Index